THE CITY IN SOUTHERN HISTORY

Kennikat Press

National University Publications

Interdisciplinary Urban Series

General Editor

Raymond A. Mohl

Florida Atlantic University

EDITED BY
BLAINE A. BROWNELL
and
DAVID R. GOLDFIELD

CONTRIBUTORS
BLAINE A. BROWNELL
CARVILLE EARLE
DAVID R. GOLDFIELD
EDWARD F. HAAS
RONALD HOFFMAN
HOWARD N. RABINOWITZ

the CITY in SOUTHERN HISTORY

The Growth of
Urban Civilization in the South

National University Publications
KENNIKAT PRESS   //   1977
Port Washington, N. Y.   //   London

Manufactured in the United States of America

Published by
Kennikat Press Corp.
Port Washington, N. Y./London

Library of Congress Cataloging in Publication Data

Main entry under title:

The City in southern history.

(Interdisciplinary urban series) (National university publications)
Includes bibliographical references and index.
1. Cities and towns—Southern States—Addresses, essays, lectures. 2. Urbanization—Southern States—Addresses, essays, lectures. I. Brownell, Blaine A. II. Goldfield, David R., 1944-
HT123.5.S6C57   301.36'2'0975   76-41235
ISBN 0-8046-9078-2

For our parents,
who wanted us to be
doctors or lawyers

ACKNOWLEDGMENTS

Working in a relatively new field of scholarly inquiry, we have benefited from the suggestions of a number of fellow workers. In a sense, this book is more a product of a nascent discipline—southern urban history—than it is of individual authors. Such talented historians as Numan V. Bartley, Charles B. Dew, Hugh Davis Graham, Louis R. Harlan, Carl V. Harris, Richard J. Hopkins, David R. Johnson, Arthur Mann, Grady McWhiney, and Walter B. Weare have taken the time and effort to analyze and criticize the essays. John Rainbolt and Dale Somers aided the initial phases of this project. Their untimely deaths robbed the historical profession in general and southern urban history in particular of bright young scholars.

Raymond A. Mohl, the editor of the series in which this book appears, deserves special praise for his early encouragement of the project. His understanding was a major reason why six historians cooperated and remained friends and colleagues over the course of several years—a unique achievement for joint efforts such as this.

The stylistic recommendations of John Parke and the typing skills of Jacksie Dickerson, Marian Harrison, Louise Oliver, Patricia Wade, and Evia Wilson made the publisher's task considerably easier. Kerry Akridge prepared most of the figures in chapter five. The proof reading and patience of our wives, Mardi and Barbara, made our job much easier.

Finally, we dedicate this book to our parents. Through them we first learned and saw the excitement of history. Although they had, initially, preferred other professions for us, they have supported our efforts in history with biased enthusiasm and devotion.

We hope that there is nothing in this book that will rekindle their earlier hopes for us.

Blaine A. Brownell
Birmingham, Alabama

David R. Goldfield
Blacksburg, Virginia

CONTENTS

THE CITY IN SOUTHERN HISTORY

1 BLAINE A. BROWNELL
DAVID R. GOLDFIELD

SOUTHERN URBAN HISTORY

The discipline of urban history has burgeoned from a mere handful of practitioners a decade ago to a legion of scholars dedicated to extracting the essence of urban civilization around the world. The reasons for this scholarly upsurge are numerous, but foremost is the simple fact that cities are important. Richard Hildreth wrote more than a century ago that American cities "are the central points from which knowledge, enterprise, and civilization stream out upon the surrounding country."[1] The city has been a crucible of change and a repository of civilization.

In a section where change has purportedly moved at the pace of a mule through a tobacco row, the study of cities should afford some insight into the character of the region. Yet the study of the urban South has proceeded much more slowly than the fabled mule. The traditional view of the South as "planter, plantation, staple crop, and the Negro, all set in a rural scene," or as a region encumbered by an "agrarian, backward status," has militated against research in southern urbanization.[2] It would appear that either southern cities are irrelevant to the history of the region or their impact has been so slight as to warrant only a brief mention. Recently, however, scholars have begun to enlarge the parochial view of the South to include an urban dimension.[3] It is the purpose of these essays to draw this scholarship together and establish a framework for the study of the urban South. The themes shaping current investigations are myriad; but the role of urban leadership, the relationship of southern cities to the national economy, and the complex patterns of urban race relations are especially significant. In these areas, as in others, we can begin by asking, "What is the South?"

SOUTHERN IDENTITY AND SOUTHERN URBAN HISTORY

For those historians—and there are many—who have generated volumes searching for the southern identity, the answers to the section's uniqueness seem as near and as distant as the land of Canaan seemed to Moses after his odyssey through the desert. Indeed, it seems as if southern historians are condemned to trek the desert of partial explanations, never to land upon the true South.[4]

For some historians, the relationship between southern and national identity is not a question of "perhaps"; it is, rather, an amply documented reality. Charles G. Sellers, Jr., stated this view succinctly: "The traditional emphasis on the South's differences is wrong historically." Southerners may well have been, and remain, simply "other Americans" whose doubts and troubles appear in sharper relief.[5] The essays in this book tend to support this view by relating the similarities between northern and southern urban development. But this does not preclude the fact that the quality of life in southern cities was often distinct from lifestyles and patterns in the cities of other regions. If differences in degree are large enough, they become differences in kind.

Any approach to the urban South must take account of the region's diversity. The area below Mason's and Dixon's line contained a variety of populations, habits, religions, soils, and landscapes that seemed, for all its statesmen's rhetoric, to defy homogenization. The region's cities reflected this heterogeneity, but it is significant that they probably differed less in any single period from one another, or from their counterparts in other sections, than the society of black belt Alabama differed from that of the Carolina mountains. Among its various cultures the South contained an urban civilization that became more uniform and consistent in its character as time passed. Regrettably, we know much more about individual southern cities than we do about this larger urban culture and the various factors that define the regional and social components of "southern cities."

In the colonial and revolutionary eras the principal southern cities were situated along the regional periphery. By the late eighteenth century, as Ronald Hoffman and Carville Earle observe, the southern pattern of urbanization resembled a distinctive configuration, a horseshoe oriented from northwest to southeast with an open end in the Carolinas and an empty core on the shoe's inside. New Orleans, Memphis, Mobile, Savannah, Charleston, Baltimore, and Louisville dominated the commerce of the region through the antebellum period, and acted as administrative centers for the settlement of the southern interior. In the late nineteenth century the perimeter of the urban South began to contract, as border state cities were integrated into the industrial cores of the Northeast and the Midwest. By the mid-twentieth century the urban South could perhaps be delimited in a new horseshoe configuration, by a line running westward from Richmond through Nashville and Memphis to Dallas, and back through Houston and New Orleans to roughly Jacksonville, Florida. The southern interior, if not fully developed, contains major cities like Atlanta and Birmingham, and the Atlantic and Gulf coasts have experienced considerable urbanization.

But if the urban South was diverse, and varied in shape and character over time, it was nevertheless indisputably "southern." What this means, precisely, lies more in the province of the cultural historian, perhaps, than in the realm of scholars who probe census data. It is probably true that the current methodologies of urban history tend to obscure regional cultural differences by concentrating on factors most readily measured and catalogued. And so we must ultimately return to the quest for the southern identity.

Ralph Ellison's classic novel about a black man's painful search for his identity has its parallel in the South. *Invisible Man,* in one sense, is a story of what W. E. B. Du Bois called the "twoness" of the black man in America: how to reconcile being black with being an American. The attainment of his visibility—his identity—did not begin until he allowed his blackness to emerge from the self-imposed exile necessitated by life in the rural South and the urban North.[6] The southerner is also torn by the "twoness" of his existence: as a southerner and as an American. Like the black man—who in many instances was or still is a southerner—the resident of the South may find reconciliation only upon asserting his "southernness." It is perhaps the only resolution for a minority in a majoritarian society.

Indeed, the southerner as a minority, or as George B. Tindall termed him, the "ethnic southerner," has been a common theme throughout the history of the region.[7] Invariably this conception of minority status has affected southern urban development. In the 1830s and 1840s southern radicals led by South Carolina's John C. Calhoun countenanced secession because they perceived the region's minority status within the Union. This same perception alarmed urban leaders sufficiently to develop a program of economic regeneration designed to achieve sectional equilibrium. After the Civil War, defeat and a continuation of minority status convinced the region's leaders—many of whom resided in cities—that the only way to salvation was through imitation of the North's economic success. Like the invisible man who suppressed his blackness, conked his hair, and attempted to survive on the terms of white society, southerners discovered by the early twentieth century that their efforts had only driven them deeper into dependence.

Today, despite the homogenization of metropolitan life brought about by McDonald's, television, and the automobile, there is still a South—that combination of what Blaine A. Brownell has characterized as "hospitality and violence, racism and tolerance, and ingenuity and fatalism." Southern cities, despite having passed through the developmental phases experienced by cities elsewhere, reflect some of the languid, unhurried, personal atmosphere that is perhaps lacking in metropolises of the North and West. Although at first glance well-scrubbed Atlanta might be mistaken for Minneapolis, and Houston may be Space City, there is a substance and quality of life forever veiled to those whose understanding rests solely on census data.

More than a century ago George Fitzhugh preached the benefits of urban growth, manufacturing, and commerce while vilifying their consequences. Fitzhugh was not confused; he wanted the benefits of capitalism and urbanization without the attendant ills. Southern cities would imitate the North, but would somehow turn out differently.[8] A similar sentiment appeared in Atlanta during the 1920s, embodied in the "Atlanta spirit," which typified the "best of the spirit of the Old South . . . with all the romance of music, beauty, poetry, idealism," and of the New South which "clasped hands with the progressive spirit and ample capital of its erstwhile enemy."[9] Much of this, of course, is chamber of commerce hyperbole. There is little poetry about Atlanta's black slums, for example. Yet, there is some validity to this mixture of old gentility and new dynamism. It does, after all, capture the "twoness" of the urban South as both part of an urban nation and part of a distinct region. Southern cities may have escaped the colonial dependence and the fawning over northern capital and expertise that marked earlier eras, but the urban South is indelibly a part of the section, perhaps much more so than Minneapolis, say, is part of the upper Midwest.

In the study of the growth of urban civilization in the South, the regional context must always be in consideration. Atlantans will tell you they are not like other Georgians, but few will claim that the Gate City is not southern. The South is diverse, to be sure; but, as Carl Degler has observed, "there is indeed an overall unity to the South that embraces the diversity."[10] Southern cities served as repositories of regional culture—including, many would argue, the primitive values and instincts of rural society—and as links between the traditional South and the contrary influences of northern capitalism and the American "mainstream." This model would help to explain, among other things, the conflict and violence so characteristic of southern cities, the evident ambiguity of the New South creed, and the role of regional cities as agents of change. It would also be among the most crucial keys for understanding southern history.

SOUTHERN URBAN LEADERSHIP

"Our greatness . . . lies not alone in punchful prosperity but equally in that public spirit, that forward-looking idealism and brotherhood, which has marked Zenith ever since its foundation by the Fathers."[11] Sinclair Lewis's George F. Babbitt was the epitome of the urban booster in an era when boosterism rivaled baseball as a national pastime. The booster was not indigenous to the 1920s, though he was perhaps more prolific and frenzied during that decade than at other times. City-building was important and delicate work throughout American history. Natural advantages and accumulations of capital were inconsequential unless translated into growth policies by an active urban leadership. Entrepreneurs were image makers, railroad builders, and rationalizers of growth, commerce, and industry. Without a heavy dose of boosterism a town would surely sink into the backwaters of American civilization.

The role of urban leadership in developing cities emerged in the colonial period when it became evident by the turn of the eighteenth century that the crown could not legislate towns into existence in Virginia. The nature of the Chesapeake economy and the indifference of the planter-merchants to town life militated against urban development. When some nodes of settlement finally blossomed into cities, urban leaders were responsible, in large part, for securing growth. The persistence and occasional gamble of Norfolk's mercantile elite transformed that community into a significant import-export center prior to the Revolution. The rapid growth of Baltimore late in the colonial period was even more impressive. Merchant-millers such as William Lux consolidated the wheat trade in the surrounding hinterland and enabled the Chesapeake city to become a leading grain and flour entrepôt. The exploitation of the hinterland and its efficacy for urban growth became the foundation of leaders' efforts to stimulate urban development.

Urban leadership was more indifferent in other colonial settlements. The planter-merchants who dominated the social, economic, and political life of Charleston provided for a lively urbanity during the "season," but abandoned the community for the remainder of the year. Their urban consciousness consisted of plotting an escape from Charleston before the first mosquitoes and after the last party. Associational activity probably consisted of dipping snuff at the St. Cecilia's Society, and when the planter-merchant discussed programs and policies, he was most likely referring to the latest directives from London.

Despite such uneven urban development and leadership, the colonial period proved educational for urban boosters. Rapid communication with the West Indies, for example, enabled Norfolk merchants to out-trade larger northern competitors. The benefit of effective transportation and communication lines was established. Wheat cultivation in the countryside stimulated the rise of flour milling in Baltimore, and greater profits for Baltimore demonstrated the salutary effects of processing industries and the necessity of courting backcountry farmers. Finally, urban merchants in the Chesapeake region took the first steps toward constructing a regional urban network by developing commercial relationships with Philadelphia businessmen.

In the antebellum era the removal of British direction and the development of a vast internal market produced profound changes in urban leadership. The range of responsibilities multiplied to include economic and physical planning, image making, and internal security and organization. Southern cities were no longer what Richard S. Alcorn has termed "island communities."[12] Instead, as David R. Goldfield asserts, they were becoming increasingly part of an integrated urban network. Devoid of British influence, states and cities had to fend for themselves. The leadership was still mercantile, but the tie to the farm was less apparent as urban entrepreneurs embarked on a series of programs and publicity campaigns to bring their communities into equal competition with cities throughout the new nation.

Organization and association were essential to antebellum southern urban leadership. Leaders used associational activity to streamline marketing procedures, provide a clearing house for information, serve as a convenient mechanism to city-building projects from railroads to hotels, and to inaugurate necessary services. Organizations from the city council to the commodity exchanges became mercantile clubs designed to promote the wealth of the leaders and their city. The planter-merchant of Charleston—a part-time urbanite—bowed before the aggressive middle class merchants of Richmond, New Orleans, and Memphis.

Perhaps the most significant accomplishment of the antebellum southern leader was the development of an urban consciousness. In a section where the planter aristocracy was the ideal, the evolution of the city as a distinct entity—both intellectually and physically—was a result of the associational activity of the civic booster. Most of all, urban consciousness illuminated the possibilities of the southern city as a cultural center, a repository of capital and expertise, and ultimately of "civilization." These attributes formed the basis of the New South's infatuation with the section's cities.

Finally, the southern urban elite, by 1860, ended the insularity of their cities' existence. Although there was no formal dialogue between southern and northern urban leaders, there was an informal exchange of ideas through commercial periodicals, newspapers, and personal correspondence. Imitation and adaptation of northern urban programs came almost matter-of-factly. Civic leaders dreamed of molding their city into another New York or London. Southern urban leaders were the reformers of their region; they sought to bring the South to economic and political parity with the North through an aggressive reordering of sectional priorities.[13] The plantation might be attractive for quiet repose, but city streets held the keys to the kingdom of wealth and power.

In the New South the urban booster became the oracle of the region. The suppression of racial unrest became a particular goal as urban leaders sought to clothe their cities in attractive raiments to lure northern capital. Booker T. Washington's Atlanta Compromise was the appropriate, businesslike approach to race relations. Atlanta, which literally rose from the ashes of defeat, became the focal point for New South rhetoric as Henry W. Grady disseminated his sermons on progress throughout the region from the pulpit of the *Atlanta Constitution*. The broad emphasis on growth and order and the specific program of railroad building, industry, and commerce remained unchanged from the antebellum period. The only difference was in intensity and scope. Urban leaders, with a national outlook, eagerly courted northern capital, expertise, and approval. By the beginning of the twentieth century, however, it became evident that southern urban leadership had accomplished considerable gains for northern urbanization, but had done little beyond cosmetic rehabilitation for their own section. The leadership in several cities began to stop running with and to the North, and concentrated on building a more solid foundation for growth at home.

The leadership in southern cities remained predominantly commercial, though the elite included a wider spectrum of middle class residents like professionals, real estate agents, and insurance brokers. The interlocking directorate which characterized the antebellum elite was less apparent in this broad middle class amalgam. The Crump machine in Memphis and the Old Regulars in New Orleans deviated from this pattern, emphasizing again the diversity of southern cities. Their programs, however, showed the same concern for developing the central business district and boosting their city's prospects to fellow citizens, prospective investors, rivals, and just about anyone who would listen. Finally, the emphasis on associational activity as the medium for city-building schemes achieved a similar prominence in the early twentieth-century urban South. In some Deep South cities in the 1920s, the Ku Klux Klan became just another civic organization for channeling the rhetoric of urban boosterism into concrete programs like prohibition and middle class morality.

City government, which struggled for identity and financial respectability in the nineteenth century, emerged as a powerful tool in the hands of the commercial-civic elite of the twentieth century, as Brownell's essay in this volume indicates. Local government with its business leadership became the vanguard for expansion of area, efficiency, and public services. To paraphrase Calvin Coolidge, the business of government was business. Image was important, and such services as education, police, and fire protection became associated with progressive cities across the nation. Access to downtown was also an important priority for civic leaders as the automobile clogged major thoroughfares.

The urban leadership, in addition to developing public services, sought to mold the minds of its constituents. Freud and amateur psychology were national fads, and it was natural for southern leaders to apply the psychological gospel to weld public opinion. Unity was important for a city's image, and slackers were unpatriotic if not downright irreverent. As one Atlanta businessman reminded citizens: "The devil was an angel in heaven until he began knocking his own town."[14]

If the Depression represented a fall from grace of sorts, the commercial-civic elite quickly readjusted its focus to remain the architect of urban growth. Just as the leadership formed partnerships with northern capital following the Civil War, boosters scrambled to Washington to secure the federal dollar and form a partnership with the government. Washington provided the money which southern cities needed to stabilize their sagging economies. Since local leaders typically controlled the allocation of such funds, civic boosters learned to live with the federal presence.

As government became centralized in Washington, urban leadership in the South, and elsewhere, began to concentrate at City Hall—and, more specifically, in the mayor's office. Running a city could no longer be accomplished through the chamber of commerce, even if its precepts remained inviolate. The accession of welfare activities, planning and zoning functions, and the attraction of large-scale commercial and industrial wealth were handled most effectively by local government officials and agencies. Moreover, these officials came to symbolize a city. Ivan Allen was Atlanta and "Chep" Morrison was New Orleans.

The cooperative spirit between federal and local leaders was shattered by the racial unrest of the late fifties and early sixties. Urban boosters found it difficult at times to maintain racial equilibrium while state administrations and campaigns resurrected the rhetoric of the antebellum fire eaters. Leaders like Allen in Atlanta and later George Seibels in Birmingham worked diligently to repair the damaged urban image and begin an era of meaningful cooperation with the black community as partners rather than as adversaries.

As if to demonstrate the new confidence in the future of the urban South to the rest of the nation, urban leaders oversaw an architectural renaissance of significant proportions. Just as the Chicago School and the Burnham Plan reflected the dynamism of Chicago, and the Empire State Building emphasized the progressive outlook of New York, southern urban boosters sought to display the soul of their cities in concrete, glass, and steel. Atlanta became the epitome of architectural boosterism. A new airport, civic center, and Peachtree Center—an effort at downtown redevelopment—have become symbols of Atlanta's progressivism. John Portman's Regency-Hyatt House has become the symbol of symbols with futuristic elevators, a dangling cocktail lounge, and a revolving dome which affords resident and visitor alike an excellent vantage from which to see what civic boosters have wrought. Other cities have become engrossed in civic centers, luxury hotels, and in the case of New Orleans, a domed stadium. Whatever the architectural merits or social morality of such dedication to the physical city, the philosophy behind such programs is the same today as it was in the nineteenth century. What benefits business, benefits the entire community.

THE URBAN SOUTH IN A NATIONAL ECONOMY

Southern cities have always been parts of the national economy. Even geographi-cally isolated trading towns related to a larger economic theater, and major southern seaports had leading roles since the eighteenth century. The economic story of the urban South, from the beginnings of colonial settlement to the third quarter of the twentieth century, is one of transformation—from dependence on a distant metropolis to a situation approaching parity.

Southern cities in the colonial period were basically creatures of British mercan-tilism. Their markets were defined by trade laws emanating from London, and their very existence was in part the result of British colonial designs. In a "typical" colonial economy, southern cities functioned as market centers for agricultural products destined for final processing in the mother metropolis. The close inter-dependence with agriculture became a characteristic feature of southern urban growth. This was especially true of the small tobacco towns of the eighteenth cen-tury which traded directly with London and Liverpool. A growing number of interior towns, rising in response to the settlement of the backcountry and to de-mands for diversified commercial crops (especially grains), traded with ports along the Atlantic coast rather than with cities in the mother country. But these internal patterns of commerce were still tied indirectly to the exigencies of a colonial economic framework.

As Earle and Hoffman demonstrate, the South's urban configuration in the seventeenth and eighteenth centuries was heavily influenced by economic factors. The decentralized economic activity encouraged by the topography of the Chesapeake region, the prevalence of nonpropertied indentured servants and capital-absorbing African slaves, and the importance of the tobacco trade—which required few urban intermediaries—all tended to discourage the rise of major com-mercial centers prior to the mid-eighteenth century. On the other hand, the economic consequences of immigration to the region and of rising European de-mands for commercial food crops stimulated the growth of southern towns and cities after the 1740s and presaged the urban development of the early nineteenth century.

The colonial economy also provided an indicator for future economic develop-ment in the form of access to market. Baltimore, with ready access to the wheat hinterland and, along with Norfolk, an excellent harbor from which to ply inter-coastal and West Indian trade, demonstrated the necessity of effective links to rural and to international markets. The favorable export trade of these cities as well as of other southern ports created considerable friction at the Constitutional Convention of 1787, when southern states attempted to include a provision requiring a two-thirds majority in both houses of Congress to enact commercial laws. Failing in their attempt to procure this feature, southern delegates secured a prohibition of export duties and a requirement that a two-thirds vote of the Senate was necessary to ratify treaties. Thus, early in the nation's history southern commercial interests feared the potential power of the federal government in dominating a national economy.[15]

Southern cities remained export-oriented in the nineteenth century, but also concentrated on developing internal markets. During this period a trend toward intraregional economic differentiation, initiated in the colonial era, achieved fruition. The lower South became dominated by a cotton economy, while cereals and tobacco characterized the development of the upper South. Cities in the region took on the characteristics of their hinterland as processing reflected the dominance of either cotton, wheat, or tobacco. Further, capital-intensive operations such as cotton plantations probably monopolized available investment capital to a greater extent than did the cultivation patterns in the upper South. Although industrial development occurred in Augusta, cities like Richmond, Louisville, and Baltimore established processing industries with greater facility. Finally, the predominance of commercial agriculture throughout the region triggered fierce intraregional competition as upper South cities attempted to secure the cotton trade as well as their own tobacco and grain hinterlands, and lower South cities planned similar forays into the upper South.

Internal transportation links became crucial in the antebellum period. Canal booms gave way to railroad construction in the constant effort to draw commerce one way or another. Though southern cities increasingly dominated their hinterlands, and some cities like New Orleans stood astride major international trade routes, they were still in a position of economic subserviency to a distant metropolis—in these cases, New York, Philadelphia, or Boston. As northern cities perfected marketing, financial, and shipping facilities, this dependence increased, even as southern cities were enjoying a lucrative reciprocal trade with the countryside. Ironically, the more extensive the transportation links and the volume of trade, the greater the dependence on northern industry and financial concerns.

A recent study by Allan R. Pred confirms the commercial predominance of the major northeastern cities between 1790 and 1840, and reveals the pronounced immaturity of the southern urban system. Larger southern centers, located generally along the regional periphery, maintained greater trade and communication with New York and other nonregional cities than they did with each other. New Orleans and Charleston, for example, both dealt extensively with New York, and to a far lesser degree with one another or with nearby cities like Mobile and Savannah. Judged by communications and trade patterns, New York was far and away the dominant American metropolis, and interurban communication and economic ties were quite weak in the South.[16]

By 1860 the regional economy was locked into a national economy whose trade patterns proceeded from the West and the South to the Northeast. Southern industry was primarily devoted to agricultural processing, and the absence of heavy manufacturing in the region (outside of a few places like Richmond) became all too apparent during the Civil War. The South's efforts at economic self-sufficiency were doomed to failure.

The urban South's subservient position in the national economy was an important issue in the secession debates. The Republican Party seemed intent on bestowing the benefits of the national economy on northern cities in the form of high protective tariffs, a transcontinental railroad, and federal funding of local projects. If the new administration pursued these policies, then southern cities, the section's economy, and slavery appeared headed for ruination. On the other hand, numerous urban leaders believed a withdrawal from the national economy would be both futile and fatal to southern economic interests.

Members of this latter group became the spokesmen for a new economic reconciliation with the North following the Civil War. Some historians have averred that the northern victory symbolized the triumph of northern capitalism. If that is so, southern cities were quick to see the implications of the war's outcome. With Richard Hathaway Edmonds generating statistics in Baltimore and Henry W. Grady spinning rhetoric in Atlanta, the New South spokesmen concocted a massive economic regeneration program predicated on northern financial and technical assistance.[17]

Despite the claims of self-sufficiency and industrial prowess advanced by spokesmen for the New South in the late nineteenth century, southern dependence on northern capital, expertise, and markets actually increased in the post-Civil War years. The region remained in what has been described as a colonial relationship to the major industrial centers of the Northeast and the Midwest, even though patterns of interurban trade and communication were expanded during the period and an active, self-conscious urban-commercial elite began to emerge.

The railroad again was the catalyst that implanted the national economy in the South. National railroad systems developed, penetrating the South. Intraregional competition became even more muted as the South participated as a unified region in the national economy. The railroad-building efforts of the 1880s revived urban growth, but solidified the commercial base of the urban South's economy. The urban South's remarkable recovery after the Civil War only allowed it to maintain its dependent relationship with the North without falling further behind.

By 1900 the urban network which had forged regional economies, and cemented the national economy, was becoming overshadowed by a new nationalizing force on the American economic scene—the corporation—and by the technological and institutional innovations that made it possible. The slow ascent of the South toward parity in the national economy in the twentieth century has been synonymous with the rise of the corporation. From the acquisition of the Tennessee Coal and Iron Company by United States Steel in 1907 to the removal of the textile industry from New England to the southern Piedmont and the increasing proliferation of national corporate headquarters and branch offices in southern cities after mid-century, the South's economy expanded and became more integrated with that of the nation as a whole. Indications are that the southern urban system grew more stable, organized, and mature between the turn of the century and 1940.

Even after the industrial "takeoff" in the region beginning in the 1920s, however, the southern economy was never devoted primarily to manufacturing. And those industries which did exist were often in areas of raw materials processing or light manufacturing which employed relatively unskilled labor and paid low industrial wages. Agriculture and commerce predominated, and before southern cities could replicate the industrial experience of their northern brethren, the nation entered upon the postindustrial age. Rising federal expenditures after 1932 (especially defense appropriations), the increase in air travel and interstate highway construction, the decentralization of the national economy, and the growth of new sophisticated industries (such as electronics and computers), led to a southern urban economy that was service-oriented, expansionist, and more capable of generating internal sources of capital. While southern cities still function as marketing and processing centers, they are increasingly financial hubs and homes of major industries, utilities, and service corporations like hotels and hospitals.

Recent statistics indicate that the southern economy of the 1970s remains relatively dependent on outside sources of capital, and the region still lags behind the rest of the country in per capita income levels and industrial production. Nevertheless, large urban-based agribusiness corporations have increasingly dominated in some areas of crop production, especially peanuts and soybeans.

But the consequences of these changes are not altogether clear. The modern communications network has penetrated virtually every nook and corner of the countryside, bringing larger doses of urban influence and generating higher levels of consumer demand. And the rising expectations which have resulted from economic improvements are beginning to clash with persistent inequities of the economic system. Certainly, it is difficult to imagine how the southern quest for prosperity, centered in cities, can succeed without a significant narrowing of the gap between rich and poor that has shaped most of southern society from the beginning.

RACE RELATIONS IN THE URBAN SOUTH

The relationship between black and white has formed one of the major themes—if not *the* major theme—of southern history. The presence of large numbers of blacks in the region has provoked an interminable debate over their condition, status, and influence. The recent quantitative epic on slavery produced by William Fogel and Stanley Engerman indicates the tenacity with which this subject seems to dominate American historiography. The more heated the historiographical crossfire, the less clear the answers to what Swedish sociologist Gunnar Myrdal termed the "American dilemma."[18]

Southern cities have not generally been the context for the debate over race. Historians have invariably placed the black man in a rural setting, and when they have moved blacks to the city it has usually been in a northern latitude. W. E. B. Du Bois pioneered the study of northern urban blacks, and focused some attention on Atlanta.[19] Richard C. Wade's admirable examination of slavery in southern cities was a piece more about an institution than about the individuals within it, and there is increasing reason to doubt his central conclusion that the southern urbanization process was inimical to slavery.[20] Fogel and Engerman have added little to the understanding of urban slavery except a few misconceptions, which Herbert G. Gutman has recently pointed out.[21] But John W. Blassingame's study on blacks in post–Civil War New Orleans is enlightening, and Zane L. Miller's work promises to be perhaps the best interpretive and comparative study of urban blacks in the South. Both Blassingame and Miller portray blacks not simply as victims manipulated by a racist society, but rather as active participants in the struggle to preserve their culture and determine their own destiny in extremely difficult circumstances.[22]

The southern city has, historically, been attractive to blacks. In the colonial and antebellum periods the city provided a refuge for fugitive slaves with its narrow streets and back alleys. The labor requirements of the cities always seemed to outstrip supply. The result was a flexibility in slavery and a limited opportunity for upward mobility among free blacks. Since there were relatively few immigrants to challenge black labor in certain trades, and since the maze of legislation designed to control slave and free black alike was adhered to haphazardly, the urban black—slave or free—faced a more flexible situation in the city than in the countryside. The antebellum city proved to be an effective preparatory school for black leadership after the Civil War.[23]

The status of urban blacks varied, of course, with their number and with the region. The so-called free people of color of lower South cities, for example, enjoyed more wealth and upward mobility than their brethren in the upper South. The light-skinned free blacks of New Orleans and Mobile especially enjoyed a modicum of status in their urban environments. The different origins and different circumstances of manumission of these lower South blacks accounted in great part for their advantage over free blacks in upper South cities. With emancipation, the free people of color lost their particular niche in Deep South urban society as freedmen crowded the cities and sparked a reaction among whites to submerge all blacks regardless of color or pre-Civil War status.

The influx of freedmen into southern cities following the war became the first phase of the Great Migration. Southern cities proved effective staging areas for young blacks on their way to better jobs and more freedom in the urban North. Despite segregation, periodic harassment, and official indifference with regard to social and public services—all legacies of the antebellum era—the southern city provided blacks with considerably more options than the impoverished and often hostile countryside. By the turn of the century a black bourgeoisie had appeared, catering to a predominantly black clientele. Although segregation was confining and often galling, it did allow urban blacks to develop their own institutions and businesses relatively free from white dominance.

Some blacks attained considerable wealth under this arrangement long before black economic power became a national battlecry. John Merrick, C. C. Spaulding, and Dr. A. M. Moore built the North Carolina Mutual Life Insurance Company into a major black business enterprise in the early twentieth century, and Dr. A. G. Gaston of Birmingham constructed a mid-century business empire encompassing everything from a funeral parlor to a radio station.[24] Such men, though, were exceptions. The extent to which the social class structure and segregation patterns in southern cities resembled conditions in the urban North is still undetermined. The rigidly segregated public schools and facilities in the urban South doubtless retarded the development of numerous promising blacks, but whether this differed ultimately from the more subtle and insidious pattern of discrimination in the North is difficult to assess.

The segregated city was particularly attractive to the commercial-civic elite.

The urban booster placed a high premium on law and order in developing a positive image and an attractive climate for investment. Segregation was an effective method of ordering the city, and the few blacks who achieved success were testimonials to the booster ethic. When blacks began to challenge the traditional racial demarcations in the 1950s, it was not merely a question of sitting in the front of the bus, it was an attack on the very fabric of southern urban life.

Martin Luther King, Jr., emerged as the leader of the challenge to southern urban racial mores. Though some have depicted Dr. King's movement as appealing to rural blacks, the Southern Christian Leadership Conference has distinctly urban origins. Atlanta's Ebenezer Baptist Church gave King his first pulpit, and Montgomery, Alabama, his national audience. When racial confrontation became racial violence in the early 1960s, it appeared as if the southern city would become perpetually etched in the American consciousness as a repressive and backward environment. The commercial-civic elite recoiled from the logical conclusion of massive resistance and cattle prods. The image makers, anxious for tourism, conventions, and investments, began to realize that antediluvian race relations were harmful to economic progress. Atlanta—the city "too busy to hate"—escaped racial unrest and advanced rapidly. Accommodation became the watchword for a new urban racial policy.

The southern city remains the most promising environment for southern blacks. The growing political clout of blacks is evident throughout the region. Atlanta's Mayor Maynard Jackson exemplifies the new black leadership emerging in the cities. Perhaps even more indicative of racial harmony, the United States Bureau of the Census reported recently that, for the first time, as many blacks are moving back to the South as are leaving it. The reasons for this reverse migration are complex, but it is sufficient to observe that such a movement would have been incomprehensible a decade ago. Finally, since the late 1960s, while southern cities have been working toward racial stability, it has become evident that cities elsewhere harbored black populations that felt as oppressed as Dr. King's followers. Worse still, apparently, conditions have not improved in the Newarks, Detroits, and Los Angeleses following the civil disturbances. In Boston, the cradle of abolitionism, the agonies over busing underscore the national scope of our racial problems.

The urban South should not, however, bask in the reflections of troubled cities in the North and West. Though southern cities have eradicated the worst aspects of a segregated society, they have not attained a racial Valhalla by any means. Chandler Davidson's study of biracial politics in the contemporary urban South challenges the view that black political participation has improved the living and working conditions of blacks. Davidson sees a new populist coalition of poor blacks and whites as the only solution to the political weakness of southern urban minorities.[25] The primacy of race as a factor of southern life—in the cities and in the countryside—seems to preclude a coalition based on class for the time being. Whites are still fleeing to the suburbs, and an undercurrent of racism still appears when black candidates seek city-wide offices. Of course, this situation is no different from what has been occurring in northern cities. Sometimes it is difficult to tell whether the South is becoming more like the North or vice versa. But cities paralyzed by a declining tax base and rising demands for social services are in dire trouble whatever their regional location.

The essays depict the brutality of the southern urban racial structure, especially in the twentieth century. Perhaps the most impressive feature of the black presence in the southern city, however, is not the harshness of white supremacy, but rather the resilience and perseverance of blacks. Both races have rubbed shoulders on southern city streets for centuries, and it would not be surprising if the urban South set the example for racial equilibrium. Measuring by the rigid segregation they encountered prior to the 1960s, southern blacks can more easily perceive significant progress in their drive for equal rights and opportunity than perhaps can their northern brethren. A new generation of white southerners regards integration as a perfectly logical fact of life, and those whites who once resisted racial change have come to accept its inevitability. As one Ku Klux Klansman sighed to Robert Coles: "Well, I pretty well have given up thinking we'll be able to stop it; I think we're headed that way, to a big, mixed population, you could put it, of all the races and nations. And here in the South it won't be the same, not any longer."[26]

THE PROSPECT OF SOUTHERN URBAN HISTORY

Southern urban history enters the field at a time of turmoil. The rapid growth of urban history, its eclectic approach to historical study, and the implementation of new methodologies have added to our understanding of the urban process while at the same time generating confusion and frustration. The specialized studies that have dissected every New England hamlet provide us with some fine examples of the application of new sources and methods, but with little feel for urban growth as a universal process. Little wonder that Eric Lampard called urban history "local history," or that Eric Hobsbawm depicted the field as "a large container with ill-defined, heterogeneous, and sometimes indiscriminate contents."[27]

The essays presented here, hopefully, do not fall into the localism excoriated by Lampard and Hobsbawm. Rather, they follow the dictum of British urban historian Lynn H. Lees that "we should produce fewer studies of whole cities and more analyses of the process of urban development."[28] While the penultimate model of urbanization does not emerge from these essays—if indeed it ever will—the authors attempt to place their periods of urban growth within a coherent framework. Further, the essays are careful to illustrate the regional, national, and at times international linkages involved in urban development. Finally, the comparative approach, both intra- and inter-regionally, enables the reader to assess southern urbanization beyond the particularistic context of a single city. The authors focus specifically on selected cities to provide detail; but the emphasis is on the broader framework which will hopefully provide guidance for future specialized studies.

One of the most difficult and fundamental questions to confront the authors, and other urban historians as well, has been the question of what is a city. Most scholars have discarded the facile census definition—any community above 2500 people—for a more sophisticated measure. Numerical thresholds explain little about a settlement, and historians, following their brethren in the other social sciences, have attempted to isolate characteristics of cityhood and to erect models to fit into particular eras. The extent and type of communications network, the degree of functional segregation, the presence of an organized commercial-civic elite, the existence of an urban consciousness, and the extent of "urbanity" (as measured by the number of service and marketing establishments in the central place), have all signified "city" to various writers.[29]

The essays emphasize the characteristics of cityhood rather than the sheer numerical status of respective settlements. Since models are always incomplete and constantly adding variables, these are hardly neat definitions of what is a city. This is no doubt appropriate since researchers have yet to discover a neat city. Even St. Thomas More's Utopia had problems. Flexibility is necessary because cities themselves are so diverse. Few would hesitate to call both Mobile and New York "urban," yet there are obviously vast differences which emphasize the inadequacy of utilizing population statistics to determine cityhood.

The singularity of cities presents additional problems for the student of southern history. In addition to isolating the facets of cityhood, the researcher must discern the characteristics of "southernness." The diversity of the region compounds the problem. Is Baltimore, for example, a southern city? Maryland, in the colonial period, shared a similar economy with Virginia, but, then again, Baltimore's growth was much more dependent on wheat than on tobacco. In the antebellum era Baltimore was a slave city, but the Baltimore and Ohio Railroad established a market that was predominantly northern. With slavery gone in the New South era, there was little to distinguish the city as "southern," if such a distinction could be made; yet, on the other hand, Richard Hathaway Edmonds published one of the New South's leading oracles, the *Manufacturers' Record,* in Baltimore.

A recent study of cities in 1890 attempted to classify American cities by region. The researchers employed three broad criteria—economic, geographic, and the direction of transportation and communications networks. More than sixty variables, obtained from sources such as the Comptroller of the Treasury, the Post Office Department, the Patent Office, and the Bureau of the Census were related to the three major categories. Despite the large data base, the researchers discovered that "some cities could not be placed into any region." They concluded that certain cities, including Baltimore and St. Louis, were actually "regional integrators," whose function was to connect the various regions into the national economy.[30]

The essayists did not find it satisfactory to assign these connector cities to a regional limbo and, therefore, usually included Baltimore in their discussions and omitted St. Louis. Such decisions result primarily from intuition and the regional role of the city in a particular period. Since even a fairly sophisticated model could not unscramble some regional affiliations, such imprecision is understandable. Moreover, it is peripheral to the major arguments of the essays. The decision to include or to exclude particular cities in the region affects primarily the population count. The focus on urban characteristics rather than on numbers alleviates the necessity to define the regional boundaries sharply. If the essential features of urbanization for a particular era are present in cities whose regional affiliation is unquestioned (i.e., Charleston, Richmond, Birmingham, or New Orleans), then the choice of peripheral cities has less relevance.

If all of this seems evasive, it is so because urban history, especially southern urban history, is still groping through methodologies and basic questions. To set parameters at this stage of historical scholarship would be premature. The pioneering work of urban histories of other regions and the special character of the South itself provide useful guidelines for future research. Some of the most effective analyses in urban historical literature have come from borrowing techniques that have been staples of other social science disciplines. Geographers offer a number of methods and theories that urban historians have found useful. Knowing the spatial configuration of a city can offer insights into the urban economy and social interaction. Allan R. Pred constructed a model for the growth of commercial cities in nineteenth-century America by analyzing the geographic location of businesses and residences, as well as depicting journey-to-work patterns—an altogether common research device of geographers.[31] Seymour J. Mandelbaum employed a spatial model for New York City in his imaginative study of the roots of Boss William Marcy Tweed's political power.[32] Finally, by employing such basic geographic-quantitative tools as the index of dissimilarity and the location quotient to determine the degree of social class segregation in early Baltimore, Richard M. Bernard has elicited a detailed picture of class structure in a developing commercial city.[33]

The application of geography to urban history has enabled historians to explore and employ little-used but nonetheless valuable sources. City directories, though limited in scope, have proved useful in social and geographic mobility studies, as well as in arranging the city by occupation categories and business locations. A major index of the movement from the colonial-commercial city to the modern metropolis has been the separation of work and residence and the attendant segregation by function. Manuscript censuses—federal, state, and local surveys—reveal a considerable amount of information about the composition of cities in the nineteenth century. Even the less specific printed census volumes of the twentieth century can be effective in charting the spatial expansion of cities, suburbanization, and the process of urban deterioration.

Municipal records are perhaps the most valuable of the recent sources. Once again the geographer's concern with space and land use becomes helpful for the historian. Sam Bass Warner, Jr., exhumed building permits as a major source for his study of the suburbanization of Boston in the streetcar era.[34] A recent survey of District of Columbia building permits from 1877 to 1949 revealed information on applications for new construction, repairs to existing buildings, elevators, signs, finances, and steam boilers. Further, the permits included the name of the property owner, the size of the lot, and the cost of construction. Research topics emanating from this single source can include neighborhood development, urban expansion, architectural changes, and varying standards of living.[35]

These sources and techniques have not, generally, been applied to historical studies of the urban South. Since the essays in this book allege a degree of commonality between southern cities and those elsewhere, studies employing the methodologies and sources of geography and other fields must be completed before the authors' conclusions based on more conventional research can be sustained. The new sources and techniques, moreover, point to an array of questions that must be answered before urban development in the South is understood by itself and in relation to other regions:

1. Has the process of assimilation and acculturation of immigrants differed in southern cities? If so, is it a function of timing, size (both of the immigrant group and of the city), race, or urban economic patterns? How did the process apply, for example, to foreign born immigrants and to those native urban newcomers who hailed from the rural South?

2. Has the composition and function of the family differed in southern cities, compared with northern urban areas? Historians, in emphasizing the unique features of southern civilization, cite the strong kinship ties in the region. What about the cities? Did they tend to reinforce or undermine these patterns? If the family functions "as an active agent in facilitating migration and adjustment to new living conditions," as Tamara K. Hareven has suggested,[36] can this family model be applied in the urban South?

3. As a value giver, the church probably stands alongside the family in importance, especially in the South. Studies have demonstrated the role of Protestant sects in northern cities in setting social welfare goals and in facilitating or obstructing immigrant assimilation during the late nineteenth and early twentieth centuries.[37] In southern cities, where Protestant denominations were and are stronger, what was their role in the urbanization process and how did it compare with that of similar groups in nonregional cities, or in New Orleans and Mobile, which had significant Roman Catholic influence? Further, how did religious institutions promote or impede the acculturation of rural blacks in the urban South, and was their role similar to that in northern black communities?

4. Geographers have outlined various stages of urban growth: expansion of downtown, segregation of function, expansion of the city with transportation technology, replication of goods and services in the suburbs, and redevelopment or deterioration of the central city.[38] Although this basic model has several variations, it has been successful in predicting suburbanization. The growth of suburbs, of course, deserves study in its own right, but its impact on cities has been significant. Historians such as Sam Bass Warner, Jr., and Kenneth T. Jackson have demonstrated the close, yet often estranged, relationship between city and suburb.[39] Race and the pastoral ideal have been two major forces generating suburban growth and urban decline. In a section where both themes have assumed the proportions of legacies, the study of city-suburb development patterns and relationships would provide further insight into regional characteristics and the comparability of southern suburbanization. Among other things, we need to examine the structures of individual southern cities in much greater detail to ascertain whether differences among cities are functions of regional location or of coincidences between existing conditions and technological possibilities.[40]

5. The recent emphasis by the new urban historians on patterns of social and geographic mobility should obviously involve the urban South as well as cities in other parts of the country. Actually, the work of Richard J. Hopkins on Atlanta

is among the best examples of the genre.[41] This approach not only exploits previously neglected sources, but provides one of the best possibilities for comparability. It may be hoped that future studies along this line will not attempt simply to duplicate those done elsewhere but will go beyond them—especially in the direction of relating mobility patterns to the dynamics of the larger urban social system.

6. The essays demonstrate that an expanding agricultural base was an essential ingredient for southern urban growth at least through the nineteenth century. What impact, in turn, did the expanding city have upon the farm? Robert P. Swierenga has asserted that rural and urban history are really two sides of the same scholarly coin, and Michael P. Conzen has examined the influence of developing Madison, Wisconsin, on the surrounding countryside.[42] With judicious use of the census and geographical aids such as plats and maps, Conzen has demonstrated the symbiotic relationship between city and country. In the South, where agriculture has not been merely a livelihood but an article of faith from John Taylor of Caroline to the Nashville Agrarians, such urban-rural connections warrant exploration in discerning whether southern cities had similar or diverse impacts on the hinterland when compared with cities in other regions. Perhaps analyses of the urban system in the South, and its relationships with the regional economy, would be one of the best approaches to this subject.

These few topics by no means exhaust the possibilities for future research, but they are among those of greatest current interest to historians. The answers to these questions have far-reaching implications for the study of southern history that transcend the contribution to urban history. Since the South has traditionally been depicted as a self-conscious region, the study of cities can aid in the ongoing debate concerning the identity of the South. But the essays include much information that points to the similarity of urban experience throughout the country. The authors, however, were constrained to discuss only the broad features of urban development in the region and point the way to future research opportunities. Comparative studies employing the sources and techniques noted earlier may reveal patterns of significant deviation from the national urban norm. Since urban history, as political historian Richard P. McCormick has observed, lends itself well to comparative analysis, future studies should employ the comparative method and take care to place the city in a regional, if not a national, context.[43]

2

CARVILLE EARLE
RONALD HOFFMAN

THE URBAN SOUTH:
THE FIRST TWO CENTURIES

Does the study of urbanization require the presence of urban communities? Or more specifically, can an urban history be written of an area that is townless? If the answer seems obvious, the seventeenth-century American South would appear to be a region inappropriate for perturbations on the subject of urbanization. Robert Beverley's remark about Virginia composed in 1704 applied, with the peculiar exception of Charleston, to the entire span of territory encompassed by Chesapeake Bay and the Savannah River. The people of Virginia, recorded Beverely, "have not any place of cohabitation among them that may reasonably bear the name of a town." And yet—and this is crucial—despite its gossamer texture, the urban history of the early South constitutes one of the most advantageous foci for exploring the region's commercial and social history. Indeed, it may be the unsurpassed perspective for meshing the South's multifaceted character.

The English had not thought it would turn out the way it did. Nor for that matter did anyone else. As the commercial and governing elites of the sixteenth- and seventeenth-century European states studied what passed for cartographic expressions of the North American continent, they thought primarily in terms of imperial control. There, locked within a vast zone whose dimensions were obscurely perceived, lay the future control of the Atlantic world. So believed the English, French, Spanish, Dutch, and Portuguese. Accepting this judgment as absolute, they correspondingly confronted a common problem—how could they effectively establish a position of dominance? And more precisely, what method of colonial settlement would best assure a posture of future commercial hegemony? Each of the competing national groups developed an array of solutions, but all of them uniformly stressed the roles to be performed by urban communities. The mercantilist Englishman's devotion to the strategic importance of urbanization found its most figurative expression in the oft repeated injunction to "plant in towns."

From the very beginning of overseas colonization, the English sponsors of the various settlement projects urged their people to locate in compact communities.

Survival could only be achieved, they advised, if the colonists established a system of towns and villages connected by a series of roads and, in the South, the extensive riverine system.[1] The consensus of opinion on this issue was clear, whether the instructions were issued by the founders in New England, the directors of the Virginia Company, or the proprietors in New York, the Jerseys, Pennsylvania, Maryland, and the Carolinas. Up to the 1650s instructions on these matters were generally buried within a range of directives, probably because the English simply assumed that towns would automatically develop. But by mid-century, with the failure of concentrated settlement evident in the Chesapeake, the English authorities became much more explicit in their orders for town planning. "You and your council," the proprietors of South Carolina told their first colonists in the late 1660s, "are to choose some fitting place whereon to build a fort under the protection of which is to be your first town . . . you are to order the people to plant in towns."[2] In Carolina the proprietors directed all who wished to settle that they must reside in towns. Indeed, so impressed were they with the commercial vitality created by towns that they even encouraged the Indians they traded with to reside in settled communities.[3] The idea remained deeply embedded in the English mind throughout the colonial period long after a system of decentralized trade had developed and prospered in regions devoid of towns. Life could not go on without towns, the English believed, and yet almost mystically life did, though how, the English could not really imagine.

The English commitment to urban life sprang from more than an exclusively commercial rationale: it derived from the basic culture of English life, and because of this they could not comprehend what they saw in some of the North American colonies. The English simply could not conceive of life, whether commercial or social, existing without towns. Even more basically, they could not conceive of civilization, as the word "urbane" implies, without towns. Certainly, this belief activated the minds of the Carolina proprietors who wrote to some prospective settlers in the 1660s: ". . . we must assure you that it is your and our concern very much to have some good towns in your plantations for otherwise you will not long continue civilized or secure, there being no place in the world either of these without them."[4] These men feared that cultural regression was a likely possibility in the New World. In fact, they already believed that a societal transformation had occurred in Maryland and Virginia where a form of barbarism had rooted, an inevitable consequence, they reasoned, because of the absence of towns. They recognized that some commercial growth had occurred in the Chesapeake, but they felt it to be of limited and transitory importance. True and enduring prosperity, they maintained, had only been established in New England, where men lived in compact towns and villages, which multiplied annually.[5]

The tenacity with which the English held their convictions about urban life developed largely because of a complex of cultural and commercial factors internal to seventeenth century England. During this period the English elite became convinced that urban life was a necessary but enormously complex process which demanded serious planning to be successful. From 1500 to 1700 a number of confusing and contradictory developments took place among the English cities. Generally, the older towns declined in wealth, though they increased in social and cultural importance, while the newer towns, particularly in the seventeenth century, underwent considerable economic and demographic expansion. By the century's end, perhaps three of every ten Englishmen lived in towns of more than one hundred houses, and of these urban dwellers one-third lived in London. Growing almost uncontrollably, London had become a phenomenon that frightened and fascinated those who watched it. Amidst all this constant change one characteristic appeared most important to English observers. For the old towns that endured and the new towns that rose, a definite correlation seemed to exist between urban growth and economic activity.[6] This development convinced the English that commercial and town development were inextricably connected.

The same held true for smaller communities. By the end of the sixteenth century, most Elizabethan towns contained three persons in five who sold consumer goods and services within and beyond each town's borders. To observers the prosperity of the towns and the surrounding regions depended largely on this pattern of interaction. Beyond the towns' obvious commercial assets, many of these communities were also emerging as social and cultural centers, particularly as the minor gentry made them their permanent residence. Churches, assembly meeting houses, libraries, and schools were increasingly being concentrated in these communities, and their presence demonstrated the acknowledged recognition of the towns' strategic role in the texture of regional life.[7]

But if towns were the essential purveyors of commercial prosperity and cultural enrichment, they were also very fragile entities, susceptible to a number of terrifying ills including fire, plague, and poverty. Because of these recognized liabilities there was always a subtle ambivalence beneath the English people's enthusiasm for town growth. They believed them the indispensable ingredient for commercial and civilized society, and yet they recoiled because of the many horrors associated with urban living—horrors which occurred repeatedly during the seventeenth century.

Fires were a constant danger. During a four-day period, September 2 to 6, 1666, a raging fire in London destroyed 13,200 homes and caused an estimated £10 million damage.[8] Similarly, the seventeenth century witnessed a dramatic rise in the extensiveness of urban poverty, not only in London but in the provincial towns as well, where at least two-thirds of the people led a precarious existence. During good years these people survived, but in times of bad trade or high prices they constituted a serious social menace. Whatever the economic situation, their numbers continued to increase, in part at least because of the relief programs implemented to serve them. The towns seemed to spawn poverty, but they alone were the essential institutions that could treat the problem as English authorities channeled grain supplies into them for relief distribution. Such cosmetic aid worked, but naturally the attraction of free food only caused a further swelling in the ranks of the urban poor. A concomitant result of this migration was the soaring death rate within the cities and towns. More died than were born there, but nonetheless their total population expanded. Finally, urban life to the English and especially to Puritan and utopian thinkers was graphically representative of the social decadence and corruption of the age. Their critiques of the city, though vastly different in substance, blamed urban life for many of the evils experienced by the English people. England's cities, according to these writers, were beyond redemption, and the New World held out the best hope for creating more perfect societies.

With much of this experience clearly in mind—the indispensable need for towns and yet the multitude of dangers involved—the men seeking to establish New World communities took great care in designing nucleated settlements. Some of them, holding high posts in London, were simultaneously involved in English city planning. During this building process there was much discussion about the size, shape, and proximity of structures and the kinds of materials to be used. Naturally, these discussions dramatically influenced the very detailed designs that were also being laid out for the New World.[9] William Penn summed up this thinking when he explained that he wanted a town "which will never be burn't."[10] Essentially, the plans that were developed, while differing in many particulars, envisioned communities consisting of farmers, merchants and craftsmen, with the amenities of social life, and the characteristics of England's most prosperous provincial towns.[11] Most designs called for large building sites with each house enjoying a fine orchard and garden. Then followed instructions as to how the town was to be laid out, including street design, wharf and warehouse locations and, in some cases, the actual designations of the various occupational services.

Besides physical construction the English designers also paid a good deal of attention to the occupational structure of the New World communities. The English had a clear-cut notion of the occupational requirements of urban life, and most settlement promoters recruited people with a variety of skills. From the cold of Puritan New England to the blistering heat of the Carolinas and the Caribbean, the communities reflected the occupational balance believed necessary to sustain a system of commercial agriculture. In conception, the societies planned were highly complex and specialized, particularly in the elaborate schemes of early Virginia where agriculture was to a great extent relegated to a secondary level. But after the failure of the Virginia Company in 1624, people with a wider range of abilities were recruited for the New World. Many of them possessed craft and mechanic talent of the rough sort calculated for a frontier environment. Their skills were representative of the dual occupational system that had developed in rural England centuries before. Indeed, as early as the fourteenth century farmers and farm laborers in certain hard-pressed areas were blending an additional vocation with farming. The spread of this practice, and the willingness of rural dwellers to accept lower wages than their urban contemporaries, naturally encouraged merchants to invest in rural industries, and by the latter part of the fifteenth century this investment pattern had been institutionalized.[12] Thus, the English colonists of the sixteenth and seventeenth centuries possessed an extensive and at times highly refined diversity of occupational skills which they and those who sponsored them believed could be put to good use in securing communities in the New World.

And yet the vision of America, so beguiling to the English, turned to disappointment almost immediately in Virginia. Believing that towns were the only conceivable form of settlement in the colony, the leadership of the Virginia Company in their instructions to their first colonists dealt briefly and without exhortation on the matter of towns. More than half-way through the instructions, the company revealed its implicit expectations by observing that the colonists should "take special care that you choose a seat for habitation that shall not be over bothered with woods near your town. . . ." Only the fifteenth of seventeen paragraphs dealt explicitly with town settlement. For the company and the settlers, town life was an article of faith. Colonizing Virginia required dwelling within towns, and that injunction needed no explication.[13]

The first colonists followed their instructions to the letter, and shortly the garrison settlement of Jamestown took shape. Other settlements followed, and their names—Bermuda City, Elizabeth City, and Charles City—displayed the English vision. These were to be towns in the modern sense of clustered communities of craftsmen, artisans, professionals, and merchants. Because they were not designed as farming villages, the Virginia Company persistently attempted to obtain immigrants with highly specialized and even anachronistic occupations. A recruitment broadside of 1610 proclaimed that the company sought

only such sufficient, honest and good artificers as Smiths, Shipwrights, Sturgeon-dressers, Joyners, Carpenters, Gardeners, Turners, Coopers, Salt-makers, Ironmen for Furnasse & hammer, Brickmakers, Brick-layers, Minerall-men, Gunfounders, Fishermen, Plough-wrights, Brewers, Sawyers, Fowlers, Vinedressers, Surgeons and Physitions for the body, and learned Divines to instruct the Colonies, and to teach the Infidels to Worship the true God.

For publication in this broadside the company had pared down a lengthier and more exotic list of Virginia's occupational needs, which included pearl drillers, collar makers, armorers, and tile makers. Here, then, were the makings of an idealized model of colonial society: one that was town based, and in which labor was infinitely divisible, with each task requiring performance by an occupational specialist.[14]

From the outset this urban society failed miserably in Virginia, because the design ignored the bulwark of all preindustrial societies—the production of food. Top-heavy with gentry and specialized craftsmen, English town society in the Chesapeake was scarce of farmers. On the basis of this disparity some historians have inferred that the Virginia Company planned to rely on the Indian population for its food supply. The Spanish colonies had already explored the possibilities of overlordship, and the English were well aware of Spanish colonization. The Indians, in any case, failed to comply, and Virginia's imbalanced labor supply and the agrarian incompetence of her settlers produced tragic consequences. Recurrent food shortages and the impoverished agricultural base contributed to fourteen years of starvation and living with what seemed perpetual shortages.[15] Eventually the company leadership amended its plans for an urban society in the Chesapeake.

Wee think it fitt, that the houses and buildings be so contrived together, as may make if not hansome Townes, yet compact and orderly villages; that this is the most proper, and successfull maner of proceedings in new Plantacons, besides those of former ages, the example of the Spaniards in the West Indies, doth fully instance.[16]

The Virginia experience taught that for survival on the frontier food production was essential, and therefore an extreme division of labor was inappropriate. In place of the specialized occupations that made up towns, the Virginia Company, as it neared the end of its life, recognized the efficacy of agricultural villages. Later venturers to Maryland, the Carolinas, and Pennsylvania, perhaps benefiting from Virginia's errors, made town planning a more explicit and sometimes a guiding aim in their colonial policy. But these lessons came too late in the Chesapeake. By 1617 Virginians had discovered tobacco, and the "weed" grew even in the streets of Jamestown. For the rest of the century tobacco dominated the economy of Virginia and Maryland, and largely because of this staple crop neither commercial towns nor compact agricultural villages succeeded in the Chesapeake.

Nearly a century after the establishment of Jamestown in 1607, there were no towns of any consequence in the Chesapeake colonies. At most, Virginians could point to Williamsburg, which showed some progress, or to the ports of Hampton and Norfolk near the mouth of the James River. In Maryland the colony's newly designated capital and largest town, Annapolis, contained about forty houses by the end of the seventeenth century. The niggardliness of urban achievement frustrated those royal officials and colonial legislators who had corresponded, debated, and passed numerous laws in an effort to promote town growth. General town acts passed the Virginia assembly in 1655, 1662, 1680, 1685, 1691, and 1705. The Maryland assembly followed suit in 1668, 1669, 1671, 1683, 1684, 1686, 1688, 1706, 1707, and 1708. But by 1710 practically all of these statutory towns had failed. An unprecedented era of settlement engineering had come to an end.[17]

Because the dispersed settlement pattern that emerged in the Chesapeake departed so radically from the English image, the area seriously engaged the attention of contemporaries. What they saw they of course deplored, but taken collectively their observations partially explain the urban growth, or the lack of it, in a tobacco economy. Their basic argument was that craftsmen and merchants were the indispensable ingredients for town life. If either element were seriously underrepresented, towns would not flourish. And this was exactly what had happened, or so they maintained. In the Chesapeake specialized merchants, they argued, were unnecessary since "all the planters in general affects the style of merchants because they all sell tobacco...."[18] With the bay and its tributaries virtually lapping at the door of many planters, the role of producer and trader had merged. As one writer observed, the Chesapeake consisted of "navigable river, creeks and inlets ... so convenient for exporting and importing goods into any part ... by water carriage that no country can compare with it."[19]

But more was involved here than simply geographic accessibility. The emergence of the planter-merchant occurred primarily because of the sheer simplicity of the early tobacco trade where commercial transactions were conducted in a very straightforward manner. Almost any illiterate planter could haggle over goods and tobacco with the ship captains or supercargoes. And even the more elaborate consignment trade, in which planters hoping for higher prices retained ownership of their tobacco until sold in English markets, only demanded that one be literate and of good reputation so that credit could be acquired in an English port. Tobacco marketing, during the colonial era, required few intermediaries between the plantation and the English ship. The crop was grown, processed, and packed on the plantations. After the arrival of the tobacco fleet in October and November, the average planter took his yearly output of 1,500 to 2,000 pounds of tobacco tightly packed into four or five hogsheads and rolled them to the nearest landing. So long as planters were assured that shipping would come up their river or creek between mid-fall and mid-spring, they gained nothing by transporting tobacco to town.[20]

The small volume of tobacco that could possibly be produced within any given trade area further impeded the development of centralized marketing facilities. Those few merchants who resided in the statutory towns found their trade orbit severely circumscribed by the bay's interlacing estuaries. As a result, the hinterlands available to these traders were limited to small peninsulas or necks characterized by dispersed plantations, low population densities, and modest tobacco outputs of several hundred to a thousand hogsheads—enough to support only a handful of full-time merchants.

The geographic accessibility to trade, the simplicity of tobacco processing and transactions, and the modest volume of local tobacco production—all these factors stunted merchant specialization and precluded town growth in the seventeenth century. Other elements, according to some commentators, were also involved, especially the "fewness of handicraftsmen."[21] But these writers, because of their preoccupation with urban-based craftsmen, invariably failed to take account of the many planters who combined agrarian pursuits with the rude crafts and mechanic skills required in an agricultural economy. In the Chesapeake a large number of planters had emigrated as indentured servants from the English counties of Gloucester and Kent where woodland laborers traditionally supplemented their small farm production with casual day labor in nearby rural industries. Living dispersed, self-reliant, and independent, these laborers competently performed for themselves and their neighbors a variety of needed tasks, though highly skilled abilities were possessed by only a talented few.[22] Contemporary descriptions of the woodland laborers read very much like those Frederick Jackson Turner would have composed in characterizing the first Chesapeake frontiersmen. John Aubery, a man who disliked the woodland folk, labeled them as "mean people who live lawless, nobody to govern them, they care for nobody, having no dependence on anybody."[23] Thus, handicraftsmen, like merchants—the basis of urban life—had few consumers to serve, because planters served themselves.

A few additional circumstances impeded the establishment of towns. In the early decades of the tidewater, urban goods and services were not in demand as they were in other colonies. Both Boston and Philadelphia grew enormously because of the heavy immigration of free families who required provisions, implements, and livestock during their colony's initial years. Within a decade of their founding both cities had achieved dominant positions never to be relinquished in colonial life.[24] This was not the case in the Chesapeake, where the majority of immigrants throughout the seventeenth century came either as servants or slaves, devoid of capital and credit, and therefore unable to exert an effective economic demand. Furthermore, servants, once their terms expired, were channeled toward planting and away from mercantile or craft pursuits. The cyclical boom-and-bust tobacco economy of the Chesapeake produced this effect. Since servants were a profitable short-term investment, importations regularly rose at the beginning of a boom when tobacco prices were climbing. But the influx of servants eventually drove up the supply of tobacco, and after four to eleven years of prosperity the glutted market caused the prices to fall. Frequently the boom's end coincided with the termination of the servants' indenture. These new freedmen had few viable economic alternatives. If they possessed some occupational skill, they knew earning a living with this talent would be difficult because of the light demand that prevailed during a depression. The best course was to establish a diversified plantation and ride out the bad years. Freedom dues made planting an even more logical, if not always desirable, choice. The dues granted him of fifty acres, corn, implements, and coarse clothing told the freedman exactly what society anticipated. And, at least, the transition from English laborer to Chesapeake planter had been rendered easy by the knowledge gained from four or more years of indentured service in the raising of tobacco, corn, hogs, and cattle.[25] The conditions produced by this pattern—scattered plantations and no substantial town settlement—were painfully evident and patently unacceptable to the English authorities. In their view, a dispersed and decentralized settlement system could not function effectively. Recognizing and acknowledging the contrary reality would be tantamount to denying a basic tenet of English culture. For them towns were customary, familiar, and indispensable in establishing lasting prosperity and in preserving the fabric of civilization. But in contrast to the English zeal for building towns, the resident planters accepted the prevailing diffuse system and only began to question its effectiveness when the tobacco economy failed them.

During the latter half of the seventeenth century a prolonged series of tobacco depressions resulted in conditions favorable for commercial town legislation. The crown authorities and the London tobacco merchants maintained that with the establishment of towns prosperity would return. The planter-dominated assemblies, wishing to acquire control over the marketing and distribution of tobacco in hope of higher prices, agreed and passed the necessary legislation. Actually, the British interests and the colonial assembly representatives had two different notions of how the urban systems should be structured, and most of the legislation enacted consisted of a compromise formula between the contending positions.[26] None of these measures worked, however, and after almost half a century of town acts the English officials reluctantly concluded that their efforts in behalf of concentrated settlements had failed. As Governor Francis Nicholson, who labored in both Chesapeake colonies, remarked, "People in these parts have been used to live separately," and "It is very difficult to bring them at once to cohabit, especially by restraint."[27] To Nicholson it was clear that ingrained habit had prevailed over statutory coercion. And with the return of good commercial conditions stimulated by the enormous expansion of the French tobacco market during the first decades of the eighteenth century, comprehensive town legislation became a dead letter in the Chesapeake.

The history of St. Mary's City, Maryland's first capital, points out the fragile character of the Chesapeake's early towns.[28] Shortly after the colony's initial wave of settlers landed in 1634, they constructed a fort in the vicinity of the future town site. Jerome Hawley, one of those present, described the surroundings as "a very commodious situation for a town, in general the land is good, the air wholesome and pleasant, the river affords a safe harbor for ships of any burthern...." Predictably, the settlers who were instructed to locate within a protected town soon scattered. Still, because resident proprietary officials elected to live there, the general area of St. Mary's continued to function as a government center with meetings and all other administrative services conducted in private homes.

In the late 1660s, with the colony's population expanding, the government purchased land in the area and initiated a modest building program. The first public structure, the state house, was completed in 1666. Several inns to provide food and lodging were also established. Governor Charles Calvert, in partial recognition of the town's development, granted a charter of incorporation to St. Mary's City in 1668 and 1671. While the grant theoretically created a form of self-government, it was primarily a device used by the proprietary officials further to consolidate their political power. For the next several years limited construction—a few more official buildings, some private homes, and several inns—continued within the city's designated hundred acres.

St. Mary's City, mainly a government center with little commerce passing through, was occasionally crowded, but normally it remained hardly different from its rural surrounding. It was not so much a town but rather a scattered assemblage of buildings devoted to political and administrative functions. During the 1680s, when the legislature designated it as one of the towns specified for the promotion of trade, the community expanded slightly. But the prevailing pattern of commerce in Maryland remained decentralized and continued to operate in its traditional manner notwithstanding the politicians' juridical directions. Hence, in the 1690s, when political pressures resulted in the capital's relocation in Annapolis, the town quickly expired. Most of the homes soon decayed or were destroyed, while the state house, after serving temporarily as a county seat, became an Anglican chapel. Within a few short decades the entire area had returned to farmland, its silent landscape devoid of any signs suggestive that once there had been a St. Mary's "City."

With the opening of the eighteenth century, not one significant commercial town existed in the Chesapeake region, though along the bay's shores and many tributaries there were numerous places—at stores, warehouses, planters' wharves— where marketing activity occurred. A few small settlements had made a beginning, but the only concentrated communities of any size were the capital towns. Two capitals had been established in the seventeenth century, Jamestown and St. Mary's City. Before both were abandoned in the 1690s, St. Mary's contained about thirty houses and Jamestown twice that number.[29] Their swift descent into oblivion illustrated their complete dependence on the political function. Less than three decades after the capital's removal from Jamestown, the town consisted "of nothing but abundance of brick rubbish, and three or four good inhabited houses...."[30] The new capitals of Annapolis and Williamsburg were, as yet, too young and raw to cut much of a figure. Five years after its founding, in 1694, Annapolis contained, according to one account,

forty dwelling houses, of [which] seven or eight . . . can afford good lodging and accommodation for strangers. There is also a State House and a free school built with brick which make a great show among a parcel of wooden houses, and the foundation of a church laid, the only brick church in Maryland. They have two market days in the week. . . .[31]

Williamsburg, in 1702 encompassed "besides the church, college and State House, together with the residence of the Bishop, some stores and houses of gentlemen and also eight ordinaries or inns together with the magazine."[32] Here were the Chesapeake's largest and most promising urban settlements. After them came several modest statutory towns. The more successful of these had been surveyed and contained fifty to one hundred lots of an acre each, arranged along streets that crossed at right angles. In most the lots sold slowly, and the majority, never getting off the ground, remained unnamed, unsurveyed "paper towns."[33] Still, a few of these areas, though not formally designated, were known and served as important centers for local business transactions.

In sum, within the seventeenth-century Chesapeake area those commercial, social, and cultural activities usually performed by the towns were instead conducted in a decentralized pattern. Merchants and planter-merchants conducted their trade from scattered landings along the tributaries of the bay. Churchgoers—Anglicans, Presbyterians, and Quakers, when they chose to attend services—gathered in the plantation houses of friends or in solitary churches near the centers of the various parishes. The one man in ten who called himself a carpenter, plasterer, tailor, blacksmith, or "physition" combined his skill with planting tobacco or corn. Practically all men lived on dispersed and slowly diversifying plantations. The men of the Chesapeake acknowledged that theirs was a rude, "mean" life. But barbaric it was not, for they perceived themselves to be tightly knit within what some referred to as a "good neighbourhood." The metropolis of London was but four weeks away; all other necessary commercial and social services were much closer, certainly within the radius of a day's ride on what one planter called "the goodness of our little horses." In such a context, life and economic growth flourished. That towns did not was a matter of supreme indifference to all but the Chesapeake's emerging political and business elite.[34]

What happened, or more properly what failed to happen, in the Chesapeake had a decisive impact on those who proposed to set up colonies in the Carolinas during the 1660s and 1670s. The Carolina proprietors thought they had learned well from the failures of previous colonial experiments. Recognizing that the towns would not grow of their own accord, they were determined to avoid the "chaotic" experience of Maryland and Virginia. Successful colonization, they reasoned, demanded that precise town planning become an explicit and leading part of colonization, and with this in mind they bombarded their colonists with orders and instructions. Their essential aim was to create agricultural villages which would also function as centers of commercial life. Their dual emphasis on the role of towns differed critically from the town forms proposed in the Chesapeake during the latter half of the seventeenth century, which were intended to be exclusively commercial in purpose. To insure that town life would prevail, the proprietors directed that the structure of town authority be written directly into the colony's basic organic law, John Locke's Fundamental Constitution of 1669.[35] The second version of the constitution, composed a year later, elaborated on these points in three separate and more detailed articles. Similarly, the instructions to the governors and councils and the temporary laws issued to manage the colony reiterated these guidelines.[36]

But from the beginning the proprietors encountered resistance. One of the first reports, sent from Carolina, informed them that "we can not possibly obey all your honors directions." Disliking the straitjacket designs, the settlers warned that if they were "not suffered to choose their own conveniences it may prove a great retarding of a speedy peopling this country."[37] Less than a year later the colony's acting governor, after promising to do his utmost in creating contiguous settlements, still admitted that "it is true that some of us have taken up the scent of better land and are very ready and earnest to follow the discovery."[38]

Naturally, the proprietors were provoked, particularly Lord Shaftesbury, their principal spokesman and the main force directing the Carolina settlement. Writing for his associates, Shaftesbury directed the colony's authorities to

be very punctual in observing the instructions you receive from us amongst which there is none of more consequence [to] the security and thriving of our settlement than that of planting in towns in which if men be not overruled their rashness and folly will expose the plantations to ruin.[39]

Again several months later he ordered the colonists: "You will in pursuance of our Constitution and instructions endeavor to accommodate things there to the advantage and settlement of plantation, one main point is the settling down together in towns."[40]

From the beginning the proprietors' hopes for Carolina were doomed. Because of the great variety of land within the coastal plain, the settlers understandably sought the good bottom land which frequently did not lie in contiguous tracts. Quickly the geographical character of the area resulted in a settlement pattern of widely scattered individual agricultural units. Shaftesbury and his partners vigorously attempted to arrest this trend. In 1674, when the colonists wrote asking for cattle because their early agricultural experiments had failed, the proprietors in a bitter letter focused on the colony's settlement pattern as the principal cause of failure:

In your letters you have been frequent in the mention of a stock of cattle, but not having paid us for tools and clothes, how do you think that we should be at so far a greater charge in cattle? . . . especially it being our design to have planters there and not graziers, for if our intentions were to stock Carolina at that rate, we could do better by Baylife and servants of our own, who would be more observant of our orders than you have been—plant in towns where we direct, take up no more lands than what they had use for nor by a scattered and large tracts of ground taken up not like to be planted these many years. . . .[41]

So wedded were the proprietors to this belief that they even discouraged pursuit of the one demonstrably proven avenue of lucrative commerce, the Indian trade, for fear that it too should have a sundering impact on the community.[42]

After 1678, when Shaftesbury fell out of crown favor and left England, the Carolina colony suffered from a lack of firm leadership. A man of lesser abilities, the earl of Craven, attempted to exert some direction, but for all practical purposes the local authorities assumed real command. Still, the old ideas hung on. In 1684 almost fourteen years after the first settlement took root, the proprietors observed:

If the inhabitants of Carolina did plant in towns and villages their lives would be more comfortable and their trade carried on and be much more secure. We have often recommended to the government there to induce the people to it but they have not minded the affair as they ought.[43]

And not until 1698, with the issuance of a new Fundamental Constitution which omitted all mention of towns, did there ultimately come some juridical recognition of the failure to promote urban growth through organic law.

Despite this failure, the Carolina settlement did survive—a success in large measure accomplished because of the proprietors' efforts to plan for town settlement. From the first arrivals the people ignored all proprietary injunctions in behalf of concentrated settlement and instead located in a spatially dispersed manner. In short, they went wherever good bottom land existed. But this dispersal did not affect the occupational structure of the colony. Early South Carolina society, in terms of occupational character, was not substantially different from that of the nucleated communities of New England or, for that matter, the seventeenth-century Chesapeake. Throughout all colonial America the prevailing occupational mosaic was similar in structure, whether the people lived in concentrated villages or scattered farmsteads. Most settlers combined their farming activities with a second trade. In South Carolina, during the first decade of settlement, over twenty-five separate occupational specialties were present.[44] Many of these trades—distilling, blockmaking, tanning, glazing—were represented by only one man, but the sheer diversity of skills suggests an operational plan of organization, a likely element considering how impressed the proprietors were with the importance of avoiding the calamity they believed had occurred in the Chesapeake. One of the earliest travelers to Carolina, Thomas Newe, composed a revealing remark in this regard. The colony's rudimentary prosperity seemed remarkable, wrote Newe to his father, "especially if we consider the first planters which were most of them tradesmen, poor and wholely ignorant of husbandry. . . ."[45] How ignorant they were of farming is debatable, but Newe's observation suggests that the colony's diversity of trades, though spatially separated, provided an essential ingredient which helped sustain the early years of growth.

Had Shaftesbury and his associates been alive by the mid-eighteenth century, they would have remained uneasy with the Carolina settlement pattern, although a few developments had occurred which would have merited their approval. One large city, Charleston, and a number of smaller urban places, both along the coast and in the backcountry, had emerged.

The Carolina coastal mercantile system consisted of six ports in North Carolina, two in South Carolina, and one in Georgia. The size and commercial character of each port depended largely, though not exclusively, on the regional economy and the geographic structure of the area served. In North Carolina, with the exception of Wilmington, none of the other ports—Edenton, New Bern, Bath, Beaufort, New Brunswick—developed into significant trading centers. Each of them commercially serviced their immediate hinterland and also performed political roles as county seats, and in New Bern's case as the colony's capital.[46] Wilmington and Brunswick were the only focal points of any large-scale trading activity. Both communities were located on the Cape Fear River, which penetrated far into the colony's interior and served as an excellent avenue for the exportation of naval stores, lumber products, and foodstuffs. Ultimately Wilmington outstripped Brunswick, though in the late colonial period it is not clear which of the two led in shipping services. Because Wilmington also played a governmental role, most colonial visitors thought it more important commercially, but the town did not establish definite urban dominance until late in the eighteenth century.[47]

Actually, what did not occur in North Carolina needs to be stressed. With a population twice as large as South Carolina—indeed, it was the fourth most populous colony by the time of the Revolution—North Carolina did not develop a single seaport of any real importance. Geographic reasons principally account for this. In the Maryland and Virginia tidewater, navigable streams enabled seagoing vessels to sail deeply into the Chesapeake district, but in the Carolinas only small craft could navigate very far into the interior because of the ubiquitous shoals. Equally important, most of the rivers that served the agriculturally rich Carolina backcountry became navigable to the coast only after passing into South Carolina. Because these rivers flowed northwest to southeast and not east to west, much of the North Carolina backcountry shipped its commodities through the ports of Georgetown and Charleston. One eighteenth-century traveler calculated that before the Revolutionary War only one-third of North Carolina's total exports went through her own ports while two-thirds went by way of Virginia or South Carolina.[48]

Charleston was the major beneficiary of this pattern. Not only did its most important river, the Cooper, flow deeply from the interior but it also gained because of the many rivers that fed into Georgetown, since that town's harbor could not accommodate ships of more than ten to twelve feet. Because of its shallow waters, Georgetown, like Savannah, became a chief deposit point within the commercial sphere controlled by Charleston. Naturally, the North Carolina merchants based in Wilmington and Brunswick strove to cut into Charleston's dominant backcountry position, and near the colonial era's end their efforts showed signs of modest success. The emergence of a more competitive price structure in the Wilmington-Brunswick area, the growth of the inland river town of Cross Creek, and the construction of an inland system of roads all helped channel some of the back-country trade into the Cape Fear area. Still the effect of these factors was limited. By the decade of the Revolution, approximately three thousand wagons plus count-less small craft laden with western goods came to Charleston annually. Yet despite the quantity of these products and their importance to the Wilmington-Brunswick merchant community the backcountry trade was of secondary value to the Charles-ton export economy.

The history of Charleston was inextricably tied to the economy and geography of South Carolina. After the initial ten years of settlement and only limited growth, Charleston in the 1680s began to expand. A traveler to South Carolina in 1682 observed that "the town which two years since had but three or four houses hath now about a hundred houses in it. . . ."[49] Charleston's exact population at this time, and for the next several decades, is unclear. A student of early American cities, whose work has been generally accepted by most colonial historians, Carl Bridenbaugh, compiled the following estimates: 1690-91, 1,100; 1700, 2,000; 1710, 3,000; 1720, 3,500. The figures are surprisingly large and indicate that early South Carolina was heavily urbanized. In 1690 the colony's entire popu-lation consisted of 3,500 to 4,000 people, and by 1700 the number of residents had risen to between 5,000 and 6,000.[50]

But the figures developed for the Charleston population must be viewed with considerable caution. Most of the city's population estimates were derived from extrapolations based on the number of families reportedly located within the city. The figure most commonly cited is that provided by the eighteenth-century his-torian John Oldmixon, who in 1708 recorded that upwards of 250 families lived in Charleston.[51] However, most students of early American cities have overlooked the fact that some of them were not year-round residents. From the very earliest period of settlement, South Carolina developed the unsavory reputation of possessing an unhealthy climate. "Carolina," a traveler later in the century re-marked, "is in the spring a paradise, in the summer a hell, and in the autumn a hospital."[52] The malaria-ridden swamps of the Carolina lowland spawned epidemics and sickness, though most people attributed these conditions to the fetid summer air. They also believed that Charleston's cool ocean breezes offered a protective haven during the perilous summer and autumn months. Actually, the brackish salt water surrounding Charleston accounted for the city's general freedom from malaria, but whatever the reason, all those who could afford the expense built residences within the city.[53] The expenses entailed were additionally justified since Charleston served as a fort in time of conflict, whether with the Spanish or the Indian tribes.

There is no method of accurately determining how many people permanently resided within Charleston during the early colonial period. Certainly, a sub-stantial reduction of Bridenbaugh's figures does not seem unreasonable, since it is clear the the colony's economy could not sustain a sizable urban community until the rapid growth of the rice and slave trades in the 1730s. Coincidentally with the expansion of those and other commercial enterprises, Charleston grew to a city of some twelve thousand people, half of whom were slaves, by the time of the

Revolution. It was by then an impressive community. As one visitor observed, Charleston "may be ranked with the first cities of British America and yearly advances in size, riches and population. . . ."[54]

Charleston's commercial growth in the eighteenth century can be accounted for by a complex of related factors. The city's modest early expansion resulted from its role as the center of a vast and highly lucrative Indian trade. The English had intense competition in this trade from the Spanish and French, both of whom enjoyed the geographical advantage of river access from their Gulf settlements to the interior Indian tribes. Yet, the English, with a strung-out network of rivers and Indian tribes to the Mississippi and beyond, dominated the southwestern region. This control resulted from the simplest of causes, as noted by one commentator in 1708: "The English trade for cloth always attracts and maintains the obedience and friendship of the Indians—they affect them most who sell best cheap."[55]

In the beginning the Indian trade consisted essentially of settlers exchanging European manufactured goods with the various tribes for deerskins and furs. As the trade expanded, deerskins became the main commodity exported, and the large numbers involved—from a norm in the mid 50,000s to on occasion over 100,000— created a strong demand for extensive storage facilities. This demand, which coincided with the inland movement of the Indian tribes by the second decade of the eighteenth century, transformed this trade from a secondary pursuit followed by individual planters to a capital-intensive industry operated by an exclusive mercantile community. The merchants who dominated the trade, whether of local origin or from England, had to possess efficient connections to dispose of their skins and, more important, credit relationships to fund the inland flow of trading goods. Naturally, the commanding position many of these traders achieved also enabled them to participate in the other commercial ventures developing in South Carolina—the rice, slave, naval stores, lumber, and provisions trades.[56]

By the early decades of the eighteenth century, Charleston had become a trading center of some importance. Though still a city of around one thousand permanent residents, from the numbers resorting there for the summer season it acquired an image of cosmopolitanism. Equally significant, the city's merchants administered an extended commercial system. In 1708 the colony's governor, Nathaniel Johnson, wrote a detailed report of the area's economy.

From this province to England are [exported] rice, pitch, tar, buck and doeskins. . . to the American Islands . . . staves, hoops, and shingles, beef, pork, rice, pitch, tar, greenwax . . . with Boston, Rhode Island, Pennsylvania, New York and Virginia to which places we export Indian slaves, light deerskins dressed, some tanned leather, pitch, tar . . . to the Madeiras (from whence we receive most of our wines) also to St. Thomas and Curacoa to which places we send the same commodities. . . . The trade of this province is certainly increased of late years, there being a greater consumption yearly of most commodities imported. And the inhabitants by a yearly addition of slaves are made the more capable of improving the produce of of the colony.[57]

For the first third of the eighteenth century, the Carolina economy continued to develop most of these trades. Charleston also became an important distribution point for the entire Caribbean trade. Because of its role in supplying the islands, Charleston developed as a reexport center. Governor James Glen, in one account, enumerated sixty-six items specifically sent to Charleston for reexport to the Caribbean. The commodities ranged from cloth, hats, and linens to metallic goods, furniture, liquors, and foods of a great variety.[58]

But the island trade, though growing, was vastly overshadowed after the 1730s by dealings in rice. Rice had in effect become king, particularly after Parliament agreed in 1730 to allow the direct exportation of rice to southern Europe. Indeed, the commitment to increased rice production, which could only be accomplished by expansion of the slave population, required South Carolina, a former exporter of provisions, to import, in Governor James Glen's words, "great quantities of bread, flour, beef, hams, bacon and other commodities."[59] Not until the settlement of the backcountry would South Carolina regain a productive capacity sufficient for the shipping of such foodstuffs abroad.

From 1724 to 1774 rice accounted for one-half to two-thirds of the total value of South Carolina's exports. Indigo, after its development in the 1740s, ultimately came to rank second, and the shipping of provisions, lumber, and naval stores from the backcountry third.[60] For Charleston's urban expansion, rice and slaves were the two fundamental ingredients. Rice required extensive storage facilities which could be employed in other trades. The two trades were also extremely profitable and thus generated incomes that enabled a prosperous standard of living to prevail in Charleston and the surrounding coastal region. On the eve of the Revolution an observer commented that

every person by diligence and application may earn a comfortable livelihood, there are few poor people in the province, except the idle or unfortunate. Nor is the number of rich people great, most of them being in what we call easy and independent circumstances. It has been remarked that there are more persons possessed of between five and ten thousand pounds sterling in the province than are to be found anywhere among the same number of people.[61]

Tied to the coastal communities there developed within the Carolinas, during the third quarter of the eighteenth century, a variety of inland towns. All were, in part, stimulated by the construction of an inland system of roads, although other factors also accounted for their growth. In North Carolina there emerged a series of midland towns—Halifax, Tarboro, Cross Creek, Campbelltown, and backcountry towns —Salisbury, Hillsborough, Charlotte, and the Moravian settlement of Salem. Contemporary descriptions attest to the thriving character of these settlements. Of Halifax one traveler wrote typically: "This place contains about fifty houses, stores are kept here to supply the country round with European and West Indian commodities for which pork, tobacco, Indian corn, wheat and lumber are taken in return."[62] Most of the other midland towns performed identical tasks in handling their region's trade and offering the needed occupational services. A few also carried out administrative and political roles. Generally, the backcountry towns duplicated these roles, but another function, the servicing of frontier immigrants, was particularly important for their growth in the rapid expansion experienced by the frontier towns.

In South Carolina, despite concerted government efforts, fewer towns developed. Because of their absence one of the colony's former governors, Robert Johnson, proposed an ambitious township scheme to populate the middle and backcountry. He suggested the establishment of townships to be settled with poor Protestant refugees from Europe. Ultimately Johnson's proposals won acceptance by the board of trade and were included in the instructions he received in 1730 when he reacquired the South Carolina governorship.

Johnson's scheme outlined ten townships of twenty thousand acres each. For defensive purposes all the townships were to contain a central town where people were to settle, much in the New England tradition. In part, the plan worked since people were attracted to South Carolina, but only one of the intended towns, Orangeburg, was permanently established. Most of them served an early defensive function and provided needed initial services, but within a few years the nucleated settlements broke down and the people dispersed.[63] And in a few cases the township directors completely ignored the town concept. James Gordon, for example, director of the creation of Queensboro township, had the proposed town site planted by his overseer.[64]

During this period the colony's authorities, in a fashion reminiscent of Shaftesbury, protested the violation of their orders, but they were no more successful in bending the colonists than their seventeenth century predecessors. Besides Orangeburg one other important inland town, Camden, did develop during the third quarter of the eighteenth century. This was an extremely important trading town, whose role has been excellently analyzed by two colonial scholars, Joseph Ernst and H. Roy Merrens. Its growth had little to do directly with the township scheme since it was not one of Governor Johnson's planned communities.[65]

The selective and generally minimal urban growth of the seventeenth and early eighteenth centuries was replaced by a wholly different pattern as an astonishing urban transformation occurred in the South after 1750. Abraham Bradley's 1796 map of the United States captured the point well. From Maryland to South Carolina there existed a vast number of urban places shaped in a very distinctive horseshoe configuration. As most travel accounts suggest, the pattern was oriented from northwest to southeast with an empty core on the shoe's inside. The barren inner core extended from the northern Virginia Piedmont through Virginia's south side and on into North Carolina's Piedmont. Travelers through this area invariably stressed the absence of towns, the abundance of isolated taverns, and the pervasiveness of tobacco culture. Surrounding this zone, the degrees of urbanization rose, though they varied substantially. The highest levels were located in the eastern coastal zone, where sizable seaport centers linked southern agriculture to foreign markets. To the west and in the backcountry moderate to high urbanization prevailed, especially from Frederick County, Maryland, south along the Great Wagon Road to the communities of western North Carolina. Significantly, the only continuous link from coastal cities to the backcountry occurred along the northern rim. In sum, the South contained a chiefly rural central zone surrounded by an urbanized periphery along the coast and in the backcountry.

The extensive nature of the South's growth was itself impressive. But the sheer number of urban places reflected more than expansion. A diverse matrix of development patterns also characterized the region. During the eighteenth century a variety of temporal, commodity, and international market changes generated a series of differing urban configurations. Each possessed its unique characteristics as part of a distinctive commercial zone. Two communities, London Town and Baltimore, located within a distance of fifty miles, were representative of the complex spectrum of experience. At its height, London Town contained no more than two hundred persons. The small size deceptively masked its vital importance as a strategic point in the international tobacco trade. From 1710 to the early 1750s London Town flourished; then it died. By the Revolution only debris and a scattering of houses remained in a place whose cargoes had once influenced market prices in England, France, and the Baltic states. Baltimore, by contrast, had over six thousand persons by the War of Independence. Its basic commodity foundation lay in wheat and flour, although a wide assortment of goods passed through the city. By century's end its fifty "capital merchant mills" would make it the leading flour market in the United States, some would say in the world. For a short time it would even bid to be the new nation's largest city. Only fifty miles apart, London Town and Baltimore capture well in their functional histories the orbit of forces that underlay the eighteenth-century urban South.

During the eighteenth century, especially in the years 1715-40, numbers of Chesapeake tobacco towns flourished, only to fall victim in the last quarter century before the Revolution to the sweeping realignment in the tobacco trade.[66] The experience of London Town was representative of the recurring pattern.[67] Founded in 1683, London Town grew dramatically between 1710 and 1750, then declined precipitously. The fundamental factors that governed this process were identical to those that influenced all of the tobacco coast's trade centers—the unique mixture of geography and international market demands that produced a distinctive settlement configuration of small nucleated communities cleaving to the Tidewater shoreline. The particular location of London Town underscores the importance of these elements. Situated a mere five miles southwest of the colonial capital at Annapolis, London Town, despite this proximity, was scarcely affected in its growth by its larger neighbor. Conjoined by the Atlantic Ocean in a taut umbilical-like arrangement to the markets of London, the town was paradoxically isolated from other Chesapeake urban centers by the intricate river courses which were characteristic of the Tidewater. For the towns of the tobacco coast, the Atlantic— some three thousand miles wide—constituted a broad avenue of access, while narrow rivers, often of less than one hundred yards, formed moats that delimited the region into a multitude of precise commercial zones.

The deep estuaries and rivers that carved up the Tidewater grossly interrupted the process of land travel. A typical journey from Williamsburg to Annapolis, a distance of 120 miles, normally required taking over a dozen ferries. So, too, a traveler from London Town to Annapolis had to cross the South River by ferry, a delay that added an hour or more to the time-distance to the capital. Several other estuaries circumscribed London Town to the south and west, creating similar barriers to land transport, although they did offer marvelous access to seagoing vessels.

The presence of the Tidewater's watercourses partially explained London Town's isolation, but other physical and marketing factors were also involved. Basically, the Chesapeake's early eighteenth-century towns were products of the unprecedented expansion in the tobacco trade that followed the opening of markets in France. In response to the new demand, output levels of tobacco soared with a wide array of differing quality levels and taste varieties soon appearing.[68] To facilitate the entire marketing process and to insure a proper price according to grade and flavor, the bay's merchants and planters strove to unify the exports of their particular sectors so as to establish a distinctive reputation. The towns, almost from the beginning, assumed this role, with each soon acquiring international recognition for the particular character of its tobacco. London Town's experience was typical. Located amidst the fertile soil of All Hallows Parish, the land surrounding the town yielded a rich tobacco grade that commanded a high price. Recognizing the importance of maintaining a standard of acknowledged excellence, the town's merchants focused their business activities exclusively on the area's hinterland. By contrast, they collectively ignored the larger land area between the South and Severn rivers, where another profitable and extensive, although slightly poorer, tobacco variety was controlled by the Annapolis merchant community.

In sum, each of the Chesapeake's tobacco towns had compelling reasons for channeling its marketing endeavors into specialized categories. Within the entire range of different tobaccos, from trash to fine sweet-scented, different economies of scale operated with profits generally possible in all but the most depressed years. And for town merchants—men whose careers existed by virtue of prestige—the concentration of their energies into a particular class of tobacco afforded them both the necessary standing and the most favorable opportunity for enlarging their personal margin of profit.[69]

Settlement within the vicinity of London Town first occurred in 1650. For the next half-century the area functioned without an urban center of any consequence. The rapidly growing population settled initially on the land contiguous to the South, West, and Rhode rivers. Later, immigrants moved inland onto the fertile upland terraces. Perhaps 90 percent of the parish families worked plantations, with tobacco as their cash crop, supplemented by corn, cattle, hogs, and horses. The remaining 10 percent, while they planted tobacco also, made their living by providing essential urban services in a nonurban setting. Dispersed widely over some eighty square miles were four or five merchants, several carpenters and coopers, so-called doctors, tailors, a blacksmith, and a plasterer. In addition, two churches and a Quaker meeting house served the region. These decentralized craftsmen, professionals, and merchants adequately met the needs of the rough-hewn planters. Despite the scattered location of planters and specialists, few residents lived further than five miles from a merchant's store where they could sell tobacco and purchase imported commodities, or from a doctor—an important functionary in a society with high mortality—or a church or meeting house. And for most of his needs, the ordinary planter possessed the crude skills and tools to make the average household repairs.[70]

But if the decentralized settlement pattern proved suitable for the frontier planter, it disconcerted and perplexed English outsiders, especially Lord Baltimore, the Maryland proprietor, who thought it a fatally flawed system. In 1683 he initiated a move to change it. Believing with absolute conviction that permanent towns were necessary to create an enduring structure for sustained economic growth, he pressured the assembly to enact a general town act officially entitled "an Act for the Advancement of Trade." The legislation directed the establishment of thirty-one statutory towns, but with most planters essentially satisfied with the existing network, few of the communities developed.[71] As one observer remarked sixteen years later: "We have not yet found the way of associating ourselves in towns and corporations . . . there are indeed several places allotted for towns but hitherto they are only titular ones. . . ."[72]

In the specific case of London Town, although there were great expectations at the outset, the achievements of the first three decades proved disappointing. The proprietor, dissatisfied with the colony's capital at St. Mary's City, considered moving his official headquarters to the vicinity of the South River. Anxious to attract the seat of government, the proponents of London Town erected a building to house the court, but their hopes were dashed in 1694 when the authorities designated Annapolis the new capital.[73]

For the next several decades London Town witnessed limited activity. Some of the town's land investors, who had long ago laid out a rudimentary street and lot plan, improved their original design in an effort to persuade the parish vestry to build a church within the community's statutory limits. But after a period of unsuccessful negotiations the vestry selected a site south of the town on the drainage divide. What commercial activity developed in London Town centered on the mercantile trade of the Burges family, the original owners of the town land. Beside the Burges's store, the only additional business involved the ferry and two or three inns that catered to travelers en route to or from the county and provincial courts in Annapolis. London Town, a sleepy little way-station at the turn of the century, contrasted sharply with the bustling community envisioned by Lord Baltimore and those planters who had purchased town lots in the 1680s and 1690s. By 1710 most of the original investors had sold out. They gave up too soon, but then again, they possessed the fatal weakness of all men: the inability to predict the future.[74]

Between 1713—the year when the French tobacco market was opened—and 1730 London Town underwent a veritable commercial revolution. That town and dozens of others like it developed from nondescript communities composed of rather lazy gaggles of buildings into small but dynamic centers of the Chesapeake tobacco trade. The most salient cause for the transformation came from Europe as the burgeoning tobacco markets discharged forces that transfigured the urban coastline of Maryland and Virginia. Within the colony the local impetus for change and growth issued almost exclusively from the merchant community. In London Town at least nine traders had established their base of operation by the mid-1720s, and the same process occurred along the length of the Chesapeake. But the crucial element involved the source of these merchants rather than their numbers. They were Englishmen with access to the capital and credit of London's more substantial mercantile houses. Patrick Sympson arrived in London Town in 1714 as the chief Maryland factor or agent for the London firm of Higginson and Bird.[75] William Chapman settled in 1716 and conducted trade on his own and for Phillip Smith, a London trader.[76] During the next several years Samuel Peele, William Nicholson, William Black, and Peter Hume established residence and rounded out the nucleus of what became known as the London affiliated merchants. A few other business-men, with credit links to Philadelphia or independent sources, also located in London Town.[77]

At the peak of its influence the scene in London Town resembled that repeated in dozens of small ports situated on the tobacco coast. About two hundred persons, white and black, resided in the town's thirty to forty houses.[78] The majority of townsmen serviced the tobacco trade; a few others were employed in running the inns and local ferries. Each year, between the end of the tobacco growing season in August and the arrival of the tobacco fleet in October and November, a spurt of brisk and sometimes frenetic activity interrupted the normal tempo of town life. In late summer while the tobacco crops were still in the fields, town merchants scoured the countryside five to ten miles around London Town observing planters' crops and negotiating their purchases. At times the merchants traveled further afield in order to acquire the several hundred hogsheads of tobacco expected by their London employers. With the purchases negotiated, the merchants arranged transportation of the crops to London Town or to accessible landings along the South River or neighboring estuaries. An added responsibility fell to Patrick Sympson, who, as chief factor for Higginson and Bird, had to coordinate the activities of other company factors scattered around the Chesapeake. By late October the arduous work of the merchants was finished in time for the arrival of the English tobacco fleet. As many as seven vessels in that fleet turned into South River and anchored in London Town's Shipping Creek. Flats lightered back and forth between the ships and the London Town shore, carrying an array of imported goods that stocked the merchants' storehouses for the coming year. Curious planters came to gape and to buy from the cornucopia of wines, clothes, shoes, buttons, thread, pins, ribbons, tools, and furniture. With equal dispatch the empty ship holds were filled with tobacco hogsheads, lightered out from the town or brought to the ships from upstream landings by flats and schooners. Sailors did most of the work, aided by the merchants' slaves, and after a sweaty day the sailors filled the inns in town, where they ate, drank, fought, and did those things sailors are wont to do. Sometimes it seemed a wonder that the fragile town survived, but as the trade became increasingly efficient, the amount of time the sailors had to spend ashore declined considerably. By mid-century ships were turned around in about two weeks, whereas earlier in the century a vessel might lie in the Chesapeake for months.[79]

It is important to recognize that London Town and communities of a similar function did not grow in any significant quantitative sense, despite the strategic importance and profitable nature of their commercial endeavors. After the mid-1720s the number of merchants within the town stabilized. Nor did the character of commerce associated with the tobacco trade attract other occupations. A variety of service and social activities present in the vicinity of London Town—grist mills, fulling mills, carpenters, coopers, schools, churches, social clubs—became more numerous in the years 1710-50, but none of these functions ever clustered within the town. As was the case in other Chesapeake centers, London Town's exportation of tobacco did not serve as a centralizing magnet. The community existed exclusively because of the role it performed—the shipping of tobacco. When London Town lost that trade, it died.[80]

At mid-century London Town began its downhill slide. The forty houses in the mid-1740s fell off to a dozen in 1765. Travelers passing through invariably referred to the town as "a small place" or "a pleasant village," with not even the hint of commerce suggested. This was not an omission or oversight on their part: all of the merchants had virtually departed. During the revolutionary era the ferry still operated, as did a few inns, but only memories and documentary evidence remained as testaments to London Town's former role as a substantial business center.[81]

A number of factors accounted for the demise of London Town and other tidewater centers of a similar character. Some historians have ascribed their death to the siltation of harbors caused by the abusive agricultural practices of planters. Although the evidence for this thesis is not overly persuasive, this is not the place either to test its accuracy or to weigh the contribution played by soil erosion. What is nonetheless clear is that another development—the changing manner in the marketing of tobacco—was of far greater significance.

It is somewhat ironic that the collapse of London Town and other ports resulted from legislation designed to provide aid for the afflicted tobacco trade of the 1740s. Since the beginning of the decade tobacco prices had been severely depressed, and in 1747 they hit bottom.[82] Faced with a grave crisis, the Maryland assembly passed a comprehensive inspection law modeled on a similar program adopted in Virginia. The measure specifically intended to improve the quality and price of tobacco by eliminating inferior grades from the marketplace. To insure the process of selection, all future tobacco exports were to be assessed at government-operated inspection warehouses. Tobacco judged poor was to be destroyed and the rest stored for export.[83]

With the passage of the tobacco inspection law of 1747, the entire focus of the tobacco trade, and its attendant marketing pattern, abruptly shifted from the existing tidewater towns to the newly mandated inspection stations. These locations now became of prime importance to merchants in both the colonies and England. London Town's fate was thus sealed when it did not secure an inspection house. Within its former trading area the assembly, possibly because of political influence, authorized three inspection stations: one on the West River, another at Taylor's Landing on the Patuxent, and a third several miles up South River.[84] Almost immediately the tobacco trade drew away from London Town, and its descent became as swift and assured as its meteoric rise nearly a half-century earlier. Soon a quiet village, London Town offered only rest to the occasional traveler to Annapolis. As the century progressed, fewer and fewer of them passed its way as the highways and travel patterns were realigned within Maryland to accommodate the explosive growth of Baltimore and the other grain ports that emerged in the 1760s.[85]

Baltimore's experience differed dramatically from London Town's. The city was located at the northwest head of the Patapsco, eighteen miles from the Chesapeake Bay's main ship channel. In the eighteenth century the Patapsco was able to accommodate ships of five hundred tons burden, but the harbor of Baltimore was shallow, and ships with a draft of over eight feet could not enter. This shallowness was not detrimental because the bulk of the city's commerce was conducted at Fells Point, a narrow strip of land extending into the Patapsco at the southeastern end of town. Here hundreds of ships could anchor safely and unload their cargoes while their crews "waited not even a twilight to fly to the polluted arms of the white, the black and the yellow harlot."[86]

The year 1729 marked the founding of Baltimore, when a town was officially established for commercial purposes on the north side of the Patapsco.[87] Growth proceeded slowly, and not until 1763 was there enough trade through the town to warrant a central market.[88] Nevertheless, compared to other Maryland ports, Baltimore had become by the 1760s a prime shipping area. Governor Sharpe's description of the town, written to Calvert in 1764 from Annapolis, presented a scene of slow but progressive development.

With respect to the growth of Baltimoretown I must observe to you that altho there is more business transacted there than at any other of our Maryland towns it is in point of both its trade and buildings almost as much inferior to Philadelphia as Dover is to London, nor do I suppose that it contains at this time more than two hundred families, it is however increasing, and will probably very soon get the start of this city.[89]

Several considerations placed the town at a competitive disadvantage in the 1760s. Because the port lacked adequate storage facilities, the merchants there could not secure outgoing cargoes as quickly as their counterparts in the more developed trading centers.[90] Nor did the town offer the purchasing market afforded by other advanced communities. "As our town is yet in its infancy," wrote William Lux, a leading Baltimore merchant, "we cannot take cargoes off at the same terms that they do in the large cities."[91] Yet, by the middle of the following year he could proudly boast, "We have about 350 houses in town and more adding every day—and we now have a pretty considerable trade. I reckon there are 70 or 80 sail of vessels loaded here yearly with tobacco, wheat, flour, flaxseed."[92]

Recognition of Baltimore's growth came in 1768 with the transfer of the county seat from Joppa to Baltimore. Joppa's residents protested bitterly, though correctly, that "none but persons blurred by their interest would endeavor a removal of the court house to promote the foreign trade of Baltimore," but their complaints were unheeded.[93] The interested parties in Baltimore defended the move on grounds that since the town had become the center of commercial transactions, it should also provide the necessary court and public services as a matter of convenience.[94] In 1772 a British customs commissioner, after inspecting Baltimore, recommended that it be made a port of entry and placed under the authority of a collector and comptroller. Such measures were necessary, he contended, because Baltimore had become "a place of considerable and extensive trade" through its dealings with England, the West Indies, and Europe. "Thirteen vessels" sailed each year between the town and Lisbon alone, according to the official, and a "great number" of other vessels plied the various colonial trades.[95]

The fundamental cause of Baltimore's rapid growth seems clear: the enormous expansion of the wheat and flour trades which began in the 1760s. The shipping, processing, and physical storage requirements necessitated by this commerce constituted the primary factors responsible for the city's accelerated development through the remainder of the century. From the mid-1760s Baltimore exported unprecedented amounts of grain to meet the huge food demands occasioned by overpopulation and cycles of poor harvest within the Atlantic community. Drawing heavily on the Pennsylvania and Maryland backcountry, Baltimore shipped approximately three million bushels in the ten-year period prior to the Revolution, with similarly high levels continuing after the war.[96]

As Baltimore endeavored to exploit the advantageous situation created by the heavy demands of the international market, the city increasingly came into competition with Philadelphia for control of their region's wheat resources. Contemporary newspapers and private correspondence afford ample evidence of their rivalry. Much of the wheat that passed through Baltimore came not only from central and western Maryland but also from contiguous similar sections in Pennsylvania, including the especially rich Susquehanna valley. An article reprinted in the *Maryland Gazette* from a Philadelphia paper explained why Pennsylvanians shipped through the Chesapeake. The author, who sounded like a disgruntled Philadelphia merchant, complained: "The distance is so great, the ferries so high, and the roads so bad from Susquehanna to Philadelphia that the countrymen to the westward of that river carry their produce to Baltimore in Maryland to the great detriment of Pennsylvania."[97]

One of the basic reasons for the dominance exerted by Baltimore over the interior, central, and western sectors of Pennsylvania involved transportation costs. William Lux, in his efforts to lure Europeans to trade through Baltimore, pointed out how the lower cost of moving goods worked to his city's advantage:

The situation of our town to an extensive back country which is now well cultivated and from which we draw large quantities of wheat, flour and flaxseed renders it fair for a place of considerable trade, [and] we can always load these articles on easier terms than at Philadelphia or New York.[98]

These lower costs resulted from the differing state of internal improvements in the two colonies. Maryland early built roads into its western areas as well as to the colony's border with Pennsylvania's central and western sections. Without the obstacle of major mountains to cross, the projects were not very difficult. By 1739 a road was underway between Maryland towns situated on the Chesapeake's northern shore and Pennsylvania's south central counties, the heart of the Susquehanna valley.[99] When other roads were built to tap this rich agricultural country, the chief beneficiary was Baltimore. The town, because of its location at the base of the Susquehanna system, enjoyed a marvelous strategic position to control the valley's trade, and with the construction of transportation facilities into that region Baltimore's penetration grew.[100] In 1770 eight roads connected the town to the valley, and one major and several minor roads led west from Baltimore to the excellent wheat country of Frederick County and the Monocacy valley.[101]

Pennsylvania, on the other hand, never constructed adequate internal improvements to secure her western resources. From the 1750s on the inhabitants of the south central counties besieged their county courts and the legislature to build roads into Philadelphia.[102] But a suitable network was not actually in operation until 1794.[103] The lack of interest shown by the Pennsylvania legislature in establishing such east-west links allowed Baltimore's merchants to control a major share of grain from the Susquehanna region throughout the latter half of the eighteenth century.

And wheat, it should be noted, although the most important commodity, was not the only export down the Patapsco. Large amounts of lumber stores and respectable levels of tobacco were also shipped. In 1750 a tobacco inspection station was erected in the town, and a second one followed in 1763.[104] Ships dropped anchor in the Patapsco in the 1750s and 1760s and advertised the price they were willing to give for tobacco.[105] Baltimore merchants also became involved in tobacco exportation, though none specialized in this crop to the exclusion of wheat. Some English traders found Baltimore one of the more desirable places to take on tobacco. During the same year that William Lux sent out five hundred hogsheads, William Molleson, a British merchant, told his purchasing agent: "I would not wish you to take tobacco from other rivers for him [Molleson's captain]. I would rather he lay a fortnight longer than not have been loaded from Elkridge and Baltimore."[106]

But crops alone do not build an extensive urban community. Capital is also needed, and as Baltimore expanded in its attempt to meet the demands of the Atlantic market, the city drew most of its capital from the traditional London sources. Significant amounts of capital also came from Philadelphia, notwithstanding the two cities' commercial rivalry. Because of the attractive profit structure of the city's grain trade, a variety of financial connections supported and complemented the interlocking commercial structure of the two provinces. Philadelphia trading houses extended credit to Baltimore merchants, established business partnerships, dispatched trade representatives, and afforded potential investors the fiscal resources of its exchange market as a mechanism for transferring the payments attendant to international transactions.[107]

Despite its impressive growth, Baltimore, it should be emphasized, could not compete equally with Philadelphia in the prerevolutionary period. In practically all cases where transportation costs were relatively equal, the higher prices and extensive storage facilities offered by Philadelphia cut deeply into Baltimore's potential commercial zone. The heavy shipments of Maryland grain from the northern portion of the Western Shore and much of the Eastern Shore to Philadelphia vividly underlined this condition. Approximately 20 percent of all wheat and flour and 50 percent of the corn exported from Philadelphia came from Maryland. Baltimore's merchants desperately wished to break Philadelphia's virtually monopolistic control over these rich grain areas, but prior to the war their efforts were largely unsuccessful. John Smith expressed the frustration felt by many a Baltimore merchant when he wrote a correspondent in Ireland that in order to fill his friend's wheat orders the best he could offer was 6/3, while in Philadelphia "wheat such as ours would sell for 7/."[108]

By the mid-1770s an increasing volume of wheat entered Baltimore from the Eastern Shore although the city did not construct the facilities necessary for seriously challenging Philadelphia until the Revolutionary War years. Baltimore, unlike Philadelphia or New York, was never closed during the war because of British occupation. Similarly, the town never suffered the widespread destruction that Norfolk experienced. Thus, the Chesapeake port became a major avenue for supplies to the Continental forces. This heavy volume of trade brought merchants and concentrations of investment capital into the city. Expanding throughout the war, Baltimore cut more deeply into the trade zone previously controlled by Philadelphia, and this pattern, continuing after the war and combining with an extended western trade, contributed to the city's sustained growth. The personal history of Robert Gilmor is typical of what happened. An English immigrant, he settled during the 1760s in Dorchester County on the Eastern Shore. There he conducted a profitable wheat and lumber trade with Philadelphia. Soon after the war started, he moved to Baltimore and formed a partnership with Thomas Russell. They in turn established close contact with Willing and Morris of Philadelphia. During the war Russell and Gilmor made considerable profits, and after the hostilities ended Gilmor, in partnership with Willing and Morris, established European offices for their firm. Gilmor's relationship with the Philadelphians soon ended, but on the basis of the contacts he had made he went on to build one of Baltimore's major mercantile houses in the early republic.[109]

From this survey several tentative conclusions may be drawn about the character of urban settlement in the early American South. Essentially, the study of urbanization encompasses five principal dimensions: time of creation, size, location, frequency, and integration into explicit regional and urban systems. This essay, by focusing on the South's export communities, has basically limited itself to the first two—creation and size. A more comprehensive approach to incorporate the other three dimensions would require an extended analysis of the interior urban network of the South that developed in the second half of the eighteenth century. This would have the virtue of being more complete; it would also, by necessity, have the liability of being superficial. And yet, it can be asserted with considerable conviction that in the entire South one central factor was common to all five dimensions. To be precise, all the region's cities, towns, and villages developed in response to a triad of local, regional, and international market forces. The case of timing, the major point of this essay, is instructive.

Three discrete time periods marked the South's early urban experience. During the seventeenth century the realities of southern life shattered England's vision of an urban-grounded colonial settlement pattern. Not until the start of the next century did urban development get underway. The pace went slowly, but by the mid-1740s some recognizable urban places existed. And then suddenly the rate accelerated impressively as towns and cities proliferated, with a few growing explosively for the remainder of the century. In each of these three stages the demand for goods and services constituted the primary controlling element.

The urban settlements envisioned by the Virginia Company, the Calverts and Shaftesbury, never got off the ground. Their grand schemes of town-oriented societies were repeatedly frustrated by irascible settlers who dispersed hither and yon. Tensions and acrimony marked the relationship between the architects of settlement and those who actually sallied forth. Believing urban settlements indispensable for permanent economic and social viability, the English sponsors first commanded, then urged, and ultimately beseeched their people to recognize what the modern world demanded. But the foremost reality of seventeenth-century America—the vast availability of land—obliterated all these elaborate programs. The New World migrants scattered; yet they endured and even prospered. They did so largely by sharing the diverse skills needed to maintain life and operate their commercial economy. Those who ventured into the southern wilderness came mainly from tough country stock, but they were more than unskilled rural folk. Many had acquired a variety of rude talents through work as day laborers in rural-based industries. They were simple farmers and rough mechanics—a useful combination for survival in early America.

In retrospect, the seventeenth century can justly be described as an epoch of coercive town planning. After the British designers recognized that towns and colonization were not inextricably connected, they attempted to impose an urban format by statutes, instructions, and threats of retribution. But other forces besides the open land and the settlers' abilities also restricted town growth. The consumption pressure exerted in the early South was limited by low population densities, the cyclical character of the tobacco economy, the low commodity demands of servant and slave immigration, and the absence of concentrated capital. No matter how loud the wails from London, urban places could not root in such a context.

But during the eighteenth century's first half, sustained urban development began in the South. Above all else, one factor was of transcendent importance in this process: the Atlantic community's expanding demand for American commodities, especially tobacco and food. In Europe and the West Indies commodity needs swelled because of population increase, economic specialization, and an interlude of peace in European affairs. First came the impressive rise in tobacco after 1713 in response to the burgeoning purchases of the French market. British merchants and factors crowded into the Chesapeake to organize the tobacco trade. They generally located in places where market transactions had traditionally been carried out in a slow and rather haphazard manner. Soon their communities became designated focal points for the conduct of business.

Still, the growth of selective urban centers between 1700 and 1750 was overshadowed by the more rapid increase of the rural population. Not until the century's middle decades did conditions noticeably change as large cities and numbers of smaller communities multiplied throughout the South, a process largely reflective of the mounting demands for foodstuffs within the Atlantic trade zone and the resultant shift by Chesapeake planters to an increased emphasis on wheat, corn, pork, and beef. The same transition occurred only slightly earlier in the Carolinas, where planters began producing rice and other food commodities for international markets. Charleston immediately became the export center for the rice trade, which expanded steadily after 1715 and swelled enormously after 1730, when London permitted direct export to Europe and the Indies.

This transition in commodity production related directly to a second dimension of the South's urban settlements—their size. In the preindustrial South a trade region's commercial crops and labor system normally determined the size and frequency of its urban places. Each staple placed a ceiling on growth which varied depending on the weight and volume of the commodity, the requirements for in-transit processing, the profit structure, and the market destination. In addition, all agrarian commercial economies require a complex of supportive services which can be performed in urban locales or on the individual units of production. These services can be executed by a variety of persons including the producer, a neighbor, servant, or slave.

For the eighteenth-century South the agrarian economies were tobacco and grains. Tobacco areas rarely generated towns of more than three hundred persons. This consistent figure resulted from the productive capacity of most tobacco-supplying zones, which could not accommodate more merchants, and the desire by most traders to unify their exports. The small volume of tobacco exported from most communities also failed to attract any complementary functions since the crop demanded no in-transit processing of the shipping tonnage. Nor did artisans and craftsmen settle in the tobacco towns. The consumption needs of small planters were limited by the cyclical fluctuations of tobacco prices. Larger planters, naturally, exerted a more steady demand, but the prerequisites of all tobacco growers could usually be supplied by persons, slave or free, living in or near the plantation. When the planter wanted something really fine, he ordered direct from England.

In contrast, the grain regions created towns and cities of varied size, some of which approached six thousand by the Revolution. The ceiling for the coastal export cities located in the wheat-producing sectors was governed primarily by price. Every time wheat rose a fraction, the distance inland from which it could be profitably shipped increased. Correspondingly, the growing exports of grain augmented the number of specialists that could be concentrated in the cities. These crops also necessitated greater handling care, in-transit processing, enlarged transport services, and more extensive storage facilities. Although Baltimore was investigated earlier as representative of this process, the expansion of Charleston in the 1760s resembled in some ways the experience of the Chesapeake port. By mid-century Charleston, because of its concentration on rice and slaves, had stopped growing. The town's exclusive commitment to this trade imposed distinct limits that operated in a manner similar to the constraints of the Tidewater tobacco economy. Initially the high demand for rice, like wheat, generated substantial requirements for land, transportation, storage, and shipping, but the raising of irrigated rice was confined to the lowland's swamps, and despite rising prices, no acreage for expansion existed after the 1740s. Charleston, as a consequence, had reached the plateau that rice, even when combined with indigo, could support, and for the next few decades the city's growth rate leveled. Then, in the 1760s its trade linkages to the Carolina wheat country of the Piedmont triggered another era of expansion. By the Revolution, Charleston's wharves so teemed with grain that the British command believed a blockade of the town would quickly bring the Carolina backcountry to its knees. In sum, the experience of Charleston paralleled the pattern that took place not only in Baltimore but in other Chesapeake ports, especially Norfolk and Alexandria, where crop characteristics determined the creation and size of urban places.

3 DAVID R. GOLDFIELD

PURSUING THE AMERICAN
URBAN DREAM:
CITIES IN THE OLD SOUTH

With independence fulfilled, the American people set out to create a viable nation. Viability to the new nation's leaders was synonymous with economic stability and growth. Beginning with Alexander Hamilton's plan for recovery, the pursuit of prosperity became a national policy that filtered down to pervade every hamlet in the country. The nineteenth century became the age of commerce; the age of canals; the age of railroads; and the age of industry. The American cornucopia burst forth with people, produce, and technology. The riches of a new continent lay open for the common man. Energy and enterprise were the keys that unlocked this bounty.

In the forty years between 1820 and 1860, the United States underwent some remarkable changes. By the latter date the outline of an emerging urban industrial giant was clearly evident. A national economy functioned in place of local and regional economies.[1] Cities were the repositories of the changes. Wealth, technology, produce, people, railroads, canals, and industry concentrated in the metropolis as if some supernatural centripetal force propelled the American dream into an urban setting. The possibilities transcended reality, but not the imagination. It was an era when one dusty street could become a metropolis and when populations would bloom overnight. Urban promotion developed into a fine art and did its best to transform dreams into reality. The cities appropriated the dream of prosperity and recognition and pursued it vigorously.

Southern cities sought the promise of American life along with their contemporaries elsewhere. Though some historians persist in viewing the Old South as "planter, plantation, staple crop, and the Negro, all set in a rural scene," southern cities are beginning to receive the study they deserve.[2] Urban biographies, monographs dealing with various aspects of antebellum southern urban life, and a spate of articles have depicted the urban South as a vibrant, progressive, and influential milieu.[3] Some southern cities during the early national period registered population gains that compared favorably with other cities. Older cities like New Orleans and Savannah increased their populations by 45 percent, while relatively new Memphis registered an impressive gain of 155 percent. Fledgling cities like Atlanta and Houston promised great advances in the future urban South.[4] Leonard P. Curry recently developed an index called the Comparative Urban Rate of Increase (CURI) by dividing the rate of increase in the urban population by the rate of increase in the total population. Curry calculated that the urban population in the South increased three and one-half times as fast as the total southern population in the first half of the nineteenth century, as compared with the northern urban growth rate of two and one-half times the entire northern population.[5]

But population statistics reveal only one aspect of urban growth in the Old South, as Curry himself acknowledged. Qualitative changes that improve and rationalize urban life are more important in revealing urban modernity than the number of inhabitants. Nineteenth-century Tokyo possessed more than three million residents but could hardly be called a city in the modern sense—without extensive commercial connections, internal organization, urban services, and civic pride. Besides, population comparisons of the South with the Northeast are unfair, since the Northeast was urbanizing faster than any other area in the world. A portion of the lower Mississippi valley was frontier well into the 1830s, postdating urban settlement in the Northeast by two centuries. Thus, population is an index of urban growth that must be employed in conjunction with other measures of development.

In nineteenth-century America the extent of a city's commercial empire and the quality of life enjoyed by its citizens were the primary measures of urban success. It was a competitive era, and both individuals and cities vied for prosperity and recognition—the fulfillment of the American dream. Internal improvements were the means to commercial empire. "In sleepless and indefatigable competition," the *Baltimore American* declared, "success is best secured by transportation."[6] When New York completed the Erie Canal in 1825 to forge the first major trade link to the West, eastern cities besieged their state governments to aid them in duplicating the feat. Imitation worked well for some, disastrously for others. Philadelphia's rail-canal line to Pittsburgh, for example, was more a caricature than a transportation facility.[7] Although the canal was the first artificial link to the trade of the West, cities looked to the railroad to secure a commercial empire.

Americans endowed the railroad with almost magical powers. The more obvious attributes of railroads—facilitating business relationships by cutting time and risks, raising property values, and stimulating subsidiary business activities—were so widely known by 1845 that few promoters bothered to regale prospective subscribers, passengers, and other patrons with such mundane information. Indeed, people believed that these aspects of the railroad arrived with the first locomotive. What was more wondrous was the manner in which the iron horse pervaded and influenced most facets of life. Railroads could attract populations, promoted "human emjoyment," were military weapons, would "kill abolition in Congress," and could generally "reorient society."[8] Ultimately the railroad assumed the status of a demigod. Senator Charles Sumner of Massachusetts, who frequently discerned divine purpose in the course of daily living, wrote in 1852: "Where railroads are not, civilization cannot be.... Under God, the railroad and the schoolmaster are the two chief agents of human improvement." A Presbyterian minister from New York went even further. He saw railroads as "the evolution of divine purposes, infinite, eternal—connecting social revolutions with the progress of Christianity and the coming reign of Christ."[9] Small wonder that communities enthusiastically embraced this iron messiah.

Both urban and rural Americans supported the cause of the railroad. In fact, it is difficult to discuss the pursuit of the American urban dream without acknowledging the contribution of rural America. Some historians have contended that the plantation was inimical to southern urban development.[10] Without commercial agriculture, though, southern cities would have been dusty outposts in the backwaters of American civilization, rather than a part of the national economy. Cooperation and mutuality of interest between city and country built railroads.

Wealthy planters and farmers of both sections invested liberally in railroad stock.[11] C. S. Tarpley, a promoter of New Orleans railroads, was a prominent Mississippi planter. Tarpley believed that a railroad connection with New Orleans would transform central Mississippi from an area of plantation monoculture to a section where small, diversified farms predominated. Henry Varnum Poor, the nation's leading railroad expert before the Civil War, emphasized the mutual benefits of railroads: "Railroads . . . are necessary to farming communities in creating a value for their products, in opening a market for them. They explain the rapid growth of cities that are the *termini* of a large number of railroads." In a similar vein Virginia's George Fitzhugh, an ardent supporter of the American urban dream, predicted that with the advent of railroads "around all these Southern cities, the country will become rich . . . [and] there will be increased property values in town and country." Fitzhugh concluded by observing that "rapid intercommunication is the distinguishing feature of modern progress."[12]

The era of "rapid intercommunication" began in a southern city when John C. Calhoun and Robert Y. Hayne promoted a railroad from Charleston to Hamburg, South Carolina. The impetus behind the scheme was a desire among Charlestonians to reassert their commercial dominance, making access to Charleston from the upland cotton regions less costly. The South Carolina Railroad, completed in 1833, covered 136 miles and was the first steam-powered railroad in the nation. Charleston, its appetite whetted, next sought rail connections to Cincinnati, the new commercial emporium of the West. In the pursuit of the American urban dream, the commerce of the West was the greatest prize. In 1836, with a charter secured, Hayne pronounced that "The South and the West—We have published the banns—if any one knows why these two should not be joined together, let him speak now, or forever after hold his peace." The outlook for Charleston's future was favorable: "The far and fertile West will pour her inexhaustible treasures into our lap." The scheme ran aground when rival cities like Louisville and Lexington objected to becoming way stations for Charleston's benefit. There were similar abortive attempts at railroad building by New Orleans and Athens, Georgia, in the 1830s.[13] The Panic of 1837 and the long depression that followed dampened southern urban enthusiasm for the railroad.

The late 1840s brought renewed interest in the railroad. The necessity of securing the trade of the West became more urgent for the South with the worsening sectional crisis following the Mexican War. Urban rivalry for the trade of the West, never a friendly competition, would now be carried on within the context of sectional conflict. Southerners in cities and on farms became alarmed at the growing economic and political strength of the North. The increasing economic dependence of the South on the North was especially distressing. In an era when the connection between wealth and power was a national axiom, the sectional crisis took on an economic emphasis. Economic weakness was an invitation to aggression. In 1851 a Portsmouth, Virginia, editor viewed the conflict as "a contest for political power as a means of securing pecuniary and commercial supremacy." The Virginia Senator R. M. T. Hunter agreed: "If we are ever to divide, it will probably be brought on by a war of commercial restriction." Southerners talked of releasing the section from "commercial vassalage."[14] If the South could cast off its economic shackles, political strength and sectional equilibrium must follow.

The trade of the West became the target for southern patriots. J. D. B. De Bow, the Old South's foremost urban booster, outlined the task for the South after the Mexican War: "A contest has been going on between North and South . . . for the wealth and commerce of the great valley of the Mississippi. We must meet our Northern competitors . . . with corresponding weapons." Cities assumed a leading role in the effort for economic independence. As George Fitzhugh stated: "We must build centres of trade, of thought, and fashion at home." The *Richmond Enquirer* volunteered the Old Domonion's cities for the cause and predicted that "building up Virginia's cities will save the South from an indelible brand of degradation."[15] The cities were to be the South's weapons against the power and influence of the North. Just as New York, Boston, and Philadelphia set the pace for their section's economic success, so the South's cities would fill a similar mission.

Railroads took on a new importance against the background of sectional strife. William M. Burwell, a Virignia urban booster and later editor of *De Bow's Review*, wrote in 1852 that railroads "will result in the rapid increase of our cities . . . and the South will be restored to her former position in the Union and render that Union more stable and firm." A writer in the *Southern Literary Messenger* in 1849 reviewed New York's success and concluded that the railroad had secured her position as the nation's commercial center. He recommended a similar course for southern cities. De Bow predicted that with efficacious rail lines New Orleans and Norfolk could command two-thirds of the nation's trade.[16] Accordingly, New Orleans civic leaders developed a railroad scheme that would reverse prevailing patterns of western trade away from northeastern cities. James Robb, a New Orleans entrepreneur, directed efforts to recapture the trade. Robb's vehicle was the Great Northern Railroad, which would terminate in Nashville, Tennessee. Norfolk embarked on a plan, also in 1851, to reach Memphis, thus securing for herself the very cotton trade New Orleans hoped to maintain.[17] The similar but conflicting aims of New Orleans and Norfolk underscored the point that rivalry was just as severe within as between the sections. Neither city, however, was able to realize its plans before secession. Only Baltimore, in the southern urban railroad-building effort of the 1850s, successfully reached the West with the completion of the Baltimore and Ohio Railroad in 1853.

The Old South, belying contentions that southerners invested only in land and in slaves, staged a prodigious railroad-building effort in the 1850s. Local interests financed most of the construction. Between 1850 and 1860 southern railroad mileage quadrupled, while northern (including western states) mileage only tripled.[18] Virginia was typical of the pattern of southern railroad-building following the Mexican War. In 1847 Virginia possessed six railroads and 270 miles of track, ranking her seventh in the nation in railroad mileage. By 1852 Virginia had doubled her railroads to fourteen and track mileage to 548 miles, though she still ranked seventh nationally. By 1858 the number of railroad companies increased to nineteen and the length of open track to 1,321 miles, placing Virginia third in the country behind only New York and Pennsylvania.[19]

Railroads were the most effective, but not the only, means to an urban commercial empire. Southern cities sought to establish direct trade with Europe and other foreign ports. The objectives were to lessen dependence on northern shipping and to attract trade from the interior. Atlantic ports such as Charleston, Savannah, and to a lesser extent Alexandria and Norfolk, enjoyed a lively trade with foreign ports prior to the Revolution. The removal of British aegis, the upsets of war, and the shift of prosperity in the section to the Gulf states precipitated a long decline in these port cities. New Orleans and Mobile became the chief export centers of the South. The trade on the Atlantic coast went primarily in one direction: north. To construct railroad lines only to see trade flow ultimately to the North would defeat the purpose of rail connections to the West. Direct trade in southern vessels would remedy the imbalance of trade and dependence on the North. "By showing our determination and ability to conduct our own foreign trade," a Portsmouth editor reasoned in 1850, "we shall soon lessen the existing disparity between the northern and southern sections of the country."[20]

Southerners searched for a qualified import-export center to challenge New York's monopoly of foreign trade. J. D. B. De Bow recommended Norfolk as the most likely Atlantic outlet to Europe. Geographic determinism was prominent in predicting urban greatness in antebellum America, and De Bow applied it to Norfolk. He noted the city's temperate climate, her fine harbor, and her position midway between North and South, as positive factors for the development of direct trade. De Bow was not partial to Norfolk, however. When it appeared that Richmond would block any attempts by Norfolk to establish connections with Europe, the editor touted Baltimore, employing the same geographic arguments he had advanced in support of Norfolk: "Baltimore possesses in its locality . . . advantages surpassing those of any city in the world."[21] Southern cities successfully developed direct trade ties with Latin American countries during the 1850s. Savannah established lumber commerce with several Caribbean islands. By the end of the decade Richmond's exports to South American ports exceeded all other United States ports, including New York.[22] But the European connection remained elusive for the Atlantic coast cities.

Although South Atlantic cities were dependent on the coastwise trade because of their inability to develop direct trade, the Gulf coast cities of Mobile and New Orleans possessed extensive commercial contacts abroad. Between 1840 and 1860

Mobile usually sent two-thirds of its cotton receipts abroad. New Orleans—the nation's premier cotton port and a constant rival to New York's supremacy as an export center—shipped, on the average, 83 percent of its cotton receipts to foreign ports. De Bow, reviewing the Crescent City's commercial progress from 1830 to 1860, declared: "No city of the world has ever advanced as a mart of commerce with gigantic and rapid strides as New Orleans." In 1830 New Orleans received $22,000,000 in southern and western produce. Thirty years later the value of produce received by the port had risen to $185 million. As cotton prosperity returned to the Mississippi valley, New Orleans bloomed again. The decade before the Civil War was indeed the golden age of river commerce.[23]

Manufacturing was a necessary but anomalous part of the American urban dream. Industry at railroad termini ensured a balance of trade for both upward and downward railroad traffic. Direct trade also benefitted from industry in that the raw materials consumed by factories created high prices for farm and mineral products, thus securing a bountiful flow of commerce necessary for direct trade. Finally, industry seemed to generate great wealth—a requisite for urban success. On the other hand, manufacturing was not necessarily synonymous with urbanization. Francis Lowell rejected the pernicious urban environment for a more pastoral setting in establishing his textile mills. Southerners like South Carolina's William Gregg and Alabama's Daniel Pratt followed Lowell's example by eschewing the urban environment for their enterprises.[24] Further, the relationship between industrialization and urbanization was not clear. Even after 1840 the great urban centers of the Northeast operated from a commercial economic base. In the West, Cincinnati by 1835 demonstrated that a city could win economic supremacy in a region without developing industry.[25]

Despite the difficulties attendant upon assessing the role of industry in pursuing the American urban dream, some southern cities believed in the necessity of industry. "A large industrial class," the Norfolk Southern Argus claimed in the 1850s, "is the greatest builder-up of a prosperous city."[26] Southerners also looked to manufacturing to diversify their economy. The Panic of 1837 devastated southern agriculture and left the South prostrate. The Southern Commercial Convention became an annual fixture in the Old South after 1837 when delegates met to devise a remedy for low cotton prices. Manufacturing was one of the solutions suggested by the convention.[27] As the South struggled through the depression, investment in manufacturing increased, and both William Gregg and Daniel Pratt inaugurated their rural-based textile mill experiments. When the sectional crisis worsened in the late 1840s, some southerners urged manufacturing as another weapon for southern economic independence. A Mobile journal declared that domestic manufacturing was "the only safe and effectual remedy against Northern oppression." A Richmond resident echoed these sentiments in 1851: "No people are independent who are compelled to rely upon others for industry."[28]

Southerners answered the call for the development of industry by establishing agricultural processing industries. Since cotton was a leading southern export, textile mills seemed an appropriate industry for the urban South. Georgia's cities were pioneers in the southern urban textile industry. Between 1828 and 1840, in response to declining agriculture and emigration to the Gulf states, urban Georgia embarked on a program to develop the state as the foremost textile center south of Massachusetts. By 1840 Georgia had nineteen textile factories, and Savannah industrialists issued a proclamation in favor of a protective tariff. Investment in manufacturing increased during the 1840s as prices dropped precipitously. By 1848 there were thirty-two cotton mills in urban Georgia, with over one-third of the manufactured product finding markets outside the state. By the mid-1850s De Bow was referring to Georgia as the "Empire State of the South," and applauded planters whose investments helped to build the mills. The return on some of these investments was remarkably high. One mill in Macon earned 17 percent semiannually on its capital. Augusta was the state's foremost textile center, though Columbus became a serious rival in the late 1840s. A new cotton factory erected in the latter city in 1845 caused one enthusiastic local editor to remark: "Columbus will, if not compare advantageously with Lowell, at least have begun the good work in such a manner as to place beyond conjecture the feasibility of the South's manufacturing her own cotton goods." By 1851 citizens had invested nearly $1,000,000 in local textile industries.[29]

In the upper South tobacco and wheat were the dominant products of the soil, and industries appeared to process these crops. Flour milling and tobacco manufacturing were most evident in Virginia. Richmond manufactured more tobacco than any other city in the world by 1860 and was among the nation's leading flour-milling centers. Richmond possessed fifty-two tobacco factories by that date, and James Thomas, Jr., its leading tobacconist, had markets throughout the country for his popular chewing brands. Richmond's Gallego flour endured voyages in excess of two months and was ideally suited for trade with South America and the Orient. In addition to processing industries, the Tredegar and Belle Isle Iron Works gave Richmond an industrial diversity that was unusual in southern cities. In the 1850s, Tredegar entrepreneur Joseph R. Anderson developed an extensive southern market for railroad locomotives. By the time of the Civil War, Richmond could well lay claim to being the "Lowell of the South."[30]

With the return of cotton prosperity in the 1850s, investments in textile industries tended to decline slightly. Nevertheless, investments in processing industries and heavier manufacturing in the upper South cities allowed the South to maintain industrial investment almost comparable to the North and West during the 1850s. While northern and western investments in manufacturing enterprises increased by 83 percent between 1850 and 1860, southern investments rose 64 percent.[31] The South, thus, was not antagonistic to manufacturing. Considering the lure of railroad investments, such an increase in industrial capitalization was impressive.

Southern cities learned their lessons well. Railroads and to a lesser extent factories and shipping were essential parts of the blueprint for fulfilling the American urban dream. In the community of cities that characterized the new urban nation of the nineteenth century, imitation was a prevailing aspect of urban growth.[32] De Bow, Fitzhugh, and Burwell educated their readers with tales of northern cities and their formulas of success. While pursuing commercial empire, and their northern competitors, southern citydwellers were undergoing changes in their daily lives.

These alterations in urban life touched everyone from the urban elite to the very poor and every institution from local government to slavery. The changes affected southern life sufficiently to transform towns to modern cities on the threshold of maturity.

Three basic features of southern urban life stood out as central to this transformation: leadership, labor, and local government. During the antebellum era urban leaders in the South emerged as spokesmen for their cities and for their section. J. D. B. De Bow epitomized the trend of southern progressive thought following the Mexican War. His *Review* alternately vilified and cajoled southerners and helped cities to set the sights for their dreams: "Once Baltimore, Richmond, Charleston, Savannah, Mobile, and New Orleans will supply all goods foreign and domestic, how easily we might cut off all dependence on the North."[33] De Bow indefatigably collected statistics on southern industry, trade, and population—never utilizing them to lull the section's cities into the false belief of a contest won, but rather to spur city dwellers and the rest of the South to greater enterprise. James Robb, a New Orleans neighbor of De Bow, represented the best of urban leadership emerging from the depression of the 1840s. Robb was the personification of the successful pursuit of the American dream in the antebellum era. He arrived penniless in New Orleans from Pennsylvania in the 1830s. Within a decade of his arrival Robb was a prominent banker and a respected member of local government. He was Louisiana's most prominent railroad promoter in the 1850s, and his singular purpose and energy were responsible for the Great Northern Railroad project. Joseph R. Anderson, born into a yeoman farmer family on the frontier of western Virginia, became one of the South's leading industrialists. By the time he was forty years old, Anderson was operating the Tredegar Iron Works in Richmond, directing a major bank in that city, promoting several railroad and canal schemes, serving on the city council, and traveling throughout the South pressing for improved rail connections between southern cities.[34]

Most southern urban leaders did not cut so wide a swath through the section as De Bow, Robb, and Anderson. They were, however, a hard-working, concerned elite, no different from urban leaders in other sections. A survey of leadership in Richmond during the two decades preceding the Civil War reveals the same pattern of elitism demonstrated in studies of northern communities by such scholars as Walter S. Glazer, Clyde Griffin, and Edward Pessen.[35] Richmond's sixty-five leaders, 2 percent of the city's heads of household, were chosen on visibility—leadership in business associations, social clubs, government, industry, and internal improvement companies. Eighty-six percent of Richmond's elite in 1850 held proprietary or professional occupations; 12 percent were small proprietors or shopkeepers (owning less than $1,000 in property); and only one leader was classified as a minor civil servant. They were a mature yet vigorous group; forty was the median age. Richmond's elite was wealthy. Three-quarters of them owned real estate, the median being $14,897. Family patterns implied stability and security. Nearly two-thirds of the leaders lived in households that ranged in size from five to nine individuals; 80 percent were married; families included, on the average, three or four children ranging from fourteen years for the average eldest child to three years for the average youngest child; and more than one-half of the leaders lodged at least one boarder under their respective roofs. Slaveholding was widespread. More than three-quarters of the elites owned slaves, though more than one-half of the slaveholders owned less than six slaves. The leaders were white, male, and native. The persistence of the elite was relatively high compared with the rest of Richmond's population. Eighty-six percent of the leaders lived in Richmond either ten years prior to 1850, ten years after 1850, or through the entire twenty-year period. Less than 40 percent of the population citywide were persisters. These figures comport with the analyses of elites in Cincinnati, Poughkeepsie, and Philadelphia, which depicted early nineteenth-century urban leadership as wealthy, established, and native.[36]

Elite studies have discovered that civic leaders formed an interlocking directorate permeating every aspect of city life that counted in guiding their city toward prosperity and recognition. Richmond leaders exhibited the pattern of common leadership as well. Forty percent of Richmond's elite served in the city government; one-fourth were prominent stockholders in railroad or canal companies; and one-third participated in charity organizations. Control of the local press was perhaps the most important aspect of the common leadership. The press was the major medium for advertising, information, and city boosterism. The editor could achieve national prominence like Thomas Ritchie of Richmond, and Horace Greeley and William Cullen Bryant of New York. Prominent southern urban journals such as the *Richmond Enquirer,* the *Charleston Mercury,* and the *New Orleans Bee* matched any northern urban press in style, content, and influence. The press was a vital tool for civic leadership in pursuit of the American urban dream. The *Norfolk Southern Argus* stated an axiom of the day when it observed: "The mighty influence of this silent teacher [the press] , pouring its lessons every day into the minds of men, it is impossible to estimate. Not all other influences combined can compare with or stand against it." Or, as George Fitzhugh put it: "The meanest newspaper in the country is worth all the libraries in Christendom."[37]

The urban press was the cheerleader for urban growth. Its editors were themselves community leaders. James A. Cowardin, editor of the *Richmond Daily Dispatch*—one of the first of the popular penny presses—was a member of the Richmond Board of Trade, vice president of the Virginia Mechanics' Institute, president of a brokerage firm, and a representative from Richmond to the Virginia House of Delegates.[38] The *Dispatch* and other urban journals urged their citizens to the offensive in pursuit of prosperity and recognition: "We hold it to be a self-evident truth," the *Dispatch* declared in a familiar paraphrase, "that no community every became great, that did not do something great themselves. Individuals may have greatness thrust upon them, communities never do." The *New Orleans Bee* warned its readers that the Crescent City could "bid adieu to much of their western trade unless they adopt more resolute measures than any now in progress."[39]

The urban press also defended cities from spurious allegations by rivals concerning health, market capabilities, and enterprise. Urban rivalry was an important theme of nineteenth-century city development. Cities jockeyed for advantage, and no detail was too small to be overlooked. Though cities constantly borrowed ideas from one another, it was more in the spirit of bitter rivalry than friendly competition. Rivalry was typically more intense within sections. The conflicts between Louisville and Lexington, New Orleans and Mobile, Savannah and Charleston, and Richmond and Norfolk were more acrimonious than contests across sectional lines. The urban press was the sentry—the city's image maker and preserver. Though "Galveston is the New York of the South," and "Augusta is the Lowell of the South," were far-fetched assertions, they were typical declarations of urban pride indulged in by the press.[40]

Richmond leadership conformed as well to the associational proclivities of urban elites everywhere. As Tocqueville observed: "These people [Americans] associate as easily as they breathe."[41] Voluntary associations were important to the process of urbanization. As a city grew, these associations rationalized growth and enabled leaders to control the development of their city with greater facility.[42] The Board of Trade was probably the earliest voluntary association formed by urban leaders, emphasizing the mercantile cast of the early nineteenth-century urban elite. In New Orleans it was the Chamber of Commerce, in Natchez the Mechanical Society, and in Richmond the Board of Trade. Whatever the name, the function in all cities was similar: to crystallize and channel business sentiment in a more orderly fashion. The Board defined urban needs, lobbied for urban interests before local and state lawmakers, and served as a clearing house for information by establishing reading rooms and libraries.

Since commerce was "the goddess of Christianity" and the key to fulfillment of the urban dream, the mercantile associations directed their efforts toward rationalizing the increasing flow of commerce to serve their customers better. Warehouse and market house facilities were important in attracting and retaining commerce. De Bow believed that one of New York's greatest commercial attributes was its commodious wharf and storage facilities which kept produce dry and intact. He suggested that New Orleans install colonnades over its wharves, but the enterprise was too expensive to implement. The Richmond Board of Trade, directed by Horace L. Kent, a dry goods merchant, and R. B. Haxall, proprietor of one of the nation's largest flour mills, successfully persuaded the city council to appropriate $3,000 to refurbish market stalls in order "to better accommodate buyers and sellers." The Board also attempted to improve coordination between railroad arrivals and city conveyances so that goods would not rot on railroad platforms or wharves.[43]

Just as the members of the Board of Trade expressed anxiety over appropriate accommodations for their customers' produce, they were also concerned about comfortable facilities for the customers themselves. Southern cities soon outgrew the shabby elegance of their old hotels. Savannah boasted of the Screven House, but simultaneously complained about the difficulty visitors faced when staying in the city. New Orleans possessed some of the most opulent hotels in the nation, and probably alone among southern cities had sufficient accommodations for the crush of fall and spring trade. Richmond's Exchange Hotel, remodeled in the late 1840s to accommodate the city's renascent prosperity, was the most impressive lodge in the state. Visitors commented on its well-appointed rooms, fine fare, and courteous service. Its French chandeliers and English broadlooms rivaled, according to contemporaries, New York's famous Astor House. Richmond's Board of Trade, however, was unhappy with the city's other hotel facilities. In 1857 the members chartered a hotel company and raised $200,000 for the new edifice, "so that our customers have the best accommodations that can be afforded."[44]

Voluntary associations were not exclusively concerned with placing customers and their goods in the most commodious surroundings. The horizon of southern urban leaders stretched far beyond nearby farm communities to encompass an urbanizing nation. They were competing against other cities, and they had to adapt their prosperity to the exigencies of a national economy. Commodity exchanges developed in nineteenth-century cities for the purpose of regulating the buying and selling of a particular crop. Exchanges were tools employed by civic leaders to rationalize economic growth. The evolution of Richmond's Tobacco Exchange demonstrates how national market mechanisms began affecting southern cities in the 1850s.

The Panic of 1857 closed Richmond's tobacco factories and created widespread unemployment. The delirium in Richmond's tobacco community resulted from the default of New York tobacco houses on their obligations to Virginia tobacco manufacturers. Richmond alone lost $1 million literally overnight.[45] The crisis embarrassingly revealed the degree of Richmond's dependence on New York as well as the deficiencies with which city leaders carried on the tobacco trade.

Richmond tobacconists called a convention which assembled in that city in December 1857, to rectify the situation. The one hundred manufacturers who attended adopted resolutions designed both to rationalize the tobacco trade within Virginia and to establish new ground rules in dealing with New York factors. The credit system received the greatest attention of the manufacturers. Urban merchants sold their tobacco on long-term credit providing for the collection of the debt in between eight to twelve months. New York merchants and factors, on the other hand, extended only short-term credit—usually four months. This meant that New York factors could call up debts before Virginia tobacconists could call in theirs, thus placing a great strain on the financial resources of the manufacturer. Also, when hard-pressed New York factors purchased manufactured tobacco on long-term credit, they would immediately dump the tobacco on the market at a price below cost, depressing the market for the manufacturers. Some of these factors went bankrupt periodically, leaving the Virginia manufacturer with a worthless long-term note. The manufacturers resolved, therefore, to limit their credits on the sale of tobacco to four months, beginning July 1, 1858.

The establishment in May 1858, of the Tobacco Exchange in Richmond was another procedure for rationalizing the tobacco trade. Tobacco merchants rather than manufacturers composed the Exchange. In addition to enforcing the resolution passed by the manufacturers, the Exchange provided that all buying and selling of tobacco was to be done only with the association. This agreement eliminated auction sales at various warehouses throughout Richmond. By creating a monopoly of sales, the tobacco buyers and merchants could set a uniform price and regulate other procedures of the trade. With the commission merchant dealing directly with the planter, greater profits and regularity would result.[46] Farmers, of course, protested the Exchange. "Corporations have no souls," stormed one farmer, "and this 'Exchange Association' is governed only by the dictates of its own interests." Another farmer condemned "*coercive* measures entered into by a *combination.*"[47] But for Richmond's tobacco merchants and manufacturers, the reforms induced by "combination" were essential to survival in a competitive national economy. Southern cities could never hope to confront the North on a basis of equality if they failed to establish a more equal economic relationship with northern cities.

Leaders devised another means besides association to rationalize urban growth: the city directory. City directories not only facilitated the process of locating businessmen, but provided an opportunity to organize the city's population between the covers of one readily accessible book. It is true that not all or even most of a city's residents found their way into the directory; but comprehensiveness was not the goal of the publication. The directory was a businessman's guide to other businessmen. In addition to names and addresses, city directories often proudly displayed the social and commercial organizations of the city, as well as a list of hotels and newspapers—items that a visitor would find useful. City directories had proved helpful in northern cities like Boston and New York in the 1830s and 1840s as these centers became international trade marts. Southern cities soon followed the northern example and published directories as well, though New Orleans's inhabitants had had the benefit of a register since the French period. The appearance of directories seemed to relate directly to urban maturation. Richmond published a directory in 1819, but it was a very modest effort. Another directory appeared in 1845, but not until 1852 did its publication become a biennial event.[48]

By 1860 city boosters in the South had articulated their cities' needs in the new urban age and had defined their cities' goals in the section and in the nation. They were ubiquitous in government, business, and society. They were cosmopolitan men, well aware of what was occurring in other cities and what should occur in theirs. As much as the railroads, urban leaders helped to dissipate the insularity of city life. The city and its residents became more wordly in their outlook. Richard D. Brown, discussing the role of associations in organizing and expanding community interests, observed that "townspeople were now members of many communities—their own organizations as well as the state and the nation."[49] Communication and interaction amongst themselves and with citydwellers elsewhere characterized the urbanizing process. Leaders met and conversed constantly—in hotel lobbies, in counting houses, on loading platforms, in parlors, and on the wharves. They talked of repealing usury laws, increasing capital in circulation, and eliminating tax burdens on merchants. These leaders set the tone for their city and created its image. In doing so, they made their urban milieu distinctive from the countryside and more similar to cities elsewhere. In a section rampant with ironies, southern cities had stronger economic ties and were more similar to northern cities on the eve of civil war than at any other time. It was, after all, a brothers' war.

Slavery was a major factor in precipitating the brothers' war and also in facilitating urban growth. The superstructure of the American urban dream—railroads, factories, and shipping—required a prodigious labor force. Labor in the urban South invariably meant slave labor. It was true that railroads and factories employed other systems of labor. Immigrants, though never a force in southern cities as they were in the North, performed a variety of tasks in the growing southern city. The Irish found work on railroad gangs and as day laborers on the numerous construction jobs offered by a growing city. Germans made an impact on the labor force in San Antonio, Baltimore, and Richmond. German domestics were beginning to replace slaves in upper South cities by the end of the antebellum era. Immigrants comprised more than 40 percent of the total population of New Orleans in 1860. German and Irish immigrants in New Orleans generally performed tasks that were deemed too dangerous for slaves, like deck and boiler work. Immigrants also worked as stevedores, screwmen, and teamsters. By the time of the Civil War a distinct labor consciousness was developing among the immigrant work force of New Orleans. The Screwmen's Benevolent Association, which included a large proportion of Irish members, struck steamboat companies successfully for higher wages in 1853.[50]

Immigrant labor proved too intractable for southerners used to a more malleable labor force. Although the inviolability of southern womanhood is one of the givens of Old South historiography, urban southerners did not hesitate to employ women in factory occupations. Travelers reported women workers in the textile plants of Athens and Columbus, Georgia. In James Thomas, Jr.'s, Richmond tobacco factory, women prepared chewing tobacco for the presses. One Richmond manufacturer even erected a dormitory for women employees similar to the accommodations for young women in Lowell, Massachusetts. The Mount Vernon Cotton Factory in Alexandria employed 150 "industrious females," with wages ranging from $12 to $17 a month—the latter figure just slightly below the national average (which included male labor). The *Alexandria Gazette* claimed that the production per hand at the textile mill surpassed that of Lowell. In Norfolk merchants employed women in their counting rooms to the satisfaction of all. The *Norfolk Southern Argus* was so impressed with the efficacy of women in industry that it suggested widespread hiring of unemployed women. Not only would this alleviate a labor shortage experienced by the city in the 1850s, but it would ease one of the city's ills—prostitution.[51] The Civil War intervened before an empirical study could confirm the *Argus's* logic.

While southerners were willing to accept and even welcome women into the work force, there were limitations to their employ. For heavier labor tasks such as work on railroads, in city streets, mines, and factories, other labor forces were necessary. Free blacks were a growing, if somewhat distrusted, labor supply in southern cities. The free black population of the urban South increased during the antebellum period, despite harassment from anxious city officials in the 1840s and 1850s. The tasks they performed were basically menial, but they were necessary to a growing urban society. Free blacks were an anomaly in southern society—not quite free, but not enslaved. The lot of the free black was unfortunate in northern cities as well. A Philadelphia judge noted in an 1837 case that the black in that city was "free, but not a freeman."[52] Blacks were often the target of rioting whites, as in Philadelphia and Washington, D. C., during the 1830s. Their civil rights gradually dwindled with each passing year. Although Cincinnati's infamous expulsion decree of 1829 found no imitators elsewhere, free blacks were no longer accepted on juries, their voting rights were curtailed, and segregation began to define social relations between the races in northern cities. Free blacks in southern cities fared about as poorly as their northern urban brethren. Both sections could point to their exceptional blacks, but they were truly exceptional. Most free blacks toiled as laborers or in service occupations such as domestic, barber, washer, or cook.[53]

Southern cities enacted laws similar to the Black Codes of the New South to restrict free black mobility. Anxiety over social intercourse between free blacks and slaves prompted these ordinances. The laws also ensured the stability of an important labor force. In Virginia cities selective enforcement of restrictions against free blacks suggests that view. When agitation for free black removal increased in the 1850s, a Richmond editor pleaded: "They are not a bad class; their labor is needed." Predictably, Richmond authorities rigorously enforced the law providing for forced labor for misdemeanor violations. The chain gang evolved from the zealous application of the forced labor law. By 1860 the gang was a common sight in Richmond streets, repairing pavement, building bridges, and maintaining the wharf.[54]

On the other hand, employers of free blacks openly violated laws requiring them positively to ascertain the status of their help—slave or free. The urban press supported the lawbreakers, contending that compliance would discourage the employment of an important labor source. The *Norfolk Southern Argus* warned that "full enforcement of such a law will act seriously detrimental to the thriving prospects of our city."[55] Businessmen came to view the free black less as a social pariah and more as an economic asset. Testimonials from urban employers depicted the free black as quite the opposite of the shiftless individual that his detractors pictured him: "They [free blacks] are more docile, less expensive, and less prone to riot than Irish laborers."[56] Figures are unavailable on the extent of free black employment in Old South cities. With an expanding economy, increased demands for labor, and more free blacks in the labor pool, it seems safe to conclude that their use and value as a labor force was growing.

Slavery was the most malleable of all urban labor systems. Since slaves vastly outnumbered free blacks in every southern city except Baltimore, cities relied heavily on slave labor for tasks ranging from streetcleaning to blacksmithing to that of factory foreman. Historians have disagreed on the impact of the urban environment on the slaves. Some have viewed urban slavery as a step toward freedom, others as a darker, harsher form of the "peculiar institution."[57] All scholars agree, however, that slavery in the cities was different in some fundamental manner from the more traditional agricultural slavery. Perhaps the most unique version of slave labor in southern cities was the slave hiring system.

Slave hiring had existed since the colonial period on farms and in towns. When slave prices began skyrocketing in the late 1840s, slave buying, especially in the upper South, became prohibitive for many prospective urban employers. Urban merchants and manufacturers found it more economical to hire their work force. As British traveler Robert Russell observed: "Were they [the hired slaves] to be bought it would require too much capital to carry on business."[58] Slave hiring was a temporary relationship more suited to factory work and seasonal construction tasks than was slave ownership. Parties could frame the hiring bonds for from one day to one year. Slave hiring became widespread in tobacco factories following the Mexican War. During the 1850s Virginia tobacco manufacturers hired 164 percent more blacks than in the previous decade. The iron industry also participated extensively in slave hiring. Tredegar Iron Works shifted to employing rather than purchasing its work force in the 1850s. Newspaper advertisements for hired slaves represented a catalog of urban employment: waitress, cook, washer, cotton factory operative, smith, drayman, and wharf personnel. Employers ranged from struggling young businessmen without property to railroad presidents. Free blacks hired slaves as well. Slave hiring thus adapted well to both situation and employer.[59]

Slave hiring was another example of a fruitful urban-rural coalition. Farmers, sometimes in small groups, supplied urban slave hiring needs.[60] Urban agents appeared by the late 1840s as slave hiring became institutionalized as an urban labor system. Commission merchants sometimes doubled as hiring agents. In addition to dealing in corn, tobacco, and wheat for their clients, they would also seek appropriate situations for their customers' slaves. By 1860 52 percent of the slaves hired in Richmond were hired through an agency. The arrangement was mutually profitable to agent and farmer. The agent received his 2.5 percent commission and sought the highest rate of hire for his client.[61]

The position of the urban slave in the hiring relationship was ambiguous. In the absence of the traditional master-slave relationship, some employers cruelly mistreated the slaves, while others allowed their hirelings wide latitude in choice of housing, pace of work, and leisure time. A few of the more talented slaves hired their own time, but this was not usual in the slave hiring system. Attempts to secure legislation fixing the responsibility of the employer generally failed. Slave hiring was a lucrative urban business, and participants in the system, though they might complain from time to time, were wary about tampering with a profitable enterprise.[62] The average rate of hire for a prime unskilled male increased from $85 to $175 per year during the fifteen years prior to secession in urban Virginia. Skilled laborers commanded $225 or more. The inflated prices prompted some enterprising individuals to purchase slaves for the express purpose of hiring them out.[63]

The prevalence of the slave hiring system in Virginia cities demonstrated that the urban environment and the institution of slavery were not antagonistic to each other. Slave hiring, in fact, underscored the flexibility and versatility of both slavery and the slave. Southerners who knew the structure of cities and the mechanisms of slavery understood that the city and slavery were well suited for each other. George Fitzhugh, Virginia's leading defender of slavery, urged the extensive employment of slave labor in cities. J. D. B. De Bow believed that southern cities could build railroads more cheaply than cities elsewhere because of the profitability of slave labor. Regardless of age or sex, slave labor proved a versatile labor source in southern cities. De Bow commented, for example, that women slaves made excellent ditchdiggers.[64] More than 70,000 slaves lived in the South's eight largest cities, and their numbers were increasing in Mobile, Savannah, and Richmond. In those cities which lost a portion of their slave population, the reasons for the decline lay not in the decreasing vitality of the institution, but rather in the increased demands for unskilled labor from the agricultural sector, which resulted in a smaller but more select urban slave force attuned to the urban economy. Slavery, far from being an albatross to urban progress, grew more valuable to city dwellers as secession approached. If, as a Wheeling journal observed, the survival of slavery was a matter of "dollars and cents," then slavery in southern cities was in robust health.[65]

The emergence of a leadership class and the ready adaptability of slavery to the exigencies of modern urban life were two important developments in the pursuit of the American urban dream by southern cities. The final and perhaps the most dramatic change affecting daily life in the southern city was the increasing role of local government in urban affairs.

The evolution of local government from a cipher to an active participant in community life was a consequence of urban growth and maturation in nineteenth-century America. As southern cities grew from frontier outposts and dusty market towns, the limitations of the small group of elites that defined community interests became apparent, even to the leaders themselves. Basic urban services such as fire, police, water, lighting, and disease prevention were necessary if a city were to carry on with the business of growth and prosperity. Few visitors and customers would be attracted to a city that was a firetrap, crime-ridden, or unhealthy. Moreover, the pressure of competition made the provision of such services prerequisites for modern urban life.

The structure of urban government in the Old South was familiar to citydwellers everywhere. The city council, a single body in some cities, a bicameral legislature in others, was the primary governing institution of the city. In the 1820s and 1830s the council typically appointed the mayor, who generally rubberstamped council decisions and presided over the city court. During the last two decades before the Civil War in a democratic wave that washed over urban America the office of mayor became elective, and the quasijudicial functions of the office gradually disappeared. The urban legislature, however, still maintained the balance of power up to secession. The council was a carefully guarded club where civic leaders could direct the progress of their community.[66]

City charters changed as well during the antebellum period. Local officials flooded state legislatures with requests either to grant routine amendments to existing city charters or to approve entirely new charters. Dividing the city into wards was a major distinction of urban status that accompanied new charters. In 1860, for example, Nashville and Louisville had eight wards, Wheeling had six wards, Petersburg had four wards, and Richmond had three wards. Ward division had little to do with population. It was, rather, the city fathers' conception of how their city should be partitioned to provide more efficient government. By 1851 all southern cities provided for universal white adult male suffrage. Thousands of new voters entered the urban political process. Although their impact on decision making and the composition of government was considerably less than their numbers warranted, the expanded electorate generated a need for a rational organization of the city. City-wide constituencies generally disappeared, and wards became the basic political units. City administrators also discovered that the ward system allowed for a more effective distribution of urban services and patronage. It was another method utilized by urban boosters to rationalize their growing cities.[67]

The city charter detailed the limits of local government power. Changes in this instrument reflected the changing needs of a maturing city. The most significant alteration—incorporation as a city—engendered greater home rule, especially in the area of taxation and debt ceiling. In the era of railroads in the 1840s and 1850s, respective state legislatures allowed cities like New Orleans, Louisville, Mobile, and Richmond to subscribe to railroads.[68] Since most southern railroads were financed locally, such charter provisions were essential to urban prosperity. The ability to levy taxes insured that the growing number of services overseen by city government could be funded.

Standing committees were another feature of expanding urban government. City officials could no longer afford to deal with problems on an ad hoc basis. A permanent bureaucracy was necessary to grapple with the troublesome aspects of daily urban life. The standing committees in southern urban government approximated those of northern cities and indicated local government's concern with almost every aspect of urban life. Alexandria, for example, possessed eight standing committees in 1860: finance and salaries, streets, lighting, real estate, public schools, claims, the poor, and fire. In the same year Natchez had a similar committee arrangement, including two additions: health and safety. Fifteen years earlier there had been half as many committees in Natchez city government.[69]

City officials proliferated with the growth of urban government. In 1856 Wheeling voters received a ballot with twenty-six offices from mayor to measurer of grain, and at least twice as many candidates. Since most cities held annual elections, the electoral process threw cities into periodic political agitations which distracted from business pursuits. With the multiplicity of offices and candidates and with major issues generally absent, emotion and personality sometimes dominated the proceedings. Baltimore's election day riots during the Know Nothing ascendancy in the 1850s, Louisville's "Bloody Monday" in 1855, and similar though less violent disturbances in New Orleans and Norfolk emphasized that nativism was a southern phenomenon too.[70]

The expanding personnel of city government resulted from the increasing need for urban services. Providing urban services was generally a mixed enterprise in nineteenth-century America—a partnership between government and citizen. This was an optimum arrangement because city funds were limited, and the private sector possessed expertise and a small amount of capital. Combined, government and citizen provided the full range of services, not always equally distributed but sufficient to improve the quality of urban life.

Disease prevention was probably the first government venture into urban services. Disease was a scourge of nineteenth-century cities, even more so in the South. Killing frosts, arriving later in that section, kept authorities vigilant for the slightest indication of the presence of disease. Since the etiology of diseases was unknown, escape was the only "cure" for epidemic outbreaks. Urban governments and their citizens therefore directed their efforts at prevention. The devastating cholera epidemic of 1832 illustrates the mechanisms of disease prevention relatively early in the antebellum period.

In 1826 the Charleston Board of Health, a government-appointed body that served in a part-time capacity, organized the Committee of Medical Police headed by a prominent Charleston physician. Its primary charge was to study epidemic diseases. When cholera first appeared in New York in mid-1832, the committee established a vigorous quarantine around the port of Charleston, much to the dismay of local businessmen. Since directives of the Board of Health, and its committee, had the force of law, the quarantine held and Charleston escaped unscathed. Unfortunately, four years later a vessel brought the disease directly to Charleston without warning. Prevention now impossible, the city government fired off a series of regulations to control the disease, empowering the Board of Health to enforce them. The city council expanded the Board, ordered inspection of all outhouses, drainage of stagnant water, erection of hospitals, and the imposition of a quarantine. Officials successfully confined the disease to the poorer sections of the city.[71] The measures approved by city government demonstrated that the leaders were aware of some link between filth and disease.

Cleanliness was indeed the primary preventive measure instituted by urban government. "Of all preventive means yet discovered," a Norfolk journal averred, "cleanliness is by far the most important."[72] The Baltimore Health Act of 1832 was a model of public health legislation and more effective than the feeble and disorganized attempts of New York City to deal with health problems. The Act required the Superintendent of Streets, a council-appointed official, to physically inspect cellars, privies, and yards. The New York measure, passed several months earlier, required only an "inquiry" into conditions in those places. Further, the model measure provided for the whitewashing of cellars and the liming of homes at public expense if residents were too poor to pay.[73] Cholera was relatively mild in Baltimore in 1832.

Savannah probably had the most unique solution to eliminating filth and "bad vapors." Between 1817 and 1820 the city placed large tracts of land surrounding the city—mostly low wetlands with fetid pools—in dry culture. The city council appointed a Dry Culture Committee to ensure that proper drainage and irrigation maintained the land in a dry, rather than in a wet state. The city government paid planters $40 an acre to grow, within a mile radius of Savannah, only crops which required dry culture. The government financed this plan in typical mixed enterprise fashion. It floated a bond issue for two-thirds of the $200,000 required to implement dry culture, and private citizens supplied the remainder. The "sanative cordon" of dry culture land around the city was Savannah's major defense against yellow fever.[74]

Most southern cities did not go to such elaborate lengths as Savannah to purify their environment. Local governments concentrated on streetcleaning—a never-ending task in the days before proper sewage facilities. Some cities solved the problem of filthy streets by allowing animals to scavenge. The animals, however, sometimes proved more dangerous to residents, especially children, than their usefulness as scavengers warranted. The *Richmond Enquirer* recommended, in 1854, a time-honored if not very neighborly method of removing offal from the streets by collecting and dumping it into the nearby James River. The city council agreed and ordered the Superintendent of Police, an elected official, to implement the suggestion. Alexandria's city council undertook a careful study of refuse disposal in other cities. The study recommended and the council implemented a plan to station garbage carts in strategic locations so that citizens would use the carts instead of the streets for refuse disposal. The council report noted that "in the cities of Philadelphia and Baltimore, this arrangement has been in operation for a series of years and fully accomplished the desired end."[75] This was another example of the community of cities.

Street drainage was another problem, especially in cities prone to yellow fever like Norfolk and New Orleans. "It is of vast importance to the trade and prosperity of Norfolk," the *Argus* warned, "to say nothing of the lives of the people, that the standing pools in our streets should be removed by the appropriate committee of the councils instantly."[76] Baltimore undertook streetcleaning operations for a time, but in the 1850s contracted for a private firm to handle housekeeping chores. Both filth and mortality rates increased.[77] Although the expense was great, proper streetcleaning, preferably under the auspices of the city government, proved profitable in the long run, as it made the streets more attractive for visitors and customers and maybe even prevented or mitigated a numbing epidemic.

But despite efforts of urban government to provide a modicum of cleanliness for its citizens, it was a losing fight. Local government lacked the manpower necessary to scour a city. Before Alexandria enacted its garbage cart law, garbage collection was left to one scavenger. Further, although the relationship between filth and disease was well known to board of health officials, the majority of citizens probably appreciated this bit of intuitive medicine only slightly. They had, after all, seen loved ones carried off when streets were clean as well as when they were dirty. Finally, streetcleaning and garbage collection efforts, because of limited personnel and funds, were selective in their application. Two citizens of Alexandria complained irately: "No garbage cart in the South End of the City. The inhabitants of that quarter pour all their slop and kitchen offal into the streets." Another citizen, identifying himself as "Health," scoffed, "What a humbug is the 'Garbage Cart' law! In some parts of the city, the garbage cart never goes—never has gone." Invariably, the business district received priority in any streetcleaning scheme. The sections that went without such services were usually the poorer, non-taxpaying districts, which, ironically were most vulnerable to disease.

Southern cities were not alone in neglecting poorer residents in disease prevention operations. In 1856 the *Boston Herald* took the local government to task for its callous disregard of the health needs of the poor: "The filthiest localities which need most of the care of the city authorities are, in general, most neglected.... [I] f a nuisance should be created on the uppercrust of the town, it would receive the attention of the powers that govern our municipality much more promptly."[78]

The dominance of businessmen in urban affairs not only led to a scanting of health measures, but hampered government efforts once epidemics were underway. Disease was bad business. A healthful image was essential to a city's prosperity. No farmer wanted to trade cotton or tobacco for yellow fever or cholera. America's cities in pursuit of their dream realized the potential of disease for wrecking their hopes in the competition for trade. Early in the century a New York journal placed the specter of epidemic in its proper catastrophic perspective: "Nothing but pestilence on the one hand, or such untoward political events as destroy our national power can prevent our becoming the first city on the western continent."[79] The mere rumor of a cholera outbreak in Richmond in 1849 sent the entire legislature fleeing northward. In 1855 the proximity of Richmond to fever-ridden Norfolk resulted in calls for the permanent removal of the capital to "some more healthy clime."[80] The urban press, consequently, spent a good deal of time both creating a healthy image and dispelling any rumors of epidemic, even if the allegations were true.

Rival city newspapers, the civic leaders' image makers and preservers, hurled allegations at each other concerning health conditions. In August, 1858, the *Augusta Dispatch* charged that the *Charleston Courier* had deliberately suppressed yellow fever statistics, and the *Dispatch* considered this suppression a "penal offense". At the same time a Norfolk paper reported that "people are fleeing [from Charleston] in every direction." Charleston sources repudiated both stories, but several months later published the following comment: "The *Courier* decided it was not necessary to report the epidemic cases, but it is now safe for any American . . . to visit in Charleston." Amid charges from rival cities that cholera was victimizing Savannah, a local journal made the following declaration: "Savannah is free from all epidemics or malignant diseases; our general health is good as usual." Two weeks later, however, the same newspaper admitted: "We have had a sickly season, but we have had no epidemic, and few deaths among our native southern population."[81] Withholding disease information might have protected business assets, but it was a disservice, even a tragedy, to other residents and travelers. For one thing, unsuspecting visitors could contract the disease. Second, since the press was virtually the city's only medium, citizens themselves could be caught in the web of epidemic. Finally, the Board of Health could not initiate control mechanisms until the disease was far advanced. When yellow fever struck Norfolk in early June 1855, Norfolk journals suppressed the information until July 30. Later investigation suggested that the frightful toll of the disease might have been lessened by prompt action of Norfolk authorities.[82]

The fear of economic disaster prompted urban leaders to suppress facts detrimental to their city's image. In 1850 a group of southern physicians estimated that the cost of disease and death in New Orleans alone totaled $45 million annually in business and in trade.[83] It took Norfolk five years to recover the population and business lost by the tragic yellow fever epidemic of 1855. The psychological damage was probably as great as the economic and human casualties. During the Norfolk epidemic all major Virginia cities, Baltimore, and New York, issued interdicts against trade from Norfolk. Wharves, streets, and business establishments became deserted. The charitable Howard Association hastily transformed Norfolk's major hotel into a hospital—which in most cases proved to be a mere way station on the route to the grave. Among those who perished were Mayor Hunter Woodis and more than half of the city's ministers and physicians. The disease left countless orphans. One man, a clergyman, recorded the passing of his wife, daughter, and sister-in-law within six days. By late summer such tragedy was commonplace. In two adjoining houses thirty-four of thirty-six residents died. During the first week in September, at the height of the pestilence, there were at least eighty deaths a day. Within a short time the supply of coffins in the city was exhausted. Ships that had once brought produce to the docks began to bring in hundreds of coffins—and still there were too few. At times survivors buried loved ones in blankets, and sometimes they placed them in common graves of forty or more victims. A resident fortunate to escape the scourge wrote sadly to a friend: "My heart sickens when I think of it. The place where my most sacred interests are located, but a short time ago, full of joy and gladness is now the scene of sorrow and distress. . . . Poor Norfolk, when will it survive the shock!"

The yellow fever epidemic shattered the prosperity of Norfolk. Time seemed to date from before or after the "summer of pestilence." Monuments to heroes of the plague, prayers of thanksgiving, and statistics of health reminded citizens of their collective tragedy. The editors of the *Norfolk Southern Argus,* upon resuming publication, wrote of a "plague spirit." In 1859 the paper admitted that the "advancement" of Norfolk was "slow, too slow." The plague had "melted away the population like snow" and had shaken the self-confidence of the city.[84]

City government, with its committees, boards of health, and special officials armed with regulations on everything from garbage collection to privy inspection was fighting a superior enemy. Nevertheless, public health was an early attempt of southern urban governments to control their city. It was a precedent for activity in other spheres of urban life. Public health, for example, demonstrated the financial versatility of city governments. General funds from the city treasury sometimes supported the health bureaucracy, but cities also employed the devices of special bond issues and taxes to secure necessary funds. Nor were southern urban governments entirely oblivious to the needs of the poor during an epidemic. Charleston, for example, divided the city into health districts in the 1850s and appointed physicians to service each district. The ordinance further required physicians to attend to the sick in the almshouse, pesthouse, workhouse, and orphanage.[85] In an era before the germ theory of disease and a period when doses of calomel and vigorous bleeding were accepted treatments of cholera, southern urban governments employed the tools and the knowledge available to them.

Disease was only the most devastating aspect of life in the maturing city; crime was an equally ubiquitous if less destructive problem that urban government grappled with. From 1830 to the Civil War, while riot became virtually an annual phenomenon in northern cities,[86] Southern cities were less prone to massive disturbances. The existence of slavery and the greater homogeneity of the southern urban population probably mitigated potential violence. During the Know Nothing campaigns in the mid-1850s, there were several serious outbreaks of mass violence, but these were exceptions to the general trend. For a section that has a reputation for being militant and prone to violent confrontation, the Old South, at least in its cities, was no more violent, probably less so, than northern counterparts. Violence in southern cities generally appeared in poorer districts, instigated by drink, sex, or both. Drunkenness was common, especially in frontier towns like Houston, but it seems more appropriate to categorize it as an affliction than as a crime.[87] The two most common crimes reported by the press in southern cities were arson and burglary. Since these actions were crimes against property, business leaders reacted vociferously, and their governments entered the crime prevention field. The crime rate in cities was probably higher than reported because, like disease, crime was bad business. As a Wheeling paper reasoned: "It is not agreeable to the feelings of any person who cherishes city pride, to have it go forth that crime exists in their midst."[88] Thus, when complaints reached a public forum the situation was serious.

Citizen unhappiness over law and order centered on the inadequacy of police protection. A Norfolk resident related his city's rising crime rate to an impotent police force and appended the following picture of anarchy: "Vice and crime are walking rampant through our streets. Our dwellings are fired by the heartless incendiary, and the privacy of our chambers invaded with impunity by the midnight burglar."[89] Southern cities, like northern cities until the end of the antebellum period, lacked a professional police force, or even any organization deserving the term "force." Though some cities like Louisville and Lexington possessed an adequate number of salaried police, even the alleged fear of slave rebellion in southern cities did not motivate local governments to establish proper police service. Even if a southern city supported a police organization, its presence offered little security to the citizenry. New Orleans police were probably the most profligate crew in the country, except for New York's finest. The police protecting Charlestonians were more of a menace to public quietude than the criminals they reputedly sought. When the police were not perpetrating crimes themselves, they usually could be found either sleeping on duty or imbibing at the local grog shop.[90] A Norfolk businessman charged that "in the past few weeks there have been a wave of burglaries. Nothing has been done to detect the perpetrators." After a particularly rampant series of robberies and assaults, another exasperated Norfolk resident asked, "Have we any police?"[91]

In some cities the answer to that query was an anguished no; so business leaders organized their own force. In June 1854, in response to a growing wave of burglaries, Alexandria civic leaders established a private night watch in the city's business district. When the cold winter months arrived, the private force proved unable to sustain its initial enthusiasm and "propertyholders" reported an increase in crime. In March 1855, the councils of Alexandria appointed a force of twelve night watchmen and named a superintendent. Following the usual urban pattern, the watchmen were less than zealous in their duty. To remedy this situation, the councilmen extended greater control over the watch by requiring the superintendent to issue a monthly report on the number of nights, with specific dates, that individual watchmen were on duty. There were no further complaints from the business community prior to secession. Alexandria remained without a day police until after the Civil War.[92]

The record of southern urban government on fire protection reveals a pattern similar to police services: early attempts at voluntary action, financial and per-formance shortcomings, and the gradual assumption by local government of fire regulations and fire fighting. Between 1830 and 1860 most southern urban govern-ments passed ordinances prohibiting the construction of wooden buildings in the downtown area. The "Fireproof Building" in Charleston, built in 1826, was the first structure in America to be deliberately planned and constructed to resist fire.[93] Businessmen favored such ordinances because of the obvious destructive capabilities of a conflagration. Further, merchants found it virtually impossible to purchase fire insurance without such ordinances. Firefighting was almost as rudi-mentary as disease control; once a fire began, given just a little wind, it would easily spread to adjacent stores and residences. As with other services, fire protection as a public service was a response to the demands of an increasingly prosperous business community.

The fire protection system in southern cities initially consisted of private, non-professional companies, or more appropriately, clubs, who competed more against themselves than against fires. Sometimes the free flow of liquor and the heat of competition, if not of the fire, provoked a general melee, though none as serious as the disturbance in Cincinnati in 1853 which prompted the formation of the nation's first public fire department. Efficiency seemed to drop as the number of volunteer companies increased. In the late 1850s Charleston possessed twenty volunteer companies, but the city's fire protection was notoriously poor. In some cases, volunteer companies merged into one association to pool resources, man-power, and equipment. The advantages in proficiency and in economic terms were numerous. The Richmond Fire Association, which included seven companies by 1850, offered fire insurance, for example. Hopefully, this arrangement inspired members to greater diligence in firefighting, though there is no evidence that fire was less of a disaster in Richmond after 1850. The New Orleans Firemen's Charitable Association, formed in 1855, fought fires on a franchise basis, receiving a contract of $70,000 from the city fathers, but with equally mediocre results.[94]

By the 1850s urban growth and the national urban competition engaged in by southern cities resulted in sufficient intolerance of fire protection laxity to warrant government action. Some cities were already involved in furnishing companies with equipment and engine houses. Mobile's well-regulated volunteer fire department of eight companies received a new hook and ladder in 1860. Alexandria in 1857 purchased a lot for one of its voluntary companies for the purpose of erecting a new house. The Wheeling city council donated, in 1858, $300 worth of hose to one volunteer group, a stone wall around the engine house of another company recently and embarrassingly destroyed by fire, and $60 for miscellaneous equipment for a third company. This civic activity ensued from a disastrous fire which destroyed the wagon factory of a prominent Wheeling citizen. The fire companies had arrived on the scene in due course, but their archaic equipment proved unequal to the task.

Richmond abandoned its volunteer system in 1858 in the interests of efficiency and inaugurated a public paid department.[95]

Fire protection improved with increased involvement of city government. Some cities even purchased steam engines to aid firefighting companies. As with wealth and police services, however, firefighting was spotty and geared toward the protection of the business district. Six or seven volunteer fire companies converging on the home of a poor resident on the city's periphery was an unusual if not improbable sight in northern or southern cities in the nineteenth century. Fire protection was inadequate regardless of section. A review of the New York City Fire Department in 1856 admitted that the Department possessed the best engines in the country, but accused the members of "rowdyism" and "inefficiency."[96] The move toward public fire departments was a beginning toward fire protection for the entire community. After the Civil War, with increased financial outlay, southern cities would build on the precedents established in the antebellum era.

The water system in southern cities reflected the inadequacy of fire protection. In New Orleans it was unsafe to drink the water until the twentieth century. There were a few southern cities, however, where it was possible to quench a thirst without seriously endangering your health. J. D. B. De Bow cited Savannah's municipal water works, replete with lead pipes, as providing a salubrious liquid refreshment. Natchez possessed a similar system which dated as far back as 1819. The Natchez Water Company was a private enterprise. Nashville also developed a water works relatively early (1833) that was municipally owned. A steam engine pumped water from the Cumberland River to a reservoir and thence to dwellings via cast iron pipes. Richmond organized a similar system at the same time, employing six pumps to raise water from the James River to a reservoir with an 11-million-gallon capacity. Iron pipes distributed the water to the rest of the city. The project cost Richmond $625,000—a good reason why not too many other southern cities were willing to take the plunge into a municipal water works.[97]

Other urban services such as street lighting and street repair were more decorative than vital to southern communities. These services, through, are essential artifacts of modern urban life. Southern cities involved in and aware of advances of competing cities across the nation, sought these attributes of modernity. Street repair demanded the city council's time and the city's money more than any other urban service.[98] This was not surprising, since streets in the urban nation resembled steeplechase courses rather than pedestrian and wheeled thoroughfares. The complaint of the *Boston Courier* in 1849 depicted a typical condition: "The sidewalks are in terrible condition and it is at great risk of life and limb that pedestrians can venture across our thoroughfares." Frederick Law Olmsted, during his travels across the Old South, repeatedly referred to the rutted quagmires that passed for streets in southern cities. A farmer visiting Alexandria after several years absence appreciated the improvement in the city's major business avenue and recalled that in the past "I expected nothing else, than the wagon would be smashed all to pieces, and the old woman too." Paved and graded streets were thus helpful to the city's interests. As an Alexandria paper noted: "There are few things which operate against a city more than bad streets, and especially when they are the principal ones."[99]

The role of local government in street repair was the familiar one of cooperation with the private sector. Individuals petitioned the appropriate council committee for street repair or paving. If the council members acceded to the request, the appropriate city official, usually the superintendent of streets or the superintendent of police, proceeded to pave the street. The city charged private property owners for this service, so that paving like other city services was nonexistent in the poorer districts of the city. Alexandria, in paving its major thoroughfare, King Street, levied a special tax on property holders fronting the street at a rate of $1.25 to $1.30 per front foot, depending on value, and issued $8,000 worth of corporate bonds. The total cost of the project was $13,000.[100] For such major projects, cities expected abutting property owners to pay for only a portion of the paving cost.

Street lighting was another service that appealed to civic leaders. It represented another attempt to rationalize urban life. Gas lighting was a sign of modernity and it impressed visitors.

The mere fact that a town is lit with gas [intoned the *Lynchburg Virginian*] is an assurance to a stranger that there is an intelligent enterprising and thrifty people, that understands its interests, appreciates the blessings of a well-organized government and is not forgetful of the comforts of home. It is a passport to public confidence and respect, a card to be admitted into the family of well-regulated cities.

It appeared as if Lynchburg were transferring the miraculous attributes of the railroad to the gas light. In 1851 Lynchburg councilmen organized the Lynchburg Gas Light Company.[101]

The extent of government involvement in lighting service varied from city to city. When Baltimore became the first American city to provide gas lighting for its streets in 1816, it was a public utility. Funding came directly from council appropriations, and administrators of the gasworks received their commissions from the city council. The city connected gas outlets upon the request and prepayment of individuals desiring the service. As with other urban services, street lighting was available only to the more affluent businesses and residences in the city. The city erected and maintained lighting fixtures in the street at public expense. The lamps, however, did not extend beyond the business core. In 1835 New Orleans lit its city with gas light by awarding a franchise to the New Orleans Gas Lighting and Banking Company headed by theater entrepreneur James H. Caldwell. Caldwell later received a gas lighting franchise from Mobile.[102]

Street lighting and paving made the southern city more attractive. The emphasis upon materialism in the mid-nineteenth century city was not so pervasive as to induce officials to ignore the more aesthetic aspects of urban life. Indeed, aesthetics and business could be mutually reinforcing. Progress and growth often meant the disappearance of open spaces. Further, population growth and the increased pace of life meant that citydwellers appreciated and needed their moments of recreation. The pastoral ideal still possessed a strong attraction, and writers like Henry David Thoreau and Ralph Waldo Emerson enshrined this ideal in their poetic prose. Description of cities, especially when written by natives, emphasized the rural aspects of urban life, as if narrating them would preserve their verdant loveliness in perpetuity. Usually these descriptions took the broadest possible perspective, thereby eliminating some of the more noisome aspects of modern life. Thus, from a building roof a Houston editor observed this view of his city in 1858:

From the feet of the beholder, the city stretches away from a mile in three directions, while in the fourth, the green prairie, dotted here and there with white houses, and covered with the beauties of spring is bounded by the timber of Bray's bayou. The young shade trees in our streets and gardens, scarcely large enough yet to attract attention from the ground, here show to a better advantage, and give the town the appearance of a forest city, the house-tops everywhere peeping out from green bowers and luxuriant colors.

In 1853 Cleveland looked like this to one observer: "On an elevated plain above the Cuyahoga, commanding a fine view of the lake and rivers, planted with groves of forest trees, interspersed with fine squares, Cleveland [is] a very desirable place for residences."[103]

The city beautiful movement as an organized national phenomenon flowered in the late nineteenth century. The antebellum decades, however, saw some cities across the nation concerned about the aesthetic qualities of their environment. Before Frederick Law Olmsted and Calvert Vaux inspired cities to imitate Central Park in the 1850s, the most common open space facilities for urban families were cemeteries. Greenwood Cemetery in Brooklyn had its southern counterpart in Greenwood Cemetery in New Orleans. Cave Hill Cemetery in Louisville was a popular park for quiet meditation and rambles through its winding pathways and "natural" pools. Probably few urban cemeteries in the nation surpassed the beauty of Richmond's Hollywood Cemetery, designed in the 1850s on a hill commanding the view of the lush James River valley and the city of Richmond.[104] Such areas, however, could not long withstand the increasing crush of weekend crowds without losing the solemnity for which the city initially designed the park.

Although southern cities did not come forth with grandiose plans similar to Central Park, they set a realistic, if modest, estimate of their citizens' recreational needs. Savannah city officials designed parks and squares with such efficiency during the 1840s that by 1850 it was the only city in the country with open spaces sufficient for the needs of its population. Olmsted himself designed parks in Baltimore, Knoxville, and Louisville following the Civil War, applying the methods of romantic planning that he had perfected in his Central Park design. In 1854 the Alexandria common council, impressed by "the importance to the City of Public Parks, and urged by similar action in almost all the cities of the Union," resolved to initiate a search for suitable park grounds. A year later, its mission accomplished, the council rejoiced that as in other cities "all classes of citizens may enjoy a pleasant walk and breathe fresh air without cost." A Norfolk newspaper registered concern that the city was behind the times in failing to prepare adequate park space, and concluded its discussion on an ecological note:

In Norfolk we have sadly neglected to promote those public improvements which take the shape of verdant interspaces in the midst of population. . . . The City would be wise to purchase appropriate areas like New York's Central Park or

Boston's Common. A few years hence will see our places of recreation closed up by masses of brick and mortar.[105]

Since parks development unlike most other urban services was entirely a public chore, some southern cities were unable to appropriate sufficient funds to design and maintain a park. There were, however, other methods of romantic planning to alleviate the strains of modern urban life. Trees, for example, were a source of enjoyment and relaxation, and were healthful besides. The demise of a venerable oak for a railroad depot or a new market house usually evoked some pangs of regret, even from city boosters. In the fall of 1849 the *Norfolk Southern Argus,* under the heading "Progress of Civilization," recorded the passing of two weathered but sturdy sycamore trees: "Yesterday the axe penetrated those ancient trees—they were doomed to be cut down because they obstructed the way where the railroad is to pass." Accordingly, southern cities sought to plant new trees to give some comfort to their residents from the summer heat, and to provide an aesthetic and healthful aspect to the city's quality of life. "Strangers and visitors to our town," the *Alexandria Gazette* observed, "notice the improved appearance of many of our streets in consequence of the beautiful shade trees that have, in recent years been planted along the sidewalks. Both for health and ornament these trees are worth double the cost of planting and rearing them." Natchez underwrote a tree nursery from the beginning of the nineteenth century. In addition, the city prompted residents to plant and to cultivate chinaberry trees in order to "contribute as well to the health as to the beauty of the city." Savannah enhanced what ordinarily would have been a monotonous gridiron street plan by lining its long streets with trees. On the widest streets the city also planted trees down the middle of the thoroughfare. Travelers visiting Savannah during the torrid summer months appreciated these leafy oases.[106]

The attempts of southern urban governments to beautify their city for reasons of health, image, and comfort, demonstrated that even beauty can be placed in a business context to work for the prosperity of the city. Poor relief, on the other hand, could not readily be justified in terms of dollars and cents. The attention of southern cities to the condition of their indigenous poor reveals a record that compares well with northern counterparts—which is to say that it was paternalistic, haphazard, and limited. Urban growth compounded the problem of poor relief by increasing the number of urban poor at a time when local government funds went toward more glamorous, and what many considered more necessary, urban services such as utilities, crime and disease control, and street repair. Further, poverty ranked about the same as disease in aiding a city's image, with the added point that rampant poverty had little effect on business. Finally, many citizens believed poverty to be synonymous with immorality, so public assistance would be contradictory. It was not surprising, therefore, that relief for the poor received a low priority from urban governments across the nation.[107]

Private voluntary associations dominated poor relief in nineteenth-century cities, with local government becoming an increasingly important financial source. Mobile, for example, possessed a Protestant orphan asylum and a Catholic orphan asylum.

The Female Benevolent Society was the major relief organization in Mobile. It owned and operated a row of twelve brick houses called the Widow's Row in order "to rescue 'the lone ones' from the pangs of poverty and desolation." The city's contribution to the poor was a charity hospital. Considering the medical treatment available to even the most wealthy citizens, the hospital probably functioned more as an almshouse than as a medical facility. In 1848 several civic leaders in Norfolk formed the Norfolk Association for the Improvement of the Condition of the Poor, modeled after an organization of the same name in New York. The founders possessed the prevailing paternalistic attitudes toward poverty and relief. They approached poor relief in much the same manner as they dealt with marketing procedures. Organized aid to the poverty-stricken was another means of rationalizing the city and bringing it in tune with the national urban community. "It has been tried in other cities and has worked well," noted one Norfolk Association member. A spokesman for the Association praised the inauguration of "a systematic plan for the judicious distribution of alms to the poor of our city." The group divided the city into districts, and its members visited the homes of the poor. In this manner "artful mendicants" could be ferreted out and dropped from the relief rolls: "*Sound discrimination* then, is the first principle of this Association. It will give to none who will not exhibit evidence of improvement from the aid afforded." The Association, whatever its biases, provided the poor of Norfolk with the city's first year-round assistance program.[108]

The almshouse was the major contribution of local government to poor relief in southern cities. This was a venerable institution established early in the nineteenth century, and before 1800 in the case of Charleston. The Overseers of the Poor, a body similar to the Board of Health, administered the almshouse. Living conditions there were primitive. In 1824 Robert Greenhow, president of the Overseers of the Poor in Richmond, observed that the poorhouse was the last resort of the poverty-stricken, most even preferring begging in the streets. Occupancy was low, rarely exceeding seventy indigents. The almshouse in Richmond, like the one in New York, also provided outdoor relief to over two hundred families. Most donations by the city consisted of wood, clothing, and some food, and were welcome supplements to hard-pressed private charity. By 1860 Richmond allotted more to the poor per capita than New York City. In Alexandria the almshouse operated by the Overseers of the Poor recorded only eighteen residents during the winter of 1854; all but four were immigrants. An Alexandria ordinance required that the Overseers collect kitchen offal for use and "benefit" of the almshouse.[109]

Poor relief in southern cities was generally seasonal. The almshouse was a year-round service, but outdoor relief and the ladies' and religious groups operated only during the winter months. Money for the poor, though, occupied an increasingly greater proportion of city expenditures. In Alexandria the budget for the Overseers of the Poor represented two percent of the city's expenditures in 1859, whereas a decade earlier the proportion was less than one-half of one percent.[110] Social welfare was not the strong suit of southern urban government. In this regard, however, it followed too well the path laid out by northern cities.

Southerners viewed education with the same suspicion as they viewed poverty.

Education was, of course, potentially dangerous as an instigator of slave unrest. Also, southerners tended to associate public education with social welfare—as an adjunct to poor relief. But southern higher education was more than adequate, with such fine institutions as the University of Virginia, and Transylvania in Lexington. As with poverty, though, southern cities recognized that general illiteracy could not be tolerated in a modern urban society. If the future of the South lay in its youth, then the concentration of population in the cities afforded singular opportunities for establishing educational facilities.

In some southern cities public education was an established tradition. The depression following the War of 1812 and the introduction of the steamboat on the Ohio River had apparently sealed Lexington's doom. Civic leaders attempted to recover prosperity by transforming Lexington into the "Athens of the West." In 1833 Lexington established its first public school. Twenty years later Lexington public schools, now numbering four, were educating 93 percent of the city's white school-age children. In Natchez the Natchez Institute, formed in 1845, monopolized nearly one-half of the city's budget.[111] When sectional animosity heightened, public education received more vocal support as southerners looked upon it as security for the future. Henry A. Wise, the irascible soon-to-be governor of Virginia, chose the topic of public schools for a July 4th oration in 1850: "The *ends* of our Republic are Liberty, Equality, and Fraternity, and they depend on *Popular Education* . . . the people universally must be trained alike in schools of one common education." The *Richmond Enquirer* was equally emphatic: "The *Public Good* demands that every white boy should be educated." "Free schools should at once be established; educate the people, no matter what it may cost," echoed George Fitzhugh.[112]

The evolution of a free school system in Norfolk followed a pattern set by cities in the North. In January 1849, the state legislature amended the Norfolk city charter, granting the councils the power to establish free schools. It was not until the spring of 1855 that councilmen authorized the levying of a capitation tax of $2 for every white male over twenty-one in order to establish a public school system. Yellow fever interrupted the free school effort, and it was not until January 1856, that the bicameral city legislature established the bureaucracy to administer the new system. The councilmen divided the city into four districts and provided for the popular election of a school commissioner for each district to compose the Board of Education. The four commissioners would then elect one of their members to the office of superintendent. Each commissioner would oversee one school in his district. Any white male child between the ages of six and twenty-one was eligible to attend. Following site selection, some construction, and staffing, the system of four schools opened in September 1858. The citizens of Norfolk responded with such enthusiasm that the rooms set aside for the schools were soon overcrowded, and a long waiting list developed.[113]

While free schools educated a future generation of urban Virginians, there was a large mass of adults who never benefited from formal education. Southern cities ran lyceums and opened libraries. Lecture series drew crowds. James Silk Buckingham, a British traveler, reported that in Mobile five hundred people listened to one of his lectures on the Middle East. Civic leaders, in conjunction with a small but helpful subsidy from the city government, engaged in their proclivity for organization by establishing mercantile library associations to provide informal adult education. The Baltimore Mercantile Library Association, organized by leading merchants in 1839, possessed six thousand volumes by the mid-1840s—the largest such establishment in the urban South. The Association included five hundred members, generating an annual revenue of $2,205. The Kentucky Mechanic's Institute opened in Louisville in 1853 and served about one thousand readers in its library by 1860. Richmond's Mechanic's Institute operated a night school for working adult males that concentrated on mechanical arts.[114]

Libraries in antebellum cities were not public in the modern sense, but usually existed on donations from local elites. City government did not usually venture into adult education, although occasionally city councils like Richmond's might donate a site for a Mechanic's Institute fair, or establish a library fund of $200 per annum.[115] Public financial resources were, of course, finite. Each city, north and south, set priorities for its services, and in this age of urban enterprise services that improved the immediate prospects of business prosperity were most likely to receive the greatest attention from city leaders who were themselves part of the mercantile elite. Thus, adult education could not compete successfully for the public dollar with street repair and lighting, fire and police protection, public health, and the city beautiful.

As the list of urban services grew and the local government participation in these services increased accordingly, the expense of rationalizing urban growth became more burdensome. For one thing, the need for urban services in the 1840s and 1850s came at a time when city governments had plunged heavily into financing railroads. The business community, which also directed the course of local government spending, believed that expenditures for railroads would eventually benefit the entire community. The logic was sound, but more immediately debts generated more debts until city officials were floating in a sea of red ink. In Wheeling, for example, city government expended $385,000 in 1853, $261,000 of this going toward railroad stock subscription. Of the $2,000,000 debt hanging over Richmond in 1857, $1,266,000 resulted from internal improvement expenditures.[116] The dilemma of these urban governments was how to reconcile soaring debt with increased demands for urban services.

Urban services were expensive. Natchez, where railroad subscription was relatively minor, resorted to bond issues to maintain educational, lighting, and street facilities. The salaries of city officials rose as their role in urban life increased. The mayor of Natchez had an annual salary of $600 in 1847; in 1859 it was $1,000. The bulk of antebellum Houston's public expenditures went toward supporting urban services, specifically street repair, salaries, and the city hospital. Education, fire and police protection, health and market control, and poor relief completed the impressive range of urban services provided by Houston—a city barely removed from the frontier.[117]

A comparison between the expenditures of Richmond in 1839 and in 1858, reveals the growth of public urban services. In the former year the city spent

$40,000 for interest on the debt; $20,000 for salaries; $9,000 for police protection; $5,000 for fire protection; $5,000 for poor relief; $4,000 for street repair; and $2,000 for public schools and the orphan asylum; total expenditures: $85,000. In the 1858 budget loans accounted for $71,000 (primarily for railroad stock subscription); interest for $125,000; water works for $45,000; gas works for $75,000; street repair for $40,000; improvements in the James River for $3,500; the market house for $2,500; the cemeteries for $3,000; fire protection for $10,000; poor relief for $11,000; salaries for city officials (including police) for $40,000; total expenditures: $826,000. Services such as water, gas lighting, cemeteries, and the market house and river improvements had not appeared in the previous budget. Some services declined as a percentage of the budget, such as poor relief and fire protection, demonstrating the presence of not only competing services but of the increasingly burdensome debt incurred by Richmond's city government. The role and fiscal power of urban government gained considerably during the two decades.[118]

City officials, confronted with the prospect of an empty treasury and a variety of urban services, concluded, not surprisingly, that their fellow citizens must share the burdens as well as the comforts of modern urban life. State governments granted cities the power of local taxation as a provision in their charters. City government, usually composed of merchants, treated that group generously when framing revenue bills. In Galveston in 1839 merchants paid a tax of $25 for the privilege of doing business, while competing peddlers and auctioneers received an assessment of $50 and $100 respectively. A capitation tax of $2 on all white males and $1 on all slaves between ten and fifty years of age was a major revenue source for Galveston in addition to the license fees. License fees, in addition to being a revenue source for the city, also were a form of business regulation. Thus, bars had to pay a license tax of $100—a prohibitive sum in that era—which eliminated the small, sleezy hideaways of vice that plagued some communities. Natchez, on the other hand, received the largest portion of its revenues from the property tax, which reached 25¢ per $100 valuation in the late antebellum period; license fees were a second major source of revenue. Mobile demonstrated the importance of property tax to a city government. In 1841, for example, receipts totaled $114,976.02. The property tax accounted for 65 percent of that figure, with license fees second at 13 percent. Charleston was one of the first cities in the country to levy an income tax. In 1816 the city taxed income received from trades and professions, except for teachers, who the council figured were too poor to pay the tax anyway. Charleston received most of its revenue, though, from the property tax, with citizens supporting the relatively high rate of $1.50 per $100 valuation.[119]

Cities continuously searched for new sources of revenue since property taxes were unpopular with civic leaders. Alexandria officials voted to lower the real estate tax in 1855 from $1.10 per $100 valuation to 90¢ while increasing the capitation tax on white male inhabitants from $1 to $1.50 and the tax rate on cows from 25¢ per $100 valuation to 50¢. The most significant differences in the new revenue bill were the additions: omnibuses—$15; boarding houses—$10; biscuit bakers—$20; loaf bread bakers—$10; horse dealers—$25; express agents—$25; and savings banks—$10. What with other license fees, there was scarcely an activity in Alexandria that escaped taxation and thus regulation. Citizens were naturally upset at the tax increases and the preferential treatment of the business community. A taxpayer in Alexandria could not see the logic of repairing the major business thoroughfare in the city while finances were so precarious. The list of taxable items which appeared on the revenue bill led "Grey Hairs" to reminisce that he could

remember when I took up the morning's paper before we sat down to breakfast, what Corporation taxes I should have to pay, in 5 minutes by the clock. To-day I undertook the annual duty, and before I got through, was peremptorily stopped and asked if I intended to keep the children and servants from their accustomed meal for *an hour* longer than usual.[120]

Richard C. Wade commented that complaints over city extravagance were a tribute to the new urban statesmanship, but citizens clearly did not appreciate the fiscal course of their leaders. A common reaction, both north and south, was to boot the spendthrifts out of office.[121] Replacements may have cut salaries and held the line on taxes and services, but it was inevitable in a growing metropolis that citizens would not stand for a regression in their more comfortable way of life. Although cities applied some services in a manner calculated to benefit one segment of the community, and although fiscal impecunity dogged some urban administrations, the southern city was a better city to live in by the end of the antebellum period.

The southern city was a part of the modern urban nation. The American city came of age in the mid-nineteenth century, and if it was an ungainly giant beset with the usual pains of rapid growth, it was the locus of the nation's economic and political power. It was a time when cities as well as individuals dreamed the American dream. Southern cities reached out with iron arms to capture the commerce of a bountiful west; their railroad depots and wharves groaned from the weight of crates, hogsheads, barrels, and bales; their citizens enjoyed the conviviality of the club, the Exchange, the counting house, and the park, as the old intimate way of life blended gracefully into the new; their visitors enjoyed elegant hotels, paved and lighted streets, commodious market houses, and informative columns at breakfast; and their civic leaders boosted their cities' prospects to anyone who would listen, and if the present was exciting with promise, the future was even more tantalizing. True, some urban streets made visitors choke from the dust or sink in the mud; disease struck without warning, often violently; taxes were high, and some services did not reach much of the population; there was poverty; and blacks—slave or free—lived in a perpetual state of uncertainty. This was not, however, a uniquely southern urban situation; it was the urban condition. Civic leaders in the urban South coped with growth with the available tools. They left problems and remnants of the primitive past to future generations who are still trying to alleviate the negative aspects of urban life.

The growth of southern cities in terms of identity and prosperity, impressive by itself, receded in magnitude in comparison with urban development on a national scale. In fact, the very success of southern cities in achieving maturity sealed their ultimate failure. While southern cities built railroads and extended their commerce beyond the region, northern cities were drawing them into an inextricable web of commercial relationships. Southern cities were victimized not by their own lethargy, slavery, or planter hegemony, but rather by national economic forces that were beyond their control by 1850. In a section where ironies grew like cotton in black soil, it was the South's irony that urban growth resulted in greater dependence on northern cities, rather than in the hoped for economic freedom.

By the end of the Mexican War, a national economy had developed with its center in New York. The Empire City had accumulated the financial and commercial expertise necessary to carry on large-scale trade enterprises—what the business historian Thomas C. Cochran termed the "Business Revolution." An early entry into the transatlantic trade following the War of 1812 and effective trade links to the West enabled New York to cultivate efficient business practices and arrangements which dispatched agents, ships, and railroad cars throughout the world. Commerce gravitated to the city, manufacturers sought its market and distributive network, specialization increased, and trade expanded.[122]

Antebellum import and export statistics indicate the centralization of trade at New York (see tables 3-1 through 3-4). The city's share of exports increased from one-fifth of the nation's total export value during the years immediately after the War of 1812 to better than one-third following the Mexican War. Boston and Philadelphia declined as export centers as the Empire City rose. Boston accounted for nearly 10 percent of the nation's exports in 1815, but only slightly more than 4 percent by 1860. In 1853 a Boston merchant complained bitterly about "the removal of commerce from Boston to New York."[123] Philadelphia's share of export value declined from almost 8 percent in 1850 to slightly above 1 percent in 1860.

Southern port cities actually fared better than New York's northern rivals. New Orleans, which challenged New York's export leadership in the 1830s, slumped slightly to 26.8 percent by 1860. Except for Mobile, southern ports experienced the same deterioration in their export trade as the northern ports. Cotton prosperity during the 1850s and the development of Mobile as an export center enabled the South to claim sectional supremacy in the export trade. The import trade, however, reflected a more serious picture of the southern urban economy.

Northern cities received the bulk of the import trade throughout the antebellum period. New York, however, monopolized an increasing share of the trade—a reflection of its financial and commercial apparatus—nearly doubling its value of imports between 1821 and 1860. Except for New Orleans, which registered only a slight gain (4.8 percent to 6.1 percent), all major ports suffered a decline in their import trade. Northern and southern ports fared just as poorly.

The coastwise trade was another indication of economic centralization, as well as of southern urban dependence. Boston, for example, received 40,000 tons of rice from south Atlantic ports in 1848; six years later the figure was 110,000 tons.[124] Savannah, through a vigorous railroad-building program in the late 1840s, became

TABLE 3-1.

Share of Total Value of Exports of Principal Ports, 1815–1860*
(Millions of Dollars)

Year	Total Value	New York		Other Northern Ports (Boston, Philadelphia)		Southern Ports (Savannah, Richmd.-Norf., New Orleans, Baltimore, Charleston, Mobile)	
1815	$52	$10	19.2%	$9	17.3%	$26	50.0%
1820	69	13	18.8%	16	23.2%	31	44.9%
1825	99	35	35.4%	22	22.2%	35	35.4%
1830	73	19	26.0%	11	15.1%	33	45.2%
1835	121	30	24.8%	13	10.7%	71	58.7%
1840	132	34	25.8%	16	12.1%	71	53.8%
1845	114	36	31.6%	13	11.4%	56	49.1%
1850	151	52	34.4%	14	9.3%	75	49.7%
1855	275	113	41.1%	34	12.4%	102	37.1%
1860	400	145	36.2%	22	5.5%	198	49.5%

*Percentages are state totals; but each port selected monopolized its state's import-export trade. The percentages do not add up to 100% because several minor ports were omitted.
Source: Secretary of the Treasury, *Reports on Commerce and Navigation,* annual reports, 1815–1860.

TABLE 3-2

Share of Total Value of Exports of Individual Ports, 1815–1860
(Millions of Dollars)

Year	Boston		Philadelphia		New Orleans		Baltimore		Charleston		Mobile*		Savannah		Richmd.-Norf.	
1815	$5	9.6%	$4	7.7%	$5	9.6%	$5	9.6%	$6	11.5%	—	—	$4	7.7%	$6	11.5%
1835	10	8.3%	3	2.5%	36	29.8%	3	2.5%	11	9.1%	7	5.8%	8	6.6%	6	5.0%
1840	10	7.6%	6	4.5%	34	25.8%	5	3.8%	10	7.6%	12	9.1%	6	4.5%	4	3.0%
1860	17	4.3%	5	1.3%	107	26.8%	9	2.3%	21	5.3%	38	9.5%	18	4.5%	5	1.3%

*No trade data available for Mobile in 1815.
Source: Secretary of the Treasury, *Reports on Commerce and Navigation,* annual reports, 1815–1860.

the South's third leading cotton port by 1860. By that date sixteen steamships were operating regularly out of the harbor, compared with only one in 1848. All vessels went coastwise to northern ports—nine of them to New York. Southern railroads and shipping lanes, developed after the Mexican War, became funnels to northern cities. As one southern entrepreneur noted: "We are mere way stations

TABLE 3-3.

Share of Total Value of Imports of Principal Ports, 1821-1860*
(Millions of Dollars)

Year	Total Value	New York		Other Northern Ports		Southern Ports	
1821	$62	$23	37.1%	$22	35.5%	$11	17.7%
1825	$96	$49	51.0%	30	31.3%	9	9.4%
1830	70	35	50.0%	18	25.7%	12	17.1%
1835	149	88	59.1%	31	20.8%	23	15.4%
1840	107	60	56.1%	24	22.4%	16	15.0%
1845	117	70	59.9%	30	25.6%	11	9.4%
1850	178	111	62.4%	42	23.6%	17	9.6%
1855	261	164	62.9%	60	23.0%	20	7.7%
1860	362	248	68.5%	55	15.2%	33	9.1%

*Import data not available prior to 1821.
Source: Secretary of the Treasury, *Reports on Commerce and Navigation*, annual reports, 1815–1860.

TABLE 3-4

Share of Total Value of Imports of Individual Cities, 1821-1860
(Millions of Dollars)

Year	Boston		Philadelphia		New Orleans		Baltimore		Charleston		Mobile*		Savannah		Richmd.-Norf.	
1821	$14	22.6%	$8	12.9%	$3	4.8%	$4	6.5%	$3	4.8%	–	–	$1	1.6%	–	–
1835	19	12.8%	12	8.1%	17	11.4%	5	3.4%	1	0.7%	–	–	–	–	–	–
1840	16	15.0%	8	7.5%	10	9.3%	4	3.7%	2	1.9%	–	–	–	–	–	–
1860	41	11.3%	14	3.9%	22	6.1%	9	2.5%	1	0.3%	–	–	–	–	–	–

*Less than 0.1 percent share of the total import trade.
Source: Secretary of the Treasury, *Reports on Commerce and Navigation*, annual reports, 1815-1860.

to Philadelphia, New York, and Boston."[125] The prevailing pattern of trade focused on the Northeast, especially on New York. Railroads, canals, and the business revolution won the West and conquered the South. New Orleans, the bellwether of southern commercial prosperity, remained an independent bastion, but she too was succumbing to the attractions of a national economy centered in New York.

The flush times enjoyed by New Orleans in the 1850s concealed a serious weakness in the city's trade network. The centralization of commerce in New York, and New Orleans's tardy entry into railroad building, were eroding the Crescent City's hinterland. While cotton receipts increased 160 percent in the 1850s, receipts of western products remained stationary despite a jump in western crop yields. More revealing was the fact that in 1820 western produce accounted for 58 percent of the total receipts at the port of New Orleans; by 1860 the figure was 23 percent. The national economy, linked by railroad lines from Atlantic ports, permanently diverted trade from the Mississippi River and New Orleans. In 1860 the superintendent of the United States Census declared: "As an outlet to the ocean for the grain trade of the west, the Mississippi River has almost ceased to be depended upon by merchants." De Bow agreed, and added with sadness that the mouth of the Mississippi "practically and commercially is more at New York and Boston than at New Orleans."[126]

The pattern of urbanization followed the pattern of trade, as New York outlasted and outbid pretenders to its economic preeminence. All roads, even for southerners, seemed to lead to the Empire City. As one southerner wrote home from a New York crowded with southern merchants in 1860: "Southern people, despite of everything said and done, buy where *they think* they can get the best assortment, and purchase at the *cheapest* rates."[127] Southern urban merchants increased their contacts with northern cities as secession approached and borrowed ideas on urban services from the collection of garbage to the installation of street lighting. The urbanization of the mid-nineteenth century produced a national urban network that complemented the national economy and transcended sectional feeling. Edmund Ruffin paraded in homespun, but profit-minded civic boosters formed packet companies to secure the latest fashions from New York.

Thus, as the sectional crisis threatened to blow the nation apart, commerce was drawing the cities of both sections closer together. Fitzhugh believed that these new commercial ties generated by a national economy would save the Union: "Heretofore, domestic weakness and danger from foreign foe has combined the States in sustaining the Union. Hereafter, the great advantages of friendly and mutual intercourse, trade and exchanges, may continue to produce a like result."[128] Others thought differently. In all southern cities, regardless of geographical location, secession divided the population. Cosmopolitan seaports such as New Orleans and Baltimore especially contained vigorous Unionist sentiment, while in Charleston secessionists prevailed. Natchez, deep in the Mississippi delta but with strong economic ties to the North, voted for Unionist delegates by almost a four-to-one margin. In general, the majority of opinion both in northern and in southern cities wished the crisis to go away.[129] The extended diorama of crisis after November 1860, was bad for business since it disrupted the free flow of commerce between North and South—a trade that had grown more intimate since the Mexican War. It was a commercial age, and commercial considerations not only weighed heavily in the minds of urban delegates but at times played a dominant role in the secession conventions.

Southern cities were caught between the two sections—economic ties pulling in both directions. At the Virginia convention urban delegates, as well as rural colleagues, expressed this dual pressure. "The question before us," a delegate from Lynchburg observed, "is not Union or disunion, but which will we join—North or South." The hinterland towns picked up the refrain: "Will Virginia join the Northern or the Southern Union—that is the True Issue."[130] The answer depended to a large extent on how Virginians viewed their commercial future. The delegates placed even slavery in this context. Two decades of bitter competition with northern and southern urban rivals caused Virginians to weigh the answer to their question carefully.

Some Virginians perceived union with the cotton South with unguarded hostility. Some urban businessmen had been complaining that the demand for slaves in the Deep South was threatening Virginia's urban economy as slave labor became scarce and expensive in her cities. On the other hand, those who profited from the domestic slave trade similarly viewed Deep South intentions with suspicion. Baltimoreans feared the potential havoc of a renewed transatlantic slave trade. The possibility of the reopening of the trade was a major reason that George Fitzhugh, one of the most prominent spokesmen for southern economic independence, opposed secession. The renewed slave trade could result in a severe loss to Virginia's economy. Alexandria and Richmond were two centers of the domestic slave trade, a business that generated $4,500,000 annually, more than the entire state's tobacco receipts.[131] The loss of that revenue could affect growth in both cities. It was not outrageous to argue, therefore, that union with the North would be the best protection for the institution of slavery.[132]

Others saw a southern confederacy as hostile to Virginia commercial interests generally. Virginia's cities dutifully sent delegates to the various southern commercial conventions, but unanimously pronounced them "abortions" or "useless." The conventions were typically forums for fire eaters rather than for commercial enterprise. Even when the delegates dropped their radical rhetoric and settled down to more fruitful discussion, Deep South rail lines and developing New Orleans or Mobile, rather than Norfolk or Richmond, seemed to dominate debate.[133] Manufacturers feared the cotton South's obsession with free trade would ruin their struggling industries, even though sentiment for a tariff was growing below Virginia. George W. Brent, delegate and Alexandria merchant, advanced a more cogent argument with respect to manufacturing. Brent argued that political considerations would force the southern confederacy into intimate economic relations with Great Britain and France. As a result, both the manufacturing and eventually the commerce of Virginia's cities would suffer gravely.[134]

Other urban Virginians assumed with equal fervor that union with the southern confederacy would insure their security and prosperity. Tredegar's Joseph R. Anderson, whose products enjoyed an extensive southern market, believed that his ironworks would enjoy a virtual monopoly in an independent South. The *Richmond Enquirer* agreed with Anderson, arguing that with the North "Virginia declines, shrivels up and finds no markets for her manufactured goods." Urban secessionists placed a different perspective on the Unionists' contentions that close economic ties with the North precluded secession. Under the heading

"Unnecessary Tolls and Tribute the Southern States Pay to the North," the *Montgomery Advertiser* related the annual cost of the South's economic dependence on the North: customs disbursed in the North—$40,000,000; profits from manufacture of southern raw materials—$30,000,000; profits from imports destined for southern market centers—$17,000,000; profits from export of southern goods—$40,000,000; profits from southern travelers—$60,000,000; profits of teachers and others in the South sent North—$5,000,000; profits of agents and brokers, and commissions—$10,000,000; capital drawn from the South—$30,000,000; total—$231,000,000. The *Advertiser* concluded: "The establishment of a new Government might cost something; but nothing in comparison to the stream of wealth that would flow to the commercial, manufacturing, and mechanical interest, by withholding this annual tribute and working ourselves."[135]

With these figures evidently fermenting in his mind, a writer in *De Bow's Review* predicted that Richmond would become "the greatest city of the Southern Union." Virginia's William M. Burwell, a leading secessionist and advocate of southern urban growth, forecast a flourishing direct trade from Norfolk with transportation lines bringing cotton through Memphis. The *Charleston Mercury* envisioned its city as the New York of the South, and added: "There are no people in the Southern States who will gain so certainly by a dissolution of the Union as the merchants of our cities. . . . Those who have ears to hear, let them hear what a calculation of dollars and cents teaches."[136] For a city, for any southern city for that matter, that had spent millions to capture the trade of the West to compete on an equal basis with northern cities, this was heady stuff.

Urban advocates of the southern confederacy argued further that the federal government under Republican control would throw its weight behind the commercial aspirations of northern cities to the neglect of the South. Distrust of Washington was not exclusively a southern phenomenon. Northern cities resented the obstacles states' rights southerners placed in the path of federal aid to harbor improvements.[137] As Republican strength grew in the 1850s, though, southern wariness of the national government changed to anxiety. The southern trade imbalance, the specter of a high tariff in a section that manufactured relatively little, and the strident economic nationalism of Republican leaders indicated that a solid factual foundation underlay these fears. If, as the *Charleston Mercury* observed, "Charleston, Mobile, and Savannah [were] suburbs of New York, Philadelphia, and Boston" *before* a Republican president occupied the White House, what could southern cities and the South generally hope for after Lincoln's election? Moreover, some Virginians believed that Washington, even prior to the existence of the Republican Party, had come under the influence of northern business and financial interests. In 1851 the *Enquirer* noted testily that while northern cities received federal aid, Richmond's James River harbor was unable to obtain a pittance from Congress. A year later a Norfolk merchant blamed his city's difficulty in obtaining direct trade with Europe on "the centralizing action of the Federal Government in favor of New York."[138] Now that the Republicans controlled the executive, northern ports would inevitably receive even greater preference. A pattern had been developing during the 1850s that portended ill for southern urban interests.

The Republican Party platform specified that the federal government would play an active and guiding role in the new national economy. Urban leaders feared a loss of federal contracts such as mail carrying and the navy under a Republican president. When the Republicans ran their first presidential race in 1856, the *Enquirer* estimated a loss of "50 or 60 million in the granting of numerous lucrative contracts," if the voters elected Fremont. Industry would also be a target for a Republican executive. An Alexandria merchant predicted that "the federal government will fetter Southern industry and pay bounties to Northern industry." Substantial federal aid and a northern route for the transcontinental railroad would accompany a Republican administration, thus effectively destroying southern dreams for a commercial empire in the Far West. Southerners were concerned that the Republicans would tip the balance of economic power irrevocably toward the North.[139]

The question of secession for Virginia's cities, and other southern cities as well, was not one of "preserving its own way of life," but rather of where best to secure the fruits of the American urban dream of commercial empire. Slavery was an important element in the secession debate because it was an integral part of the urban economy. Slaveholding per se was irrelevant to secession. The votes of Virginia's urban delegates on secession reflected their perception of the American urban dream. There were two secession votes: one defeated on April 4 and one passed on April 17 after Lincoln's call for troops made secession a fait accompli. In the April 4 voting the twelve urban delegates divided their vote with four ayes, six nays, and two absent. On April 17, there were seven ayes and five nays. Wheeling rarely dealt with southern markets, and 90 percent of Norfolk's trade was with northern ports. On the April 4 vote, one Norfolk delegate was absent and one voted against secession. On the April 17 vote the two delegates split. Wheeling's two delegates never cast a ballot for secession. Lynchburg, the Old Dominion's major interior market, had the least direct commercial relations with the North. The city was also the eastern terminus of the Virginia and Tennessee Railroad, a line extending to Memphis. Its two delegates voted aye on both occasions. Unionist sentiment prevailed in Alexandria, though not so strongly as in Norfolk or Wheeling. Alexandria's delegate George W. Brent, an outspoken critic of the cotton confederacy's economic policies, cast ballots against both secession ordinances. Petersburg's Thomas Branch personally opposed secession, but pressure from constituents who hoped for a flourishing cotton trade via the Virginia and Tennessee Railroad induced him to vote for secession on both occasions. Richmond possessed the widest market of all Virginia cities, and its equally close connections with southern and northern market centers divided the city and its four delegates. On the first ballot Richmond's delegates voted three to one against secession, and on the second three to one for secession. The result implied that market orientation, i.e., where best to pursue the urban dream, might have influenced secession sentiment, as the rhetoric suggests. Other variables such as slaveholding, geographic location (Tidewater vs. trans-Allegheny, for example), property holding, age, and political party do not seem to form as distinctive a pattern as market orientation.[140] A detailed correlation analysis of urban votes in all secession conventions would reveal the validity of this hypothesis.

Southern cities encountered a variety of fates in the Civil War, from a business-as-usual atmosphere prevailing throughout most of the war in New Orleans, to the chaos and confusion in Richmond, to the stark destruction in Atlanta. Their resurrection after the war was by no means immediate, but in the process of rehabilitation southern cities became enshrined in the pantheon of the New South—a creed developed primarily by urban southerners. The foundation for this new urban hope, though, lay solidly within the Old South. Wilbur J. Cash first expounded the theory of the continuity of southern history. The urban South's pursuit of the American urban dream not only remained viable through the Civil War, but emerged with a new dignity and place in southern society. The railroads, the street lights, and, above all, the urban consciousness were there in 1865 as southern cities renewed their quest for what was to become in the ensuing decades an impossible dream.

4 HOWARD N. RABINOWITZ

CONTINUITY AND CHANGE: SOUTHERN URBAN DEVELOPMENT, 1860–1900

During the late nineteenth century northern cities were radically transformed. The wrenching experience of Civil War and Reconstruction might have similarly affected their southern counterparts. Instead, continuity between urban development in the Old South and the New was more noteworthy than change.[1]

The continuing efforts of urban boosters to alter the basic character of southern life and to bring their communities into line with those of the North met with only limited success. Economic realities, the pull of the past, and northern competition proved too great to overcome. This is not to say that there was no change, only that in most aspects the closing years of the century witnessed the playing out of old themes in new circumstances. First, though continuing to exercise a disproportionate influence in their region, southern cities still lagged behind those in the North in size, numbers, municipal services, and wealth. Second, manufacturing gained a greater place in local economies, but as in the antebellum period, commercial and administrative functions of cities remained more important than in the North. And third, urban dwellers remained preoccupied with disciplining their growing black populations, now free rather than slave.

The main difference between antebellum and postbellum urbanization was the filling in of the urban network through the growth of important interior southern cities, a development which considerably rearranged the rank order distribution of cities that had existed in 1860. Before the Civil War the ten largest cities in what soon would be the Confederate South were river or seaports located on the perimeter of the region east of the Mississippi River. By 1900, however, the top ten included Atlanta, San Antonio, and Houston, while Dallas and Birmingham ranked eleventh and twelfth. Whereas in 1860 Virginia had four of the twelve largest cities and Texas none, by 1900 Virginia had two and Texas three. These inland cities, unlike the Old South's largest towns, owed their growth not to a choice water location but rather to the postbellum expansion of the region's railroad system. Older river ports like Memphis, Richmond, and Nashville and the ocean port of Norfolk were able to keep pace because of their railroad connections, while New Orleans,

Mobile, Savannah, and Charleston were among the established coastal cities that lost ground because of changes in transportation patterns. New Orleans, for example, remained the South's largest city throughout the period, but the sharply diminished gap between it and the next four largest cities in 1900 revealed the growing maturation of the urban system that had occurred since 1860.

As suggested by table 4-1, individual cities might rise or fall in spectacular fashion but there was no sudden change in the overall hierarchy. Gradual change

TABLE 4-1.
Largest Southern Cities, 1860-1900

1860		1870		1880	
New Orleans	168,675	New Orleans	191,418	New Orleans	216,090
Charleston	40,519	Richmond	51,038	Richmond	63,600
Richmond	37,910	Charleston	48,956	Charleston	49,984
Mobile	29,258	Memphis	40,226	Nashville	43,350
Memphis	22,623	Mobile	32,034	Atlanta	37,409
Savannah	22,292	Savannah	28,235	Memphis	33,592
Petersburg, Va.	18,266	Nashville	25,865	Savannah	30,709
Nashville	16,988	Atlanta	21,789	Mobile	29,132
Norfolk	14,620	Norfolk	19,229	Galveston	22,248
Alexandria	12,652	Petersburg, Va.	18,950	Norfolk	21,966

1890		1900	
New Orleans	242,039	New Orleans	287,104
Richmond	81,338	Memphis	102,320
Nashville	76,168	Atlanta	89,872
Atlanta	65,533	Richmond	85,050
Memphis	64,495	Nashville	80,865
Charleston	54,955	Charleston	55,807
Savannah	43,189	Savannah	54,244
Dallas	38,067	San Antonio	53,321
San Antonio	37,673	Norfolk	46,624
Norfolk	34,871	Houston	44,633

also characterized internal developments that included the expansion of municipal services and the control of urban blacks. Both the internal and external dimensions of southern urbanization can be divided into four chronological periods. From 1860 to 1865 wartime conditions determined the character of urban life. During the subsequent eight years southern cities with varied degrees of success sought to recover from the effects of the war. This effort was cut short by the Panic of 1873, whose economic aftereffects restricted growth and progress until the end of the decade. The last twenty years of the century brought sustained urban expansion and prosperity that was only briefly undercut by the Panic of 1893 and the subsequent depression.

1860-1865

No event has received more attention among southern historians than the Civil War. Often termed a watershed in southern history, its impact has been seen as especially great on urban development. In his study of the South during Reconstruction, E. Merton Coulter emphasized the damage to southern cities during the war. In Columbia, South Carolina, "everything in the business district had been swept away and two-thirds of the rest of the city was gone." Atlanta "was now as famous for its utter destruction as it had been for its rapid growth and Savannah would mourn six blocks of ruins." Richmond, Selma, Fredricksburg, Petersburg, and Charleston were also singled out—"And so the story went; towns and villages throughout the fought-over Confederacy had their scars to show." In similar fashion Thomas Wertenbaker concluded that at the end of the war Norfolk "like all Southern towns was prostrate." She had escaped complete destruction, "but her commerce was at a low ebb, her tributary railroads broken, her finances deranged, her streets out of repair, her citizens impoverished."[2]

At first glance, comparative census data for the North and South support the claim that the war seriously hindered postbellum southern urban growth. A closer look, however, buttresses T. Lynn Smith's view that "it is doubtful that the twenty years of war and reconstruction greatly retarded the development of urban centers in the South."[3] In 1860 the eleven states had 54, or 13.8 percent, of the nation's 392 urban centers; ten years later the same states had 67, or only 10.1 percent, of the 663 urban centers. Yet, this decline in the South's percentage of the nation's towns was part of a long-term decline that antedated the war. From a high point of 17.8 percent in 1830 that percentage had dropped to 16.8 percent in 1840, then 15.3 percent in 1850, and finally to the figure of 1860. The region's share of places with more than ten thousand people had dropped even more sharply from 18.9 percent in 1840 to 11.8 percent in 1860.[4]

Five years of fighting accelerated the growing gap between the extent of urbanization in the North and the South, but it did not prevent the accretion of the southern urban population. By 1870 8.6 percent of the region's population was listed as urban, as compared to 7.1 percent in 1860. Because of the undercount of southern urban blacks in 1870, the actual increase was no doubt greater; but it was still far less than the jump in the national percentage from 19.8 percent to 25.7 percent.[5]

Many cities suffered because of the disruption of their traditional trade routes, damage to their agricultural hinterlands, ruinous inflation and speculation, decline of public services, and loss of men to the war effort. But for most there were offsetting benefits, and for many the war definitely contributed to urban growth. Generalizations about a "prostrate South" are risky. Galveston and Houston, for example, were hurt by the Union blockade, but San Antonio flourished as a result of its secure inland position and its role as a military and supply center for the Confederacy. Charleston, Savannah, and Mobile lost a major share of the cotton trade, but the occupation of New Orleans and Memphis by Union troops in 1862 allowed cotton merchants in those cities to prosper. As Gerald Capers concluded about Memphis, "Few Southern towns suffered as little from the four years of war."[6] Even some cities which experienced much destruction and disruption quickly recovered. The outstanding example was Atlanta. By 1864 the city had doubled its 1860 population to over twenty thousand. As a military headquarters and manufacturing, supply, and medical center, it was among the three most important Confederate cities. The much publicized "destruction" of the city in 1864 did little to hinder its path to regional dominance, in part because the extent of the damage itself has been exaggerated. On arriving in the city in November 1865, Sidney Andrews, surprised to find less devastation than he had expected, wrote, ". . . the City Hall and the Medical College and all the churches, and many of the handsomer and more stylish private dwellings and nearly all the houses of the middling and poorer classes were spared."[7]

1865-1873

The first postwar years are usually divided into the eras of Presidential Reconstruction (1865 to 1867) and Radical or Congressional Reconstruction (1867 to 1877), but in terms of urban development the years from 1865 to the onset of the Panic of 1873 form a more natural unit. In all but their treatment of blacks, southern cities reacted very similarly, whether Radicals or former Confederates were in control.

The primary tasks of the first postwar years were to rebuild urban economies on a sound basis, to repair the damage of the war, and to cope with the increased number of rural migrants, especially blacks drawn to the cities by rural dislocation and urban prosperity.

The task of postwar recovery was greatest for the older port cities, especially New Orleans and Charleston. Even before the Civil War these two cities had seen their once lofty positions challenged by competing towns and especially by the intrusion of interior railroad development. Their comparative decline continued in the early postwar years. Along with Mobile, both cities were plagued by obstructions still blocking their harbors. Charleston also suffered from the destruction of the 104-mile rail link to Savannah that remained out of operation until March 1870. But these port cities were hurt most by changes in the cotton trade. As they had done during and before the war, postbellum cotton factors initially continued to sell the cotton of inland producers and to supply them with imported goods and credit. Already on the eve of the war, however, improved rail connections had threatened the traditional role of the seaport factor. Farmers in western Georgia and northern Alabama had new markets for their crops and could choose among Charleston, Savannah, and Norfolk on the Atlantic; Mobile, New Orleans, and Pensacola on the Gulf; or widely scattered interior towns like Augusta, Macon, Montgomery, and Memphis. And in the first decade after the war, new rail links which greatly expanded the small overland trade to the North by way of Memphis seriously hurt the Gulf ports. The growth of east-west railroads south of the Ohio River also drew cotton to the Atlantic ports. While Charleston and Savannah continued to be destinations, they were already being challenged by Norfolk. Norfolk greatly benefited by the swift repair of both the Seaboard and Roanoke and the Norfolk and Petersburg railroads, which by 1874 had made the city the third cotton port behind New Orleans and Galveston.[8]

As elsewhere in the United States during this period, the railroad meant success or failure for communities of all sizes. Equipment was worn out and thousands of "Sherman's hairpins" (rails twisted around trees) bore testimony to the numerous gaps in the system. Nonetheless, John Stover reports that between 1865 and 1870 the lines were rebuilt and placed in operation. As early as 1866 "southern rail recovery was so advanced that nearly every state had new railroad projects in mind and in some cases work had actually begun."[9]

This railroad recovery spurred the growth of interior towns and altered their economies. Between 1860 and 1870 Montgomery grew by 19.7 percent, Augusta by 23.2 percent, Macon by 31.1 percent, Natchez by 37 percent, Memphis by 77.8 percent, and Selma, Shreveport, Vicksburg, and Little Rock by whopping percentages of 104 percent, 110 percent, 171 percent, and 232 percent, respectively. Each of these attracted more merchants and bankers, who eventually took over the credit and supply functions of the port factor.[10] Dallas, for example, opened its first bank in 1868; by 1872 Atlanta had ten banks, none of which had existed at the end of the war.[11] And of course, interior merchants like the Lehman brothers in Montgomery began to purchase local cotton themselves. They added cotton gins, storage facilities, and large compresses so that the cotton could be readied for market locally before being sent on through bills of lading to the seaports or directly to the North overland. The coastal factors still remained important, but their days were clearly numbered. To survive they would have to turn to new ways of doing business.[12]

Railroads had already begun to alter trade routes and determine urban growth in the antebellum period, but there was a major difference in the postwar period. Before the war extensive subscriptions of money by individual cities enabled many of them to control railroads. Augusta determined the policy of the Georgia Railroad; Savannah, the Central of Georgia; Charleston, the South Carolina; and Mobile, Richmond, Norfolk, and New Orleans each had a special railroad to secure the western trade. James Russell has concluded, however, that "never again would Southern cities have such opportunities. . . . After the Civil War, the cost of building a railroad rose far beyond the means of most cities."[13] Until the Panic of 1873 cities nonetheless sought to continue the earlier policy. Atlanta businessmen pressed the city council to subscribe to a number of railroads; the first postwar city government in Montgomery bought $500,000 worth of stock in the South and North Railroad.[14] In the first eight years after the war most cities, though, were content to lure railroads to town with limited capital subscriptions, tax breaks, and free rights of way. And the tactic worked. In 1870 Dallas was a sleepy Texas town in the middle of nowhere with a population of 2,960. Then in 1872 the Houston and Texas Central Railroad came to town, followed the next year by the Texas and Pacific Railway. By 1880 the town had over 10,000 people.[15]

But it was Atlanta, "the Chicago of the South," that benefited most from the railroad in the immediate postwar years. Again we can see the antebellum roots of postbellum developments. During the antebellum period Atlanta, originally called Terminus, had emerged as "an incidental byproduct of a railroad system constructed to promote the prosperity of other towns."[16] By the eve of the war it was connected by five railroads to major cities of the North, West, and South. Less than a year after Sherman had left the city in flames, all five railroads were in active operation.[17] A local editor could rightfully claim in the fall of 1866 that Atlanta "is the radiating point for Northern and Western trade coming Southward, and is the gate through which passes Southern trade and travel going northward."[18] Trade with the Midwest quickly revived after the war, and the city was also one of those that profited from the changes in the nature of the cotton trade. Atlanta's prosperity was further stimulated by the influx of northerners and others interested in making money and from an active trade with nearby country stores. Its designation as the headquarters of the Third Military District under Congressional Reconstruction in 1867 and as the state capital in 1868 also spurred growth.

Known for their fervent boosterism even then, Atlantans were not content to simply let prosperity come—they went out and grabbed it. In 1865 Whitelaw Reid compared Atlanta to the former capital of the Confederacy. "The burnt district of Richmond was hardly more thoroughly destroyed than the central part of Atlanta, yet with all the advantages of proximity to the North, abundant capital, and the influx of business and money from above the Potomac, Richmond was not half so rebuilt as Atlanta."[19] In order to attract the wagon trade of nearby farmers, Atlantans quickly rebuilt the public market in 1866; in order to secure the capital, they promised to provide free of charge for ten years any necessary state buildings. And flushed by their manufacturing success during the war, they actively sought to encourage industry. The Atlanta Rolling Mill was back in operation by 1866, and within five years after the war there were 74 manufacturing establishments, more than ever before, producing goods valued at over $2 million annually. Sparked by an impressive construction boom, Atlanta real estate increased in value from $2,752,650 in 1860 to $5,328,450 in 1866 and then to $8,972,562 in 1870.[20]

Other southern cities drew on their wartime experiences and memory of the antebellum industrial crusade in the hope of diversifying their basically commercial economies. Augusta, which had prospered during the war as a supplier of cotton goods and weapons to the Confederate army, sought to capitalize on its water power, sufficient venture capital, close proximity to the cotton fields, and abundance of cheap labor. City officials and businessmen believed that their community could become the "Lowell of the South" if they enlarged the old canal used since 1845 to supply water power to local mills. A majority of the voters approved the project in October 1871, and the city purchased the necessary dredging equipment, awarded a contract to a private contractor, and arranged for the importation of several hundred Chinese laborers to assist in digging the canal. After several years of labor the project was completed in 1875 at a cost of almost $1 million. With the aid of northern and local capital, cotton mills, a flour mill, an ice factory, a silk mill, an iron works, and other major industries were built along the banks of the enlarged canal. The new establishments in turn stimulated additional growth.[21]

Nevertheless, during the years from 1865 to 1873, advances in manufacturing were less important than the massive effort to improve the quality of urban life by providing residents needed services. Spurred on by the local press, there came an unprecedented building program that left in its wake new waterworks, streetcars, bridges, city halls, market houses, and paved streets.[22] Though still leaving southern cities behind their northern counterparts, this period of construction helped to close the gap and to prepare the way for further gains in the 1880s.

Much of this activity was financed directly by the cities. Prior to the war city income derived primarily from wharfage, license fees, bond issues, and special taxes. After 1860 the ad valorem tax on property was the chief source of regular income, although an increasing number of cities sought to fund major projects through the issuance of bonds. Between 1866 and 1873 Atlanta tax receipts grew from $80,000 to $300,000, thanks largely to the doubling in the value of city property. During roughly the same period the value of bonds issued by the city amounted to an estimated $100,000 more than the total revenue gained from taxes.[23] This was part of a national trend. In fifteen principal American cities the city bonded debt increased 271 percent from 1866 to 1875. The larger part of the increase took place from 1870 to 1873.[24]

The cities used the money primarily to improve intraurban communication. The major expenses in Houston were for streets and bridges; in Atlanta, they consumed 32 percent of the budget between 1868 and 1873. Other large chunks of money went to new public buildings. Montgomery, Atlanta, and Houston were among the many cities which rebuilt or erected new public markets and city halls. Municipal water works were built in Norfolk, Montgomery, and Atlanta.[25] And by 1873 almost every southern city had inaugurated a public school system, a further contribution to local construction booms.

The private sector also contributed to the postwar building surge. In addition to impressive new commercial buildings, there were great hotels like Atlanta's six-story Kimball House and theaters like New Orleans's Grand Opera House. Everywhere private gas companies received charters and began tearing up the streets to lay their pipes. But most important to urban life was the appearance of horse-drawn streetcars. Only New Orleans and Mobile had had streetcars prior to 1861. The Civil War delayed the installation of systems in the other large cities, but did not seriously interfere with their subsequent adoption.[26] In 1865 streetcars began operating in Richmond, Charleston, and Memphis, giving the former Confederate states a total of five of the nation's forty-eight cities with lines. All major cities had street railways by 1870, most by 1866. Aside from the five already mentioned, the list includes Nashville (1866), Savannah (1869), Atlanta (1871), Norfolk (1870), Houston (1868), and Dallas (1873).[27] The streetcar systems not only provided needed construction work but encouraged the extension of city boundaries, the creation of economic subcenters, and the sorting out of the population. Nevertheless, it was not until the appearance during the late 1880s of the steam dummy and the electric car that urban mass transit began to have its greatest effect on urban life.

On the eve of the Panic of 1873, local boosters could take pride in the recovery and prosperity of their cities. There were still complaints about muddy streets, inadequate water, insufficient police protection, and high freight rates, but clearly there was much ground for optimism. By 1873 most white urban dwellers could also express satisfaction with the way in which they had handled their "Negro problem."

One of the consequences of emancipation and the end of the war was a marked cityward movement of large numbers of rural blacks, even though the great majority remained in the countryside. The antebellum trend towards the thinning out of black urban populations was reversed. According to U. S. Census data, between 1860 and 1870 Atlanta's black population grew from 1,939 to 9,929, and the percentage of the black population from 20 percent to 46 percent. In 1860 Richmond's 14,275 blacks constituted 38 percent of the city's population; in 1870, 23,110, or 45 percent of the residents were black. Nor did federal censuses tell the true story of the immediate postwar years. The 1870 censuses greatly underestimated the number of urban black southerners, and by that date there had already been some exodus to the countryside. According to the *Nashville Dispatch,* for example, there were 10,744 freedmen in Nashville in 1865 as compared to the prewar figure of less than 4,000; the 1870 census, however, counted only 9,709 blacks, who nevertheless represented 38 percent of the city's population as compared to 23 percent in 1860. And in Atlanta local censuses conducted in 1867 and 1869 recorded 9,288 and 13,184 blacks.[28]

Rural blacks came to the cities for a variety of reasons. For some the cities as headquarters for the federal forces represented safety from the violence and intimidation of the countryside. Others came for the welfare and educational services provided by the army, the Freedmen's Bureau, and northern missionary societies. No doubt, others were drawn by the attractions of city life and the simple desire to exercise their new freedom of movement. Whatever the motivation, most realized that in the antebellum period the cities had been better places for blacks than the rural areas.

Local whites were horrified and dismayed by the influx of blacks. They believed that the blacks were needed in the countryside and that city life would be harmful to them. Most important, they felt that the blacks would constitute a threat to public order. "Our advice to them is to go into the country and cultivate the soil, the employment God designed them for and which they must do or starve," declared the *Montgomery Daily Ledger* in 1865. Its editor added, the city was "intended for white people." To the *Raleigh Daily Sentinel,* "Nothing can be more deleterious to the black race as their strong proclivity to congregate in the towns. The temptation to idleness, viciousness, and crime are tenfold what they are in the country."[29]

Such views were common in the antebellum period. But now the blacks, no longer slaves, were even more difficult to control. The first postwar local governments elected by white suffrage under Presidential Reconstruction consisted primarily of former Confederates, often members of the wartime administrations. Together with the help of the Freedmen's Bureau and the army, they sought to prevent additional migration or to export blacks to the countryside. When this policy had little effect, city officials did as little as possible for the blacks, preferring to concentrate on the needs of the whites. The antebellum policy of excluding blacks from schools and welfare services was initially continued. Increasingly, however, the federal authorities forced city governments to assume responsibility for needy blacks, though they were cared for in segregated facilities. Little else was done by local officials from 1865 to 1867 to ease the transition of the freedmen from slavery to freedom.[30]

With the onset of Congressional Reconstruction in 1867, conditions for urban blacks began to improve. In most areas the governments appointed by military commanders or elected by black and white suffrage replaced the old policy of exclusion with a new one of separate, though allegedly equal, treatment. Throughout the urban South separate black militia companies were formed; blacks were admitted to segregated almshouses, institutions for the blind, deaf, and dumb, insane asylums, and hospitals; and by 1873 Republican governments had either organized segregated public school systems or, as in Atlanta, provided separate accommodations for blacks in what had been all-white systems. Only in New Orleans was an effort made to "mix the races", but even there the extent of integration was never great.[31]

The shift from exclusion to segregation also affected black access to public accommodations. The new streetcar systems in Nashville and Richmond, for example, initially excluded blacks. By the early 1870s black protests in these two cities, New Orleans, Charleston, Mobile, and elsewhere had forced streetcar companies at first to permit blacks to ride on the platforms of the cars, then in separate cars, and finally in the same cars as whites.[32] The extent of integration within the cars, however, remains a subject of controversy. Recent research has also modified the views of C. Vann Woodward concerning the prevalence of integration in other forms of public accommodation. Rather than the flexible system of race relations portrayed by Woodward, it seems that by 1873 the urban landscape for blacks was dominated by segregated galleries in the theaters; exclusion from leading hotels, restaurants, and bars and segregated access in others; segregated or no waiting rooms in railroad stations; and second-class or smoking cars on the railroads.[33] It must be remembered, however, that contrary to current assumptions, segregation generally marked an improvement for blacks, for what it replaced was not integration but exclusion. Meanwhile, a combination of white hostility and black voluntary action produced separate Negro churches, fraternal and benevolent societies, and residential segregation that by 1873 had helped to create separate black and white worlds within most southern communities. Black neighborhoods with their own institutions, such as Atlanta's Shermantown or Summer Hill and Nashville's Black Bottom or Rocktown, were located on the fringe of the still compact cities near railroad tracks, industrial sites, and contaminated streams on land considered unfit for white habitation.

The determination of whites to keep blacks "in their place" and the absence of nonagrarian skills among most blacks similarly produced a distinct occupational structure in which blacks were confined mainly to unskilled and semiskilled jobs. The low pay of these jobs and their scattered location contributed to the low quality and segregated character of Negro housing. Although the number of Atlanta blacks with property worth $1,000 or more increased from 4 in 1866 to 45 by 1874, the mass of blacks were mired at the bottom of the economic ladder. In 1870 76.1 percent of the city's black males sixteen and over were classified as unskilled as compared to 16.8 percent of their white counterparts.[34] This concentration was repeated throughout the urban South and increased as the period waned.

Although most whites were willing to accept the shift from exclusion to segregation, they were less satisfied with the specter of Negro officeholders. During these early years native whites spent as much time, energy, and newspaper space on trying to "redeem" their local governments from the control of white "carpetbaggers," "scalawags," and their black allies as they did in trying to rebuild their cities. Often the two problems went together, as when the *Montgomery Daily Advertiser* urged the defeat of the local Radical administration for fear that otherwise the Democratic state government would move the Alabama capital to another city.[35]

Using gerrymandering, restrictive voting laws, and the less subtle means of vote fraud and intimidation, southern whites usually needed little time to redeem their cities. In the first popular elections under universal manhood suffrage, many cities, including Norfolk, Savannah, Memphis, and Richmond, immediately came under Conservative or Democratic control, while in Atlanta, an independent Democratic mayor elected with Radical support confronted a Democratic-controlled city council. In others, including New Orleans and Nashville, brief periods of Republican hegemony had ended by 1873. Redemption did not occur in Houston until 1874, and Raleigh and Montgomery until 1875. In only a handful of other cities, including Jackson, Mississippi, and Chattanooga, did Republicans continue in power until the late 1880s.[36]

The extent of black officeholding varied. No black served as mayor of a major city, but with the exception of a few cities like Savannah, the Reconstruction city councils did include some blacks, though never a majority. Black councilmen like William Finch of Atlanta, Holland Thompson of Montgomery, and James H. Harris of Raleigh used their considerable influence to secure schools and greater relief aid for blacks and to provide improved services for Negro neighborhoods. Thompson and Harris also pressed successfully for the appointment of Negro police and the establishment of segregated fire companies.[37] Few other cities had Negro policemen during the period, but with the notable exceptions of Atlanta and Richmond, most cities had Negro firemen.

Redemption in places like New Orleans, Atlanta, and Montgomery meant the end of Negro officeholding in nonfederal jobs until the twentieth century. Elsewhere, as in Richmond's Jackson Ward and Raleigh's Second and Fourth wards, the gerrymandering that prevented Republican control of the cities permitted the election of Negro councilmen until the turn of the century. These black politicians, however, were no longer able to help their black constituents to the extent their counterparts had during Reconstruction.

1873-1879

The celebration over urban Redemption was quickly tempered by growing nationwide financial difficulties. Although the Panic of 1873 and the subsequent six years of depression severely hurt the North, the South suffered more. In part, this was because southern cities were "traditionally low in capital with substantial credit advanced to the agricultural regions."[38] More important was the crippling effect on the region's railroads and on the cities whose lifelines they had become. John Stover's survey of postbellum southern railroads concluded that as a result of their financial position on the eve of the panic, southern railroads suffered more than northern lines.[39] Though Stover's subject states included Kentucky and excluded Texas and Arkansas, his findings apply to the conditions in the eleven states of the former Confederacy.

By November 1873, 55 railroads in Stover's ten states had defaulted on interest on their bonds. Within three years 45 percent of the 127 major southern lines were in default of their bond coupons, and the figure was 50 percent or more in Virginia, Florida, Alabama, and Louisiana; in the rest of the country less than one-fourth of the lines were in default. Default usually led to receivership, and together they greatly restricted the amount of new railroad construction. The depressed conditions of the 1870s thus accelerated the decline of the South's share in the nation's railroad mileage. That share had shrunk from nearly one-third of the total in 1861, to little more than one-fourth in 1865, and to one-fifth in 1873. By 1880 the 14,811 miles in the southern states constituted less than 16 percent of the national total. The shortage of funds also led to a decline in the quality of equipment, roadbeds, and service. And, finally, many of the bankrupt locally owned southern railroads fell into northern hands. Of the 45 major roads in Stover's ten states in 1870-1871, only 19 percent of the traceable members of the boards of directors came from the North, whereas in 1880-1881 37 percent of the directors were northerners and nearly half the companies had northern presidents, compared to less than one-sixth ten years before.[40]

Internally the period from 1873 to 1880 was one of belt tightening in payment for the heady expansion of the early postwar years. With the economic downturn, cities had increasing difficulty in maintaining municipal services and in paying the interest on their bonded debt. The collection of the newly levied property taxes became even more difficult than in the past.[41] In an unsuccessful effort at social pressure, newspapers listed the names of residents owing taxes, but even Nashville Mayor Thomas A. Kercheval could be found among his city's defaulters. The combination of national depression, overspending, and tax evasion forced Houston's officials to arrange compromises with that city's creditors in 1875, 1881, and 1888. They were able to fund a consolidated debt at a lower interest in return for cutting expenditures and raising taxes. Montgomery's Republican newspaper in November 1873, called upon the voters "who desire economy in city government" to turn out the Democratic-controlled council because it had allowed the floating debt to rise from $20,000 to $70,000. The voters answered the call, and the new Republican council along with the reelected Republican mayor cut city expenses from

$180,887 in 1873 to $144,874 in 1874. Because revenue for 1874 was only $143,832, the call for retrenchment was renewed. In response, the council eliminated one city office, consolidated several others, and reduced most salaries.[42] The little town of Greensboro lagged behind its larger counterparts in the timing of its expansion and contraction but provides an excellent example of what was happening in cities throughout the region during the 1870s. In 1874 Mayor Cyrus Mendenhall was elected to the first of three consecutive terms as mayor in response to pleas for better services. Under Mendenhall charter amendments were passed tripling the property tax rate and increasing the poll tax from $2 to $3. As other cities had done prior to 1873, the city under Mendenhall constructed a new market house, set up a mayor's court, improved the streets, gave free vaccinations, and levied new taxes to support a public school system. But by 1877 hard times had arrived in Greensboro, and a taxpayer revolt defeated Mendenhall. Silas Dodson was elected on a platform promising retrenchment and economy. Reelected annually from 1877 to 1882, Dodson cut taxes in half, causing city income to fall substantially and city services to decline greatly.[43]

For several cities the economic troubles of the 1870s were made even worse by the ravage of disease. In 1873, for example, epidemics of cholera in Nashville and yellow fever in Montgomery drained city finances and interfered with trade.[44] But hardest hit by the economic repercussions were New Orleans and Memphis. Though New Orleans remained the South's largest city throughout the period, its postbellum rate of growth was seriously slowed by a number of problems. Hurt most by the impact of the railroad, she also suffered from the absence of a populous local market area and the effects of the Civil War on the cotton trade. Throughout her history the epidemic-plagued Crescent City had also suffered from frequent quarantines that brought commerce to a standstill. After the war yellow fever visited the city in 1873 and more severely in 1878. In the latter year thousands fled for their lives, leaving behind 3,977 dead. Throughout the South cities closed their doors to New Orleans trade lest the disease be spread. Not until the late 1880s would there be an economic revival, some eight years after the city's more healthful competitors again had begun to prosper.[45]

The importance of a healthy environment to urban growth was even more evident in Memphis which, unlike New Orleans, had been prospering in the postwar period. Blessed by a choice river location and the coming of the railroads, the Bluff City became the largest inland cotton market with a population that grew from 22,623 in 1860 to 40,226 ten years later. Through the early 1870s it looked like nothing would impede the city's rise to regional dominance, but in 1878 its longtime disregard for sanitation and the poverty of its growing lower class population finally took its toll. The city had endured frequent yellow fever epidemics, but in 1878-1879 the dreaded disease killed approximately 5,800 people, nearly half of them Irish. Meanwhile the wealthy fled, many of whom, especially Germans, settled permanently in St. Louis. Unable to meet its financial obligations, the battered city lost its corporate status, and its legal name was changed to "Taxing District of Shelby County." It was governed by two sets of commissioners made up equally of appointed and elected members which became a model for future commission governments. By 1880 the population had shrunk to 33,592. As Gerald Capers observed, there were "two cities . . . one which existed prior to the pestilence, and a second metropolis which sprang up like a fungus growth on the ruins of the first."[46]

While a few places such as Richmond, Atlanta, Nashville, and the young Texas towns did comparatively well during the 1870s, for most of the urban South the decade was a disaster. Without the prosperous first three years the debacle would have been even worse. Cursed by an unhealthy location like New Orleans and Memphis, Mobile saw its population reduced from 32,034 to 29,132. Savannah grew by less than 2,500 and Knoxville by under 1,100. A slight increase in the South's urban population resulted in the percentage of urban dwellers rising from 8.6 percent in 1870 to only 8.68 percent ten years later. Meanwhile outside the South the urban population had grown by about 4 million people, and the percentage of the nation's urban dwellers had grown from 25.7 percent to 28.2 percent.[47]

While slower population growth and rising unemployment weakened the tax base and forced city governments to cut basic services, private companies were also failing to live up to the requirements of their franchises. The chief victims were the poor and the middle class. In 1875 the Montgomery Street Railway Company discontinued service after less than a year in business; in 1876 two Nashville streetcar lines increased their fares from 5¢ to 10¢. By 1881 the Houston Gas Light Company had laid 10 miles of mains on the city's 200 miles of streets but only in the most lucrative areas.[48] Neither private nor municipal waterworks extended their lines into poorer neighborhoods, continuing instead to supply the central business districts and better residential areas. Most cities remained without any sewer systems, and the early efforts at street paving languished. In 1880 less than a third of Charleston and only 94 of New Orleans's 566 miles of streets were paved.[49] Houstonians with no paving called Galvestonians "sandlappers"; the latter with half of their 200 miles of streets paved called their upstart rivals "mud turtles."[50] To a northern visitor Mobile looked "dilapidated and hopeless," and the business district of Charleston remained in the ruins left by the war.[51] Even in Atlanta where the decade of the 1870s had begun so favorably, the decline in municipal services took its toll, especially after local businessmen in 1874 pushed through a new charter framed so as to help pay off the city debt and not incur a new one. The value of trade and real estate rose very slightly, and as in other cities "retrenchment and reform" replaced "enterprise and progress" as the slogan of the day. Arriving in Atlanta in 1878, George Campbell was "disappointed to find that it is not at all a pretty or nice town; very inferior in amenities to all the other Southern towns I have seen. It is, in fact, a new brick town built with no trees in the streets, but abundant mud." By 1880 only 3 of Atlanta's 100 miles of streets were paved, all downtown. And by 1883 the less than 20 miles of water pipes proved inadequate to save from fire the city's most visible symbol of progress, the Kimball House hotel.[52] Only the city's mild climate and high elevation protected it from the ravage of disease, for as yet there was no adequate sewer system or sanitation service.

1879-1900

The trouble of the 1870s was largely forgotten in the boom years that followed. The period from 1880 to 1892 was one of rapid urban growth throughout the country, and this time the South led the way. Whereas in 1880 8.6 percent of southerners qualified as urban, by 1890, after an increase of 49 percent the figure stood at 12.8 percent. During the decade the national percentage had climbed from 28.2 percent to 35.1 percent, a gain of only 25 percent. Urban growth continued during the 1890s, though it was less marked because of the Panic of 1893 and the economic hard times that followed. By 1900 14.8 percent of southerners were urban as compared to 39.7 percent of the nation as a whole.[53]

An infusion of northern capital and capitalists helped pull the railroads out of the depression and thus aided local merchants who had been suffering from erratic service and high freight rates. Of crucial importance was the organization in October 1875, of the Southern Railway and Steamship Association. Open to any southern railroad south of the Ohio and Potomac rivers and east of the Mississippi, it had twenty-seven members in 1877. Thanks to the efficiency of this new pooling arrangement, freight rates to eastern cities declined from 1875 to 1887. Rates from New York, Boston, or Baltimore to Atlanta, for example, were reduced roughly one-third between 1876 and 1884. As Stover concluded, "The rationalization of the freight rate structure plus the mere passage of time brought a degree of prosperity to the Southern railroads." There was no new default among major railroads after 1878, and new construction increased in 1879 and 1880. As early as 1877 the northern press was noting the first indication of an economic recovery in the South.[54]

During the 1880s American railroads added more mileage than in any other decade in history. This time the South outpaced the nationwide growth; while the increase in mileage for the nation was 79 percent, Stover's ten southern states increased their rail network by 98 percent.[55] Had his sample included Texas rather than Kentucky, the percentage increase would have been even greater. During the decade the Lone Star State led the entire country in miles constructed with 5,934; its 1880 total of 2,697 had already placed it first in the South in total mileage. Georgia ranked second in miles added, while Alabama almost doubled her total trackage, and Florida's almost quadrupled. Though Virginia, South Carolina, and Tennessee lagged behind, each of them still built more new lines in the decade than all of New England.[56] Some of this expansion was due to the construction of entirely new roads like the Georgia Pacific and the Louisville, New Orleans, and Texas, but most of it was due to the activities of the eleven largest companies of 1880. New construction slowed in the 1890s, especially after 1893, yet the southern rate of increase remained slightly greater than the national average, with Texas, Georgia, Louisiana, Florida, and Alabama in the forefront. By 1900 Florida had jumped from last in total trackage in the region to fifth.[57]

The last twenty years of the century also brought increased consolidation of the southern lines, first as a result of the prosperity of the 1880s and then because of the numerous receiverships prompted by the economic downturn of the 1890s. Though coming later in the South than in the North, that process of consolidation was essentially completed by 1900. In 1890 there were 58 lines over 100 miles in length; by 1900 there were only 31. By 1900 three-fourths of the mileage in the South outside of Texas was controlled by five corporations: Southern Railway, Louisville and Nashville, Atlantic Coast Line, Seaboard Air Line, and Illinois Central. All five were controlled by northern bankers. Indeed, the expansion and consolidation of southern railroads had been accomplished by a steady increase in northern capital and management. In 1880 37 percent of the directors of the 45 major lines in Stover's ten states had come from the North. In 1890 58 major lines drew 47 percent of the board members from the North and 36 of the presidents were northerners, including the heads of 9 of the 12 longest lines. By 1900 over 60 percent of the directors of the major lines came from the North, as did 58 percent of the presidents. Throughout the period the extent of northern control was even greater than it seemed, for southerners operated only the shortest lines over which the larger railroads through leases, stock ownership, and other financial ties exerted significant influence.[58]

The expansion, consolidation, and infusion of northern capital greatly improved the southern rail system. Certainly without consolidation and northern influence, the switch by southern railroads to the northern 4-foot, 8½-inch gauge in 1886 would have been delayed several years. By 1900 there was better service, more efficient interchange of traffic, better equipment, and lower rates than there had been in the past, although in none of these areas had the southern railroads attained parity with the North.

The urban impact of these railroad developments cannot be overestimated. T. Lynn Smith concluded that the perfecting of rail transportation in the last quarter of the nineteenth century was probably the most important factor in determining the precise locations for concentrations of population in the South. As a result, "By 1900 important towns were aligned along the principal railways like beads on a string."[59] Or, as John Stover concluded about the railroad boom of the 1880s, "Expansion and economic growth came most definitely to those cities such as Atlanta and Memphis, which were served by newly built railroads." Memphis, whose population rose 92 percent from 33,592 in 1880 to 64,495 in 1890, gained seven new railroads in the dozen years after 1880, while new lines enhanced Atlanta's position as the South's major rail center and helped swell its population from 37,400 to 65,533.[60] With the aid of better railroad transportation, Chattanooga grew from 12,892 to 29,100; Knoxville from 9,693 to 22,535; Houston from 16,513 to 27,557; San Antonio from 20,550 to 37,673; and Dallas from 10,358 to 38,067. The expansion of the Norfolk and Western Railroad into the rich Virginia and West Virginia coal fields had by 1885 allowed coal to replace cotton as Norfolk's chief export and helped increase the population from 21,966 to 34,871, well above the percentage increase for other coastal cities.[61] By 1900 the penetration of Florida by rail had almost quadrupled the population of Jacksonville from the 1880 figure of 7,650, and Tampa had grown from 720 to 15,839.

Most noteworthy was the growth of Birmingham, no more than a cornfield in

1870. Two northern real estate speculators, attracted by the rich iron deposits of northern Alabama's Jefferson County, founded the town in 1871. Realizing the site's potential, the Louisville and Nashville Railroad completed the South and North Alabama Railroad to Decatur, making a junction with the Alabama and Chattanooga near Birmingham. L & N officials invested in real estate and in the town's new iron mills, ran special trains for prospective investors, and provided lower rates for southern pig iron.[62] Because of a cholera epidemic and the effects of the Panic of 1873, growth was slow: there were only 3,086 inhabitants in 1880. But the town was linked to Atlanta by the Georgia Pacific in 1883, and a plethora of new lines soon connected the once isolated community with the major cities of the North and South. By 1890 the population was 26,178, and ten years later it had climbed to 38,414, on its way to the almost unbelievable figure of 132,685 in 1910.

After 1880 railroad penetration and industrial development went hand in hand. In 1880 the southern states produced approximately one-sixteenth of the nation's pig iron. By 1890, thanks to Birmingham and her sister towns of Anniston, Sheffield, and Bessemer, Alabama was producing nearly one-tenth of the nation's pig iron, and the South accounted for nearly one-fifth of the 10,307,000 tons in the country.[63] The iron mines and later the steel mills of Birmingham dominated the economic as well as the physical landscape of the community. By 1900 there were 282 manufacturing plants employing 7,000 workers who produced goods valued at more than $12 million. Around the city there were numerous coke ovens, blast furnaces, rolling mills, iron foundries, and machine shops in addition to the newly erected steel mill. The products of the mills went north on the city's eight railroad lines, which also helped distribute the products of the city's more than fifty different kinds of noniron related manufacturing enterprises.[64]

Of the ten largest cities in the South, only Memphis approached Birmingham in the debt owed to manufacturing. Here too the most spectacular phase of the city's industrialization coincided with the railroad expansion of the 1880s. In 1880 there was $2,313,975 invested in manufacturing establishments that turned out products valued at $4,413,422; by 1890 the respective figures were $9,357,821 and $13,244,538. The increase in invested capital from 1880 to 1890 was 304 percent while the increases in Nashville, Atlanta, and Richmond were 154 percent, 285.2 percent, and 142.4 percent. Memphis experienced a similar comparative advantage in the growth of value of her manufactured goods. Though slowed by the Panic of 1893, the rate of investment in manufacturing continued to increase. The city's major industry until the turn of the century was the production of lumber. Second largest was the manufacture of cottonseed products, which began in the 1880s. In addition, other types of minor manufacturing included beer, snuff, printing and publishing, drugs, and pharmaceutical supplies.[65]

Throughout the South other communities sought to build their post-1880 economies around industry. Richmond was clearly the tobacco capital of the nation, with more than fifty factories in operation by 1880, while its rich hinterland also provided resources for its flour mills and iron and steel foundries. Steamboats ran regularly between the city and Norfolk, New York, Baltimore, and

Philadelphia. It was the terminus of six railroads, nearly all parts of trunk lines which connected Richmond with principal markets throughout the country.[66] But just as Birmingham took its place in the production of iron, and cities like Norfolk challenged its flour milling leadership, by the end of the century the new tobacco towns of North Carolina had replaced Richmond and used production of the noxious weed to catapult themselves from obscurity to urban prominence. From 1880 to 1900 Winston grew from 443 to 10,008, and the Dukes of Durham had pushed their town's population to 6,679 after having been entirely omitted from the census of 1870. To the south Tampa had grown "from an isolated gulf coastal town of sandbeds, small merchants and cattlemen to a thriving commercial port city" after the beginning of the cigar industry in 1885.[67]

Much local manufacturing centered around cotton. Memphis, for example, became the country's leading producer of cottonseed oil. Montgomery was typical of many of the medium sized interior towns. One local firm produced cottonseed oil, another manufactured cotton presses and other machinery, and a third operated a cotton press.[68] Cotton presses were especially important to the economy of interior towns because newer and larger presses meant tighter packing of cotton, allowing more cotton to be sent by rail without transshipment in the port cities.

Montgomery also had a textile mill, a type of facility which southerners increasingly sought during the 1880s. In the 1870s the South had no more than 6 percent of the nation's cotton textile spindles and looms, and processed no more than one-tenth of the cotton manufactured in the nation; by 1890 the South had one-eighth of the nation's spindles, and southern mills were using nearly one-third as much cotton as northern mills.[69] The Atlanta International Cotton Exposition held in the fall of 1881 gave southern textile manufacturing a boost. In its wake there appeared a veritable cotton mill crusade, allegedly aimed at providing jobs for needy white workers but with more than passing interest in profits and town building. The stimulus of the mills, usually financed and often controlled by northerners, helped increase the populations of numerous North Carolina towns: between 1880 and 1900 Greensboro grew from 2,105 to 10,035; Charlotte from 7,094 to 18,091; and Gastonia from 236 to 4,610. By employing as textile workers the wives of men who worked in the city's furniture factories, High Point, unlisted in 1870, grew to 4,163 by 1900.

The effort of Raleigh to get a textile mill indicates the importance of the facility as an element in urban rivalry and urban imperialism, but it also points out that not everyone was equally enthusiastic about the quest. "How about that cotton factory?" chided the *Raleigh Daily Constitution* in urging local businessmen to "awake from your lethargy" in 1875. "Wilmington has one, Charlotte is thinking about establishing one and Raleigh should not be behind the times." Thirteen years later civic leaders were still trying to bring a factory to the city. "What is to become of Raleigh unless we do something to increase its business?" bemoaned the *State Chronicle.*[70] Finally in 1891 a mill began operating, soon followed by two others.

Southerners like Atlanta's Henry W. Grady pointed with pride to southern gains in manufacturing. Yet the gilt of New South imagery obscured the core of Old South realities. As C. Vann Woodward has demonstrated, the South by running fast had, despite considerable progress, merely succeeded in standing still in its race with the North. In 1860 the South had 17.2 percent of the manufacturing establishments in the country and 11.5 percent of the capital; by 1904 the respective figures were 15.3 percent and 11 percent. The value of manufactures rose from 10.3 percent of the total value produced in the United States to 10.5 percent. In 1900 the proportion of people in southern states east of the Mississippi engaged in manufacturing was about the proportion in all the states east of the Mississippi in 1850.[71]

The antebellum dream of a balanced economy secured by a strong manufacturing base that would free the region from dependence upon the North remained unfulfilled. As before, commerce was the lifeblood of most southern cities, which continued to depend primarily on an exchange of goods with their agrarian hinterlands. Atlanta, for example, tried mightily to become a manufacturing center. In addition to hosting the Exposition of 1881, city businessmen and officials supported construction of the Georgia Pacific to Birmingham in search of cheap fuel, and in 1886 had the city chosen as the site for the Georgia Institute of Technology. As a result, the city added about twenty new factories during the 1880s. Yet by 1890 the city's 410 industries employed 8,684 workers with an annual value of products of only slightly more than $13 million. Whereas in 1880 34 percent of the employed male workers were in trade and transportation and 28.5 percent in manufacturing, ten years later the respective figures were only 38.6 percent and 31.5 percent.[72] Manufacturing lagged in the city initially because of the absence of water power and later because of the inability to get cheap coal for steam power under freight discrimination. Above all, there was the lack of investment capital, as local businessmen preferred the rich rewards of commerce and railroad speculation.

Elsewhere the story was similar. In 1890 42 percent of the employed males in the 50 largest American cities worked in manufacturing, 30.3 percent in trade and transportation, and 24.9 percent in professional and personal services. Yet of the 6 cities of the former Confederacy in the sample, only Richmond with 38.4 percent of its employed males in manufacturing even approached the big city mean; the other 5 cities ranged from 28.5 percent in New Orleans to 33.6 percent in Nashville. Each city naturally exceeded the mean for percentages of service and trade and transportation workers.[73] Cities like Memphis and Augusta used manufacturing to encourage growth, but their respective economies clearly depended on their positions as the first and second largest inland cotton markets in the country. The value of manufactured goods in Memphis, for example, had increased to $18 million by 1900, but during the 1890s the city's annual trade was estimated at $200 million. The production of cigars helped Tampa, but without the trade of its growing agricultural hinterland, the export of phosphate discovered nearby in 1883, and its role as the major embarkation and supply port during the Spanish-American War, its growth would have been minimal.[74] And, as in the case of sugar refining in New Orleans, tobacco manufacturing in Richmond, or furniture making in Memphis, manufacturing usually was itself commerce-related.

The extent to which commercial and service-oriented pursuits continued to dominate the life of southern cities is also evident in the pattern of political leadership.

In northern cities during the last twenty years of the century, the old commercial elites which had governed throughout the nineteenth century were being replaced by professional politicians. And in major industrial centers like Pittsburgh, manufacturers figured prominently in the nationwide urban reform opposition generally led by lawyers. But although cities like New Orleans and Augusta were controlled for many years by professional politicians, it was the merchants who generally ran the southern city governments or spearheaded the reformers. Nashville, for example, enjoyed a marked increase in the importance of manufacturing during the postbellum period, but only one manufacturer, the owner of a hardware firm, was elected mayor and then not until 1898. Of the thirty members of the city council in 1878, only two were manufacturers; four years later there were none. In both years the majority of councilmen were merchants and petty tradesmen.[75] Not until 1902 did control of government in Houston shift from mercantilist hands, and then the recipients were lawyers rather than manufacturers. Even in the mill town of Greensboro, the manufacturers had a minority share of the power. By the turn of the century political leadership "was in the hands of a small oligarchy of bankers, large merchants, industrialists, influential editors and professional men." Not until 1910 was there a definite shift of power from commercial elements to manufacturers. Surprisingly, even in Birmingham commercial interests controlled the government and eventually triumphed over industrialists outside the city.[76] Throughout the South merchant-dominated chambers of commerce and boards of trade were the most powerful institutions in urban life.

The success of trade, the stimulus of manufacturing, and the general return to prosperity in the nation after 1880 allowed the southern cities to return to the task of extending and modernizing municipal services. By the last decade of the century, however, it was evident that there was an important difference between this period of expansion and that of the 1870s. As Harold Platt has written about Houston, "Reconstruction officials possessed an unrestrained spending authority and an uncertain ability to collect revenues. Administrations in the 90s mainly faced decisions on how to allocate insufficient but predictable amounts of income."[77] Southern cities were clearly less inclined than northern cities to spend public funds for urban improvements. In 1902 every southern city over 25,000 had a tax levy per capita below the national average of $12.89 for the 160 cities with that population. Only 7 of the 21 southern cities—New Orleans, Richmond, San Antonio, Houston, Dallas, Galveston, and Fort Worth—came within two dollars of that figure. And whereas the total debt per capita for the 160 cities was $62.04, only 8 of the southern cities—Richmond, Charleston, Norfolk, Houston, Mobile, Galveston, Fort Worth, and Montgomery—exceeded that average.[78] While some of the gap between public spending in the North and South was due to the great number of poor people, particularly blacks, in southern cities, it was due more to the twin desires to keep spending low and to give tax breaks to manufacturing concerns.

Within the confines of limited budgets, the municipal governments sought to improve their urban plants. By 1902 the high rates charged by electric light companies led five of the cities—Nashville, Little Rock, Jacksonville, Galveston, and

Fort Worth—to join the fourteen northern cities with more than 25,000 people that had erected municipally owned electric light plants. Jacksonville, Galveston, and Fort Worth constructed municipal waterworks, while Dallas, Montgomery, New Orleans, and in 1903, Memphis officials purchased private companies that had been poorly supplying their cities with water. In the case of Memphis, the result was a 20 percent decline in rates.[79] Nevertheless, by the end of the century water mains were still confined largely to the better sections of town and the downtown area, and most citizens relied on cisterns and wells. Often there was insufficient pressure with which to fight fires, and pure water did not become a reality until after 1900. Slaughterhouses and tanneries were inadequately regulated and, as was true of individuals, dumped their waste directly into the streams, wells, or rivers that furnished the water. A letter writer in Nashville described the town's drinking water in 1890 as "warm and thick," and visitors unaccustomed to it were advised to flee to the suburbs for a purer version.[80]

Prompted by the yellow fever epidemic of 1878, most cities sought to prevent contamination of their water supplies. Businessmen in towns like Mobile, Memphis, and New Orleans had learned the economic costs of disease and took the lead in urging improved sanitation measures. Their counterparts in healthier cities like Atlanta sought improvements in public health in order to maintain prosperity rather than to regain it. Memphis, Atlanta, and New Orleans had by 1879 greatly strengthened the powers of their boards of health. They also concentrated on sewerage and waste disposal. But here again the better neighborhoods were the chief beneficiaries.[81] Memphis had the most ambitious program. From 1878 to 1899 the city constructed approximately 45 miles of sewers; from 1898 to 1901 an additional 98 miles were added. In New Orleans, however, it took the deaths of almost four hundred people from yellow fever between 1897 and 1899 to force the city to purchase the franchise of the dormant sewage company and to begin laying sewer pipes in 1903.[82]

Together with the installation of sewers, the paving of streets received the bulk of municipal expenditures. The little town of Tampa, whose population went from 720 in 1880 to nearly 6,000 in 1890, approved bonds totaling $95,000 in 1889 for streets and sewers and then approved an additional $100,000 two years later. Despite significant advances in paving over the previous twenty years, by the turn of the century few southern cities had more than half their streets paved. By 1902 New Orleans had more than doubled its mileage of paved streets, but that still left almost 500 of the city's 700 miles of streets unpaved; Atlanta's paved street mileage had increased from 3 to 63.4, but that left 140 miles of streets unpaved; about one-tenth of Memphis streets were paved.[83] In each case it was the downtown and better residential areas that avoided the dust and mud that plagued most urban residents.

The urban South also continued to lag behind the rest of the country in the quality of education offered its children, though again significant gains occurred in the closing years of the century. The decade of the 1880s was especially noteworthy as the number of schools in Richmond rose from eleven to eighteen and Nashville added five to its total of nine. The number of Norfolk schools rose from

6 in 1874 to 10 by 1893 and 15 in 1902.[84] By 1902 almost all school buildings were owned by the cities rather than rented, as had been the case earlier in the period, and everyone of the towns over 25,000 had at least one high school. When compared to northern cities of comparable population, however, southern cities were still far behind in the percentage of children enrolled, number of schools and school rooms, and numbers and salaries of teachers. Whereas in 1902 the 160 cities with over 25,000 population spent an average of $4.37 per capita on their schools, New Orleans spent $1.74; Memphis, $1.61; Atlanta, $1.90; and Charleston, $1.41. Houston with $3.68 led the South, Fort Worth and Dallas being the only two others spending more than $3 per person. Nor were southern towns fertile ground for learning outside of the classroom. Of the 29 cities with more than 25,000 people that had no public library in 1902, 12 were in the South; and those cities with libraries generally had fewer books in them than did northern cities of comparable size.[85]

Law enforcement and fire protection followed the same pattern. Important strides were made in professionalization, the integration of new technological advances, and numbers of men. By the 1870s police forces of the major cities were uniformed and more efficiently deployed, and by the early 1890s patrol wagons and modern communications systems, already common in the North, enjoyed widespread use. Throughout the South new city jails bore testimony both to the period's expensive public works efforts and the desire for greater security against lawbreakers. During the same period full-time paid firemen replaced the volunteer fire companies, though often, as in New Orleans, not until after 1890. Increasingly the new firemen benefited from better alarm systems and fire fighting equipment. Yet, as in the North, political favoritism greatly influenced police and fire department appointments.[86] And because of low funding, southern cities were probably less adequately protected than their northern counterparts.

City administrations had the most success in adding publicly owned parkland that provided aesthetic and recreational benefits to their communities. Though well underway in the North since the 1850s, the park movement had only slightly affected the South as late as the 1870s. As of 1880 there were no public parks in Norfolk, Chattanooga, or Montgomery; Charleston had 33 acres of parks; Memphis, 4 acres; and Atlanta, about 3 acres. Only New Orleans, with 659 acres, ranked with northern cities. Although the amount of parkland in New Orleans dropped to 522 acres during the subsequent two decades, other southern cities made remarkable gains. By 1902 Norfolk had 95 acres, much of it reclaimed from marshland; Atlanta, 155 acres; Charleston, 449 acres; and San Antonio, 294 acres. With a late spurt of acquisition, Memphis produced the most spectacular change. As of 1898 the city had only 30 acres of parks; by 1902 it had 782 acres, including the much publicized Riverside and Overton parks.[87]

After 1880 city governments also moved more aggressively to ensure that private companies provided needed services to residents. Unlike the financially troubled water companies, most utility and all traction operations remained in private hands. Exceptions included the municipally owned electric plants already mentioned and the gas works in Richmond, one of the five municipally owned in the entire country in 1902.[88] As in the rest of the nation, the service provided by these companies and the rates they charged were major issues in local politics. Because of the high stakes, franchise owners and seekers became actively involved in politics. In Houston between 1874 and 1888 twenty-one of the seventy mayors and aldermen were connected with a franchised corporation; in Greensboro, the head of the waterworks company was on the board of aldermen waterworks committee.[89] Elsewhere presidents of streetcar and gas companies served as heads of council franchise or streets committees. And their companies contributed generously to candidates for office. City administrations at first were hesitant to regulate closely these companies, but increasingly, especially after the Panic of 1893, urban reformers in cities like Houston, New Orleans, and Augusta joined their northern counterparts in demanding greater regulation. The earlier policy of defending the public interest by liberally granting franchises to competing companies was replaced by the acceptance of supervised monopolies.[90]

This shift was aided, especially after 1893, by the kind of expansion and consolidation in privately owned municipal services that characterized the railroad system. Similarly, by 1900 northern capitalists owned most of the traction and utility corporations.

By the turn of the century the "natural monopolies" of telegraph and telephone which had arrived in most southern cities by the late 1870s were under the control of Western Union and the Bell System. Likewise, the twenty-year competition within the gas and electric light industries had left one company in each field in control of a given city. As in so many other areas of southern life, the loser was frequently a local outfit; the winner, either northern-owned or northern-financed. New Orleans, for example, chartered three electric light companies, two of them owned by local residents. By 1897 the northern-owned Edison Electric Company had absorbed one of its local rivals and had driven the other out of business. In the early 1890s the economic difficulties of two competing Houston electric light companies resulted in their merger into Citizens Electric Company, financed by outside capitalists. Smaller towns exhibited the same tendency. The locally owned Tampa Electric Company, formed in 1887, was taken over in the 1890s by the Boston firm of Stone and Webster.[91]

The most significant franchised enterprise of the closing twenty years of the century was the street railway. Telephones remained very much the playthings of the rich and the successful businessmen (1,641 phones in New Orleans in 1898);[92] electric lights illuminated the downtown areas and homes of the very rich; even gas and water left the lives of many urban residents unaffected. But for all but the very poor the streetcar was an indispensable part of urban life. As in the rest of the country, the period from the mid-1880s until the Panic of 1893 witnessed a tremendous surge in the installation of the first streetcar systems in cities like Raleigh, Natchez, and Baton Rouge, or the reinstallation in cities like Montgomery where systems had failed during the hard times of the 1870s. Installations were especially frequent in towns of less than 10,000, for which streetcars became a symbol of urban maturity. Furthermore, the South took the lead in the electrification of the lines. The first electric streetcar in regular operation appeared on

Montgomery streets in 1886, and two years later successful service on hilly Richmond streets "proved, even more conclusively than Montgomery, that the electric railway was practical." By 1890 several southern towns were among the fifty-one cities with electrified lines, though New Orleans and Norfolk were among those dragging their feet.[93]

As with the other utilities, the rapid expansion of the streetcars during the 1880s and 1890s attracted northern financiers. During the 1890s the Memphis streetcar network expanded from 30 to 70 miles through the consolidation of the different lines into the Memphis Street Railway Company. Consolidation also meant a shift from mule to electricity. Then in 1905 the system was sold to a northern syndicate. Representing associates in Omaha, Nebraska, E. A. Allen and O. M. Carter purchased Houston's two streetcar lines and converted them to electric power in 1891. Ten years later, after several receiverships, the Stone-Webster syndicate of Boston assumed control. In Tampa, where Stone and Webster owned the electric company, it was the New York-financed Light and Power Company that forced the locally owned Tampa Street Railway into bankruptcy in 1894.[94]

The electric streetcar and the steam dummies which also appeared on southern streets after the mid-1880s greatly affected the lives of city residents. As in the North, they contributed to the sorting out of the population by race and income and helped to usher in the golden age of the downtown area. The entry of the lines into previously isolated areas of the city sparked a housing construction boom. Housing advertisements now identified neighborhoods in terms of their proximity to the streetcars. In 1882 the *Nashville Banner* observed that the six-month-old Fatherland Streetrailway had "brought into prominence that hitherto comparatively inaccessible but most beautiful portion of the city known as the East End." The following year it noted that in North and East Nashville "immense numbers of small cottages are being built within a short walk of the 'tramways.'"[95] Even those too poor to ride the cars regularly to work could take them to pleasure grounds like Atlanta's Ponce de Leon Springs or Nashville's Glenwood Park that the lines operated to increase their ridership.

The streetcar's greatest impact was on the boundaries of the metropolitan area. The expansion of the lines resulted in the development of numerous communities on the rim of the city. In 1891 the *Richmond Dispatch* noted that "men of means seeking villa sites; mechanics desiring cheap lots; people who delight in roominess and ample acreage have ... encircled Richmond and Manchester with built up suburbs." The previous year the *Nashville Banner* carried a full-page advertisement for the sale of lots in "Waverly Place, the Suburban Gem." Located 20 or 25 miles from the heart of the city, Waverly offered to the "wealthy and professional classes" as well as the "man of moderate means" "all the quiet of the country with the advantage of proximity to the business center of a big city, by means of quick motor transportation." The streetcar was also responsible for the growth of Ghent outside Norfolk. In a short period of time it changed from farmland to "one of the most exclusive residential sections of Norfolk." Often operation of the street railway and suburban land development were directly connected. O. M. Carter and his American Loan and Trust Company of Omaha purchased the Houston City Railway in 1890 to ensure that his suburban community, Houston Heights, would be linked by rapid transit to the city.[96]

Increasingly the cities sought to annex the surrounding areas. Annexation was urged on the ground of assuring better sanitation for the entire metropolitan area, raising the tax base of the city, and making suburbanites pay for the use of city services such as maintenance of streets and police protection. "In plain words tax dodging through the use of a trolley line should be abolished," said the *Birmingham Age-Herald* in 1900. "Suburbs should not be built up at the expense of cities. . . . If one avails himself of the advantages of a city in the earning of his daily bread, he should share the burdens of that city."[97] Urban boosters also called for annexation so that the federal census would show a great increase over the previous decade. It was no accident that annexation efforts usually appeared just before a new census was scheduled. In 1879 the *Nashville Daily American,* while stressing the sanitary advantages of annexation, noted the success of annexation in St. Louis and "the tendency of large cities" to prosper. Ten years later the *Nashville Banner* pointed to Chicago and Cincinnati to argue that "the bigger the town the stronger it draws people and capital." By taking in the "populous suburbs," Nashville would have "the population of a great city." The failure of annexation efforts in 1889 no doubt left Nashville boosters feeling like their unsuccessful counterparts in Birmingham in 1899. "The city," the *Age-Herald* said, pointing to the forthcoming census, "stands before the world belittled by cramped confines."[98]

Suburban dwellers were divided on the issue of annexation; but by the 1890s they were more attracted by improved city services—water, schools, sewage, etc.—than repelled by an expected increase in their taxes. Some annexations had already taken place. Nashville annexed Edgefield across from it on the Cumberland River in 1880; by that year Jefferson City, Lafayette, Carrollton, and Algiers, once suburbs, had been incorporated into New Orleans. The great surge in annexations, however, came after the mid-1880s. Norfolk annexed Brambleton in 1886 and Atlantic City in 1890. Houston added South Houston in 1890, Houston Heights in 1891, and Deer Park in 1893. After much resistance from the surrounding communities, Memphis enlarged its 4½ square miles to 16 square miles and added 30,000 people to its population through annexation in January 1899. Even towns like Greensboro, which added South Greensboro in 1891, kept pace with their bigger rivals. The big lure was city schools, and the end result was the quadrupling of Greensboro's area to four square miles and the addition of about 3,000 people.[99] Meanwhile Birmingham, through a series of small annexations in 1873, 1883, and 1889, took in some adjacent residential areas so that the city limits had grown from 1.4 square miles in 1871 to 3 square miles. In 1895 the city added North and South Highlands, but opposition from the industrialists outside the city prevented annexation of the major furnaces and rolling mills. The industrialists continued to thwart the desire of city officials, downtown business interests, and city and suburban residents who supported the Greater Birmingham Movement organized in 1898. Unsuccessful at annexing all the surrounding suburbs in time for the 1900 census, the Greater Birmingham advocates finally got their wish in 1910. The city expanded to 48 square miles and added approximately 72,000 people.[100] Few cities made as spectacular use of annexation as Birmingham, but throughout the South these annexations contributed greatly to the growth in urban population.

The horizontal expansion of the cities which kept pace with developments in the North was not matched by a vertical expansion. The less expansive economies of southern cities and their less congested cores meant that downtown skylines were still of human scale. In 1900 the Memphis business district consisted mostly of old four-story brick buildings. The highest structures were the eight-story Randolph Building and the eleven story Porter Building. Neither Nashville nor Norfolk had a building over seven stories, though plans were soon announced for a thirteen-story one in the former and a twelve-story edifice in the latter.[101] Significantly, they were to be banks. But in 1900 large office buildings did not dominate the skylines. Rather, it was the new union railroad stations, hotels, theaters, YMCAs, government buildings, and churches. On business streets such as Nashville's Second Avenue or Montgomery's Commerce Street, one could enjoy the finest period of American storefront architecture—two- and three-story commercial buildings erected after 1880 with concern for scale and design that was sorely lacking in subsequent years. In a further concession to the urban aesthetic, most cities during the first decade of the twentieth century began placing utility wires underground.

By 1900 southern cities had more to offer their residents in terms of services, attractions, and economic well-being than they did twenty years before. Yet, the fruits of progress were not equally distributed. The primary beneficiaries were the commercial elites who saw to it that the downtowns and the residential areas in which they lived received the lion's share of urban improvements. Members of the working class and especially the poor often suffered from the low priority given to their needs.

Unlike their counterparts in the North, comparatively few of the lower class workers were foreign immigrants. The small number of immigrants has often led historians incorrectly to minimize their impact on southern life. The Irish played a significant role in southern urban politics and as laborers, particularly in Memphis, Richmond, and New Orleans.[102] Jewish merchants, usually of German descent, figured prominently in business affairs and politics; there was a "Jewish seat" on the Atlanta board of education, and both the Radical and Redeemer mayors of Montgomery were Jewish.[103] And at the end of the century New Orleans received a large number of Italian immigrants.[104] Nevertheless, despite white attempts to encourage foreign immigration as an alternative to dependence on Negro labor, the percentage of foreign born in southern cities dropped sharply between 1860 and 1900. In Richmond the decline was from 13 percent to 3.4 percent; Charleston, 15.5 percent to 4.6 percent; Savannah, 21 percent to 6.3 percent; New Orleans, 38 percent to 10 percent. Not on the map in 1860, the new town of Birmingham had only 5 percent foreign born in 1900, when Pittsburgh, its chief rival for iron and steel supremacy, had 26.4 percent.[105]

A larger share of the urban working class was composed of native whites, many of whom had migrated to the cities from the depressed rural areas. Studies of San Antonio, Birmingham, and Atlanta indicate that as a group they enjoyed only limited social mobility during the prosperous closing years of the century; in

Atlanta even the foreign element outstripped them.[106] These were the people who worked in the mines or iron works of Birmingham; the cotton mills of Greensboro, Augusta, and Gastonia; the tobacco factories of Richmond and Durham; and on the docks of New Orleans, Savannah, and Charleston. Their wages low, they inhabited the growing tenement districts of the expanding cities, moving apart physically from the commercial elites and the middle classes, just as they were being left behind economically.[107]

The lower class whites found comfort in the frequent assurances of their "betters" that they were superior to the Negroes. And not surprisingly, blacks benefited least from the urban growth of the last two decades of the century. By 1900 only 17.2 percent of the South's blacks lived in cities, but they comprised 30.9 percent of the total urban population. Their percentage of the population in the major cities ranged from lows of 14.1 percent in San Antonio and 27.1 percent in New Orleans to highs of 56.5 percent in Charleston and 51.8 percent in Savannah. Not until after 1900 did the percentage of blacks in the urban population of southern cities decline for the first time since 1860, as significant numbers migrated to the North.[108] Blacks who did leave prior to 1900 enjoyed greater opportunities in the northern cities than those who remained behind. The last twenty years of the century witnessed the improvement of black prospects for economic success in the North, a decline in the extent of legally enforced segregation, and a greater role for blacks in politics.[109] The economic, social, and political trends for blacks in the South ran in the opposite direction.

For most southern blacks the closing years of the century meant continued economic hardship. The great majority of black workers were disproportionately represented in menial jobs, and black women, unlike their white counterparts, formed a significant part of their race's work force. Out of Nashville's work force of 8,100 black males in 1890, 1,107 were employed as servants and 2,566 as unskilled laborers. Yet only 56 whites were employed as servants and 676 as laborers out of a total work force of 14,847. There were 991 white carpenters and joiners; only 198 blacks were in those skilled positions. Of the 6,609 employed black women, 2,465 were laundresses and 3,372 were servants; of the 2,989 white women, 104 were laundresses and 378 were servants.[110] Outside of the cotton mills, blacks comprised a large part of the unskilled factory workers and were in great demand as day laborers for such hazardous occupations as well digging or sewer building. The streets, docks, and railyards throughout the urban South were filled with black workers.

Blacks were hindered by their lack of skills, but many were clearly confined to the low paying, unskilled jobs because of their race. Throughout the South jobs in cotton mills, for example, were reserved for whites. Much of the opposition to blacks in skilled positions came from white workers, though organized labor sometimes sought to incorporate blacks. Often the Knights of Labor and the local unions which preceded them permitted blacks in their unions, usually in segregated branches. In 1888 the Richmond Knights of Labor had twenty-three white and thirty black assemblies. New Orleans, described by David Bennetts as "most certainly the best organized city in the South," witnessed united action by black and white union members that resulted in increased wages, shorter work days, and improved conditions for most workers. Collapse of the city's general strike, the first in the nation, in 1892 and the depression of the 1890s brought an end to "labor's golden era in New Orleans" and also ended racial cooperation.[111] By the mid-1890s white union and nonunion labor in New Orleans, as elsewhere in the urban South, was committed to blocking black access to skilled positions. The replacement of the Knights by the racist American Federation of Labor spelled the doom of prospects for a revived biracial alliance.

At the same time that the ranks of the black unskilled were increasing, there emerged a small business and professional class. Even in the 1870s there had been a class of successful blacks, but many of them, like the Atlanta barber Robert Yancy or the dentist Frederick Badger, had a white clientele.[112] By the end of the century, however, a black elite of undertakers, barbers, lawyers, teachers, grocers, and doctors serving primarily a black clientele had risen to prominence in southern cities. Black business districts along Raleigh's Hargett Street or Nashville's Fourth Avenue announced their presence. Yet as an 1899 survey of Negro businessmen in the South suggests, the range of black businessmen was limited. Better than 40 percent were either grocers, general merchandise dealers, or barbers with $500 or more invested; the next two highest groups were printers and undertakers. In Atlanta groceries comprised more than one-third of the sixty-one Negro businesses in the city of sufficient size to be noticed.[113] Nevertheless, there had emerged a group on the other end of the economic scale from the mass of blacks. As of 1891 Richmond blacks owned real estate valued at $968,736; four years later there were six blacks who owned more than $10,000 worth of property in the city's largely black Jackson Ward. By 1886 the combined wealth of Nashville's black population was approximately $1 million, with seventeen individuals worth more than $10,000. More than half of that $1 million was owned by only forty-four families.[114]

The great poverty of the black masses plus the racism of whites encouraged the earlier trend towards segregated neighborhoods. Though ward statistics for most cities suggest a high degree of residential integration, a street-by-street survey reveals that in cities such as Richmond, Montgomery, Raleigh, and Atlanta the great majority of whites and blacks lived on totally segregated blocks. Because of racial discrimination, even members of the black elite were confined to black neighborhoods among lower class dwellings as on Atlanta's Wheat Street. The few whites in black neighborhoods came primarily from three groups with limited mobility: laborers, widows, and grocers. Most blacks in predominantly white areas lived in the rear of fashionable white streets and served whites as laundresses, gardeners, and handymen.[115]

The combination of large poor black populations and significant numbers of lower class whites meant that southern cities generally had a lower percentage of home ownership than their northern counterparts. Of the 420 cities and towns of 8,000 to 100,000 populations in 1890, 12 had a rate of home tenancy less than 40 percent; none were in the South; but of the 18 cities with a percentage of home tenancy above 80 percent, 11 were in the South. Birmingham ranked highest with 89.84 percent, Norfolk was third with 85.62 percent, and Macon was fourth with

84.6 percent. Overall, the percentage of families who were tenants was greatest in the south central and south Atlantic sections of the country.[116]

The black areas of the cities shared little in the expansion of municipal services during the 1880s and 1890s. Water mains, sewer lines, paved streets, and regular garbage collection rarely reached into black neighborhoods. Neither electricity nor gas illuminated their houses. In Richmond the fire chief unsuccessfully pleaded for a fire station to protect the largely wooden homes of Jackson Ward, while in Atlanta, Spelman Seminary's Union Hall burned down because fire engines had a two-mile run over rough roads to get there. Major black institutions like Atlanta University were not served by streetcars. When streetcar service existed, it was unsatisfactory. Richmond's Jackson Ward had twenty-minute service on a single-track line; nearby white areas had five and ten minute service on double-track lines. In Algiers, a heavily black section of New Orleans, mule cars were still running in 1907, fourteen years after the rest of the city's lines had begun to be electrified.[117]

Other services were available to blacks on a separate but unequal basis. By the 1890s city hospitals and local almshouses in Atlanta and Nashville offered inadequate segregated accommodations to blacks. During the 1880s local black protests finally succeeded in securing the appointment of black teachers in most black schools as the expansion of the white schools provided jobs for the white teachers and scores on teacher exams demonstrated that the blacks were qualified. Only Charleston and New Orleans seem to have lagged behind the other cities. Even this triumph for blacks had its price, since the black teachers received considerably lower salaries than white instructors.[118]

By the 1890s the first Jim Crow statutes were being passed, enforcing segregation in a variety of public accommodations. But even without the passage of laws, de facto segregation or exclusion had become further entrenched during the 1880s in public and private parks, theaters, zoos, and other places of public amusements. The dummy streetcars for example that appeared in Nashville, Atlanta, and Montgomery after the mid-1880s were segregated. Jim Crow streetcar legislation passed in Georgia in 1891 and elsewhere after 1900 removed whatever flexibility there had previously been.[119]

Despite widespread de facto and increasingly de jure segregation, whites were not satisifed until they had removed the blacks from the political arena. As noted earlier, while Redemption had generally been quickly achieved, blacks remained active in city government in several major southern cities. Though the cases were certainly atypical, blacks were regularly elected to city councils in Nashville and Jackson, Mississippi, until the late 1880s, and in Richmond and Raleigh until the turn of the century. During the 1890s fusion movements returned white and black Republicans to office in a number of North Carolina cities, a development that had taken place in Jacksonville in 1887.[120]

Black councilmen had limited power, as revealed by their assignment to unimportant committees or to none at all, but they were often able to help their constituents. Nashville's leading black politician, J. C. Napier, was instrumental in the opening of new black schools and the hiring of black teachers, while his councilmate from 1883 to 1885, C. C. Gowdey, secured free water for some Negro neighborhoods and pushed through the organization of a regular black fire company of which he immediately became captain. The four Negro councilmen in Jacksonville in 1887 saw to it that almost half of the police force was black, as were the municipal judge and one of the three police commissioners. Richmond's black councilmen secured improved streets and better lighting in Jackson Ward, the dispensing of coal to the Negro poor, the opening of the first black night school, the appropriation of money for the Negro militia companies, and construction of a separate armory.[121]

Blacks temporarily increased their influence by combining with other groups like the Knights of Labor in Richmond, Mobile, and Jacksonville during the mid-1880s or the Populists in North Carolina cities during the 1890s.[122] But whites came to be more concerned about the role of blacks in the Prohibition and local option campaigns, fixtures of local politics in the late 1880s. Liquor was an emotional issue that divided both communities and the Democratic Party. Even in Atlanta where blacks were prevented by the use of the white primary, poll tax, and manipulation of the election procedures from winning public office, the issue of prohibition made them a pivotal force in local politics. From 1885 to 1888 Atlanta witnessed a series of referenda or campaigns in which Prohibition was the chief issue. Blacks unsuccessfully sought to play off the wets against the drys to win concessions, but the victors never kept their promises, and the net effect was to increase white desires to eliminate totally the black vote. During Richmond's local option campaign of 1885, a local newspaper feared that Prohibition would be "forced upon white men by negro votes"; three years later a "race war" in Jackson was attributed to bad feelings generated by a local option election.[123]

Thus, throughout the urban South white Democrats became interested in disfranchisement even before the rise of Populism. The bidding for the Negro vote in Prohibition campaigns or when independents challenged incumbent Democratic administrations severely upset local elites. The only remedy was to remove the Negro voter, since containment, though successful, was not enough. As they had done during Reconstruction, the urban dwellers turned to the state legislatures for help. And help soon came! Jackson Democrats, who finally ousted their Republican mayor in 1888, secured an amended charter in 1890 which included "changes [in the] wards so as to give perpetual control of the board of aldermen to the white people."[124] The same year the legislature passed the Mississippi Plan, the first clear-cut statewide disfranchisement program in the nation. In 1889 Tennessee passed new voting and registration laws that applied only to Nashville, Memphis, Chattanooga, Knoxville, and their counties in order "to practically exclude the vote of illiterate negroes." The heart of the laws was adoption of the nonpartisan Australian ballot that barred the practice of aiding voters as they selected their candidates from an alphabetically arranged list. This law, plus tighter registration requirements and a $2 poll tax enacted in 1890, was responsible for the reduction of voting blacks to less than 250 in the 1890 Nashville municipal election.[125] But even after the passage in Florida in 1889 of an Australian ballot, multiple-ballot-box system, poll tax, and other restrictions, blacks still were being elected to the council in Jacksonville after the turn of the century.[126] By then, however, with the notable exception of Memphis, the passage of disfranchising legislation throughout the South had largely eliminated the black urban voter as a factor in any kind of election. And as a further reminder to blacks of their inferior position in southern cities, race riots occurred in Wilmington, North Carolina, in 1898 and in New Orleans in 1900.[127]

Postbellum cities failed to fulfill the antebellum dreams chronicled by Professor Goldfield. Cotton remained king, northern control of the region was extended, southern urban populations continued to experience a quality of life inferior to that of their northern counterparts, and race was still "the central theme of Southern history." There is no denying the validity of C. Vann Woodward's conclusion that "the Southern people remained throughout the rise of the 'New South' overwhelmingly a country people, by far the most rural section of the country."[128] Between 1860 and 1900 the proportion of urban dwellers in the South grew from 7.1 percent to 14.8 percent, as compared to a shift from 19.9 percent to 39 percent in the nation at-large, and the region's share of the nation's urban places grew from 13.8 percent to 15.7 percent, but by 1900 the South had none of the country's eleven cities with over 300,000 people and only two of the twenty-seven cities with between 100,000 and 300,000.[129] Nonetheless, only if Woodward is speaking in statistical terms is it true that after the urban boom of the 1880s "the sum total of urbanization in the South was comparatively unimportant."[130] The founding of Birmingham and Miami meant that by 1900 every one of today's major southern cities had been established; their arrival, plus the growth of the young Texas towns, spelled the end of the hierarchy of cities that had existed in 1860.

Furthermore, as in earlier southern history, postbellum cities played a role far greater than their limited share of the total population would suggest. Certainly, the expansion of the rail network during the period was tied to the growth of the region's cities, and the South's agriculture depended upon urban marketing. Nor should the impact of urban leaders on the political life of the region be forgotten. Norfolk's Gilbert Walker, Knoxville's William Brownlow, and Raleigh's William Holden were only three of the Reconstruction governors with urban roots. Later, as Woodward himself acknowledges, "Southern progressivism was essentially urban and middle class in nature."[131] Birmingham produced Governor Braxton Bragg Comer; Atlanta, the future governor and secretary of the interior Hoke Smith; Jacksonville, Governor Napoleon B. Broward and Senator Duncan Fletcher; and Houston, future presidential adviser Colonel E. M. House. Meanwhile, the Raleigh editor and future secretary of the navy Josephus Daniels and the Atlanta editor Henry W. Grady exercised great influence as spokesmen of the New South. Despite all the just attention given to the colorful southern agrarian leaders, it should be remembered that the cities were overrepresented among southern political leaders everywhere but in the state legislatures.

Southern cities were also at the core of the momentous decisions that occurred in the area of race relations. As had been the case in the antebellum period, it proved more difficult for whites to control blacks in the cities than in the rural areas. It is not surprising therefore that much of the early stimulus for disfranchisement came from southern cities and that most of the Jim Crow legislation was aimed at urban blacks.

And if urban services and amenities still left much to be desired, southern cities had at least made noteworthy strides toward the day when the bluster of urban boosters would match the reality of southern urban life. Yet, that time was still far in the future, and the changes in southern urban life between 1860 and 1900 would pale next to those of the twentieth century. Only then, as well, would colonial dependence on northern cities cease and the forces of racial moderation triumph.

5

BLAINE A. BROWNELL

THE URBAN SOUTH COMES OF AGE, 1900-1940

Every historical period is a watershed of sorts. In the American South the years from 1900 to 1940 linked an earlier era of social and economic recovery—when the region's cities struggled to keep up with their burgeoning northern counterparts—with the mid-century era of pronounced sectional urbanization. The period was not a culmination but a transition in which a modern urban framework appeared in the nation's most rural region.

Like most periods in American history, the early twentieth century was a time of change, even in the presumably somnolent South; and change was concentrated in the cities. Novelist Ellen Glasgow found these developments both fascinating and disquieting. From the vantage point of her native Richmond, she wrote in 1922:

Everywhere people were pushing one another into the slums or the country. Everywhere the past was going out with the times and the future was coming on in a torrent.... To add more and more numbers; to build higher and higher; to push harder and harder; and particularly to improve what had already been added or built or pushed—these impulses had united at last into a frenzied activity. And while the building and the pushing and the improving went on, the village grew into the town, the town grew into the city, and the city grew into the country.[1]

Such impulses seemed destined to transform the face of the region.

Virtually every significant southern city (with a few exceptions like Miami) had been established by the turn of the century. The next forty years witnessed a pronounced rate of urban population growth, territorial expansion, and economic development, along with increased spatial differentiation and social fragmentation. As northern urban centers confronted an array of problems arising from industrialization, intensive land use, technological development, and the arrival of native and foreign born immigrant masses, southern cities faced some of the same difficulties in a different context; for the South was moving gradually from an agricultural to an industrial economy, and hundreds of thousands of southerners were wrenched from a preurban to an urban existence. In the process, the cities that had struggled to their feet in the post-Reconstruction years came of age in the first half of the twentieth century.

Between 1900 and 1940 a complex and relatively more stable urban system—marked by increasing levels of urban interrelationship and interdependence—emerged in the South. But the outlines and details of this system remain indistinct, primarily because so little research has been done on the patterns involved. This system appears more compact and articulated than it had been in times past. It included those cities in the former Confederate states, but not peripheral centers like Baltimore, Washington, St. Louis, or Louisville, which had been increasingly drawn into the northeastern and midwestern industrial orbits in the nineteenth century. As the twentieth century wore on, cities in western Texas and southern Florida, and perhaps also those of Arkansas and northern Virginia, were drawn by ties of communication and economic development into other urban systems. And at least two southern urban subsystems appear to have developed, one in the Southeast and one in the Southwest. What actually happened can only be guessed at for the moment, but available evidence tends to support this very tentative model.

Southern cities expanded considerably during the first three decades of the century, with the greatest rates of growth occurring between 1900 and 1910. Population increase dropped off during the depression years, though it did not stop altogether, as it did in many other areas of the country. In fact, the overall rate of southern urban growth was more than three times that of twenty-one selected northeastern and midwestern states, while the comparative rates of regional population increase were about the same. (See table 5-1.) The dozen largest cities in the

TABLE 5-1.

Rates of Population Increase in Selected Southern and Northern States 1900–1940

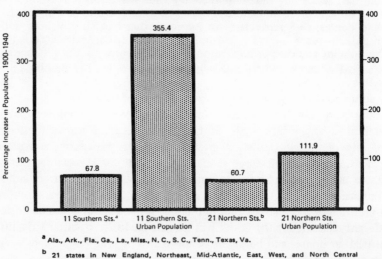

a Ala., Ark., Fla., Ga., La., Miss., N. C., S. C., Tenn., Texas, Va.

b 21 states in New England, Northeast, Mid-Atlantic, East, West, and North Central Census Regions.

South also expanded at a pace which exceeded the growth rates of the largest northern metropolises and a dozen comparable medium-sized northern cities. (See table 5-2.)[2]

Urban growth rates were, to some extent, the functions of varying city sizes. Southern centers were much smaller than cities like New York, Chicago, or Philadelphia, and thus more likely to double and triple their populations during the period. On the other hand, medium-sized cities in the North, which like most of their southern counterparts had reached a population of 100,000 by 1910, also fell behind the southern urban growth rate. This suggests that the South may have been in an earlier, different, and perhaps more active stage of urban development in the period, comparable to that which the North experienced in the late nineteenth century. But this difference in stages of urban growth is not very accurately expressed by the notion of a forty- or fifty-year lag in urbanization, since so many other factors besides population increase are involved.

TABLE 5-2.

Rates of Population Increase, 1900–1940: Southern and Northern Cities

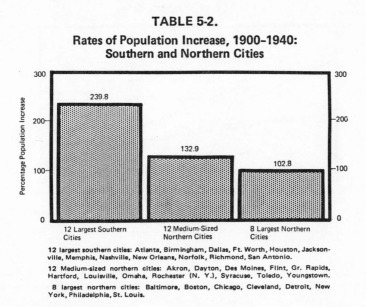

12 largest southern cities: Atlanta, Birmingham, Dallas, Ft. Worth, Houston, Jacksonville, Memphis, Nashville, New Orleans, Norfolk, Richmond, San Antonio.

12 Medium-sized northern cities: Akron, Dayton, Des Moines, Flint, Gr. Rapids, Hartford, Louisville, Omaha, Rochester (N. Y.), Syracuse, Toledo, Youngstown.

8 largest northern cities: Baltimore, Boston, Chicago, Cleveland, Detroit, New York, Philadelphia, St. Louis.

The growth rate for the dozen largest southern cities reached a peak for these years in 1910. (See table 5-3.) Migration to the cities obviously accounted for a good part of this increase, though it was also due to successful annexations that added outlying populations as well as territory. A rate of almost 60 percent could not be sustained for the next two decades: urban population growth declined to a level consistent with that in the North during the decade after 1910, but rose again during the 1920s. By 1940 the dozen largest southern cities were still expanding.

The metropolitan areas of these dozen cities also gained rapidly in population, a measure which is doubtless more revealing of the actual character of population growth, since it applied not only to the central cities—defined by political boundaries—but also to the immediately surrounding areas. Even with the annexations that padded the municipal population counts in 1910, metropolitan areas expanded by 40 percent, indicating a sizable net immigration to southern metropolises in the first decade of the century. (See table 5-4.) As in the case of central cities, the metropolitan rate of increase dropped after 1910, picked up in the 1920s, and declined again during the 1930s. But by 1940 these southern metropolitan areas were expanding at a rate more than three times that of their northern brethren—an average population growth of more than 35 percent per decade. A comparison of the central city and metropolitan area figures reveals the importance of annexation among the major regional urban centers, and the considerable population decentralization that was underway in all cities during this period.

TABLE 5-3.

Comparative Rates of Population Growth, 1900-1940: Southern and Northern Cities

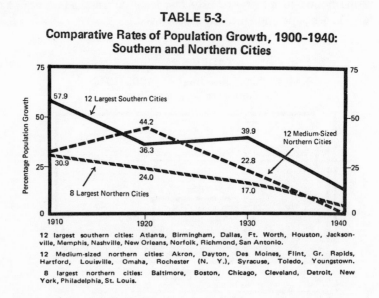

12 largest southern cities: Atlanta, Birmingham, Dallas, Ft. Worth, Houston, Jacksonville, Memphis, Nashville, New Orleans, Norfolk, Richmond, San Antonio.

12 Medium-sized northern cities: Akron, Dayton, Des Moines, Flint, Gr. Rapids, Hartford, Louisville, Omaha, Rochester (N. Y.), Syracuse, Toledo, Youngstown.

8 largest northern cities: Baltimore, Boston, Chicago, Cleveland, Detroit, New York, Philadelphia, St. Louis.

The rank-size order of major southern cities was quite unstable at the beginning of the century, suggesting either the absence of a regional urban system or the immaturity of such a system. The rank-size order of 1900 was highly scrambled forty years later—with fluctuations along the way. (See table 5-5.) New Orleans remained the largest metropolis throughout the period. Memphis and Atlanta registered respective populations of 102,320 and 89,872 in 1900, while Houston, Dallas, and Birmingham gave little indication of their later growth. The first ten years of the century witnessed the continued growth of Atlanta, the meteoric rise of Birmingham (due substantially to annexation), and the precipitous decline of Charleston and Savannah, but none of the urban development destined to occur in the Southwest. During the 1920s Houston eclipsed Atlanta in size and Dallas outdistanced Birmingham. Accompanying this spectacular urban growth—fueled by the black gold of the Texas oil fields and rising agricultural trade—was the appearance of a southwestern urban subsystem, centered primarily on Houston and increasingly on Dallas–Fort Worth. Likewise, Atlanta was dominant in a southeastern subsystem that included the secondary cities of Birmingham and Memphis. Atlanta was not nearly so dominant in this period as she became after mid-century. In fact, Atlanta and Birmingham were ardent competitors in the census race, and some contemporaries believed that Birmingham's industrial base destined it for ultimate urban superiority. If the rank-size order of the southeastern and southwestern cities is considered separately, a relative stability emerges within the two subsystems.

Rank-size order is, of course, only one among many indicators of urban systems. What is needed is a detailed analysis of major patterns of urban interrelationship, including economic and transportation ties and interurban communication and population movements. What rank-size order suggests, along with scattered data

TABLE 5-4.

Comparative Rates of Population Growth in Standard Metropolitan Areas,* 1900–1940

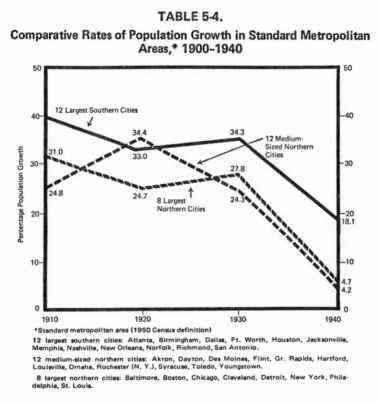

*Standard metropolitan area (1950 Census definition)

12 largest southern cities: Atlanta, Birmingham, Dallas, Ft. Worth, Houston, Jacksonville, Memphis, Nashville, New Orleans, Norfolk, Richmond, San Antonio.

12 medium-sized northern cities: Akron, Dayton, Des Moines, Flint, Gr. Rapids, Hartford, Louisville, Omaha, Rochester (N. Y.), Syracuse, Toledo, Youngstown.

8 largest northern cities: Baltimore, Boston, Chicago, Cleveland, Detroit, New York, Philadelphia, St. Louis.

from other sources, is that the first forty years of the century witnessed considerable changes in the previous patterns of regional urbanization. Older seaports like Charleston, Savannah, and Mobile, and inland market towns like Augusta and Montgomery were rapidly displaced by cities tied to expanding economic activities—steel, oil, finance—and to developing transportation networks. By 1940 the urban rank order was more stable: the dominant metropolises had forged their way to the front, followed closely by a new group of secondary market centers

(Chattanooga, Knoxville, Charlotte, and Shreveport among them). This more stable and articulated system was, in all probability, constituted of at least two major subsystems, one dominated by Atlanta in the Southeast and the other by Houston and Dallas in the Southwest. New Orleans was the major port which anchored the southern periphery of the regional urban system, and functioned as a truly dominant and "national" city for much of the period. New Orleans and Memphis possibly served to connect the various channels of trade and communication in the major subsystems.

The southern urban system hardly achieved complete stability in these years, since continued change was in the offing. During the 1940s southern metropolitan

TABLE 5-5.

Rank-Size Order of Twenty-Five Largest Southern Cities, 1900–1940

Rank	1900	1920	1940
1	New Orleans	New Orleans	New Orleans
2	Memphis	Atlanta	Houston
3	Atlanta	Birmingham	Atlanta
4	Richmond	Richmond	Dallas
5	Nashville	Memphis	Memphis
6	Charleston	San Antonio	Birmingham
7	Savannah	Dallas	San Antonio
8	San Antonio	Houston	Richmond
9	Norfolk	Nashville	Fort Worth
10	Houston	Norfolk	Jacksonville
11	Dallas	Fort Worth	Miami
12	Augusta	Jacksonville	Nashville
13	Mobile	Savannah	Norfolk
14	Birmingham	Knoxville	Chattanooga
15	Galveston	El Paso	Knoxville
16	Knoxville	Charleston	Tampa
17	Montgomery	Mobile	Charlotte
18	Chattanooga	Chattanooga	Shreveport
19	Jacksonville	Portsmouth	El Paso
20	Fort Worth	Macon	Savannah
21	Macon	Augusta	Austin
22	Austin	Tampa	Winston-Salem
23	Roanoke	Roanoke	Mobile
24	Columbia	Winston-Salem	Montgomery
25	Waco	Charlotte	Charleston

areas exceeded by 50 percent the national average rate of metropolitan growth; and Atlanta and the major Texas cities (not to mention Miami) grew even more dominant. But the urban system which emerged over the first forty years of the century did provide a structural framework for the significant urban expansion after 1940.

In 1900 about 15 percent of the population of the "census" South (which included Delaware, Maryland, and the District of Columbia) resided in places of 2,500 or more people, a figure which rose to 24 percent in 1920 and to about 30 percent in 1930. Smaller market towns, and the mill villages of the Piedmont sections, accounted for a substantial portion of the southern urban population (only 34 percent of southern urban dwellers resided in cities of 100,000 or more people in 1930). Indeed, the growth rate of the largest southern cities was significantly less than that for the region as a whole, indicating the population increases registered by scores of small towns from Virginia to Texas. On the other hand, the number of southern urban areas in the list of the nation's largest doubled between 1920 and 1940—from seven to fourteen. And the larger cities of the region dominated, and indeed, determined, the configuration and character of the emerging regional urban system.

THE URBAN ECONOMY

The southern urban economy, according to most observers, existed in a dependent, "colonial" relationship with the heavily industrialized North through the late nineteenth century—a condition which applied with even greater force to the regional agricultural sector. This relationship continued into the twentieth century, with the South supplying northern industry with raw materials and human resources and depending on other sections for capital resources, technical expertise, and manufactured goods. The industries which existed in southern cities and towns were often engaged in the first- or second-stage processing of agricultural products rather than in the more sophisticated types of manufacturing, and employed workers who were relatively unskilled when compared with those of the North. But the relationship was changing, with the South assuming more initiative in its economic affairs, especially in the provision of local capital for new industrial operations. And the wholesale and retail sectors of the southern urban economy grew more extensive and prosperous through the 1920s.

By 1910 most of the larger cities of the Southeast (Atlanta, Birmingham, Nashville, and New Orleans) contained a higher percentage of their workers in the manufacturing and mechanical category of the census than in commercial jobs. As George B. Tindall has observed, the 1920s was a "takeoff" period for southern industry. The migration of the New England textile industry to the southern Piedmont, the increased availability of hydroelectric power in the Southeast, and the discovery of oil in the Southwest combined to make this decade "a period during which industry and urbanization rapidly altered the face of the land."[3]

In 1929 eleven southern states (including Kentucky but not Texas) accounted for 13.2 percent of the nation's wage earners in manufacturing (compared with almost 50 percent in the Northeast), and these employees comprised 31.4 percent of the regional work force. The number of production workers in southern industries rose by 99 percent between 1899 and 1919, and by an additional 16 percent during the 1920s. Between the turn of the century and 1939, the increase in production workers amounted to 140 percent.

The southern urban economy was, however, primarily commercial. The South received less than one-fourth of its income from manufacturing in 1929, even though its rate of urbanization exceeded that for the nation as a whole. The region consistently ranked lowest in per capita wealth (though this was due in part to the higher proportion of agricultural workers), and the real wages of southern workers in 1930 not only lagged behind those of workers in other regions but actually de-clined after 1914. Cheap labor was—at least in the minds of many southern busi-nessmen—a principal drawing card for outside industry throughout the period.

The growth of southern cities in the first half of the twentieth century thus took place within a largely agricultural and commercial economic framework. But growth was obvious enough, both in the development of the region's cities and in their economies. For one thing, both larger southern cities and smaller market towns increased the degree of economic integration with their hinterlands. Patterns of intraregional trade grew even more regular, and the processing and marketing services available in the cities became more sophisticated. Southern chambers of commerce periodically dispatched delegations to farm areas and smaller towns in competition for business, and the greater centralization of commercial and financial activities in the larger cities was crucial in the emergence of the regional urban system.

That significant developments occurred in the southern urban economy during the early twentieth century is further indicated by an examination of the rank order distribution of regional cities. The distribution pattern of the twenty-five largest southern urban areas in 1900 (including the Texas and Florida cities) suggests a relatively immature urban system with little or, at most, moderate inter-dependence among cities. (See table 5-6.) New Orleans played the role of a "pri-

TABLE 5-6.

Rank Order Distribution of Twenty-Five Largest Southern Cities, 1900

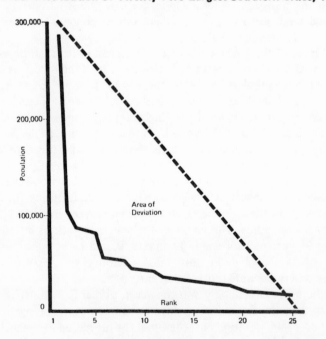

mate" city, eclipsing the other urban areas, which were grouped closely together in a rank order pattern often encountered in economically developing regions. It is, in fact, what urban geographers term a pattern of "intermediate distribution." The southern urban system deviated significantly from the optimum distribution of cities encountered in developed industrial economies. Forty years later the rank order of many cities had shifted, but they were much more evenly allocated along the spectrum from the largest to the smallest. (See table 5-7.) By 1940, in short, southern cities had become larger, and they were parts of a discernible hierarchy of urban places. (See table 5-8.) This transition from an intermediate to a more linear rank order distribution provides only a very theoretical framework for the evaluation of the southern urban economy. But the transition implies significant functional changes in patterns of regional urban interdependence—communication, trade, finance, and economic relationships in general. It implies a more mature and developed regional economy and reflects, in part, the significant rate of urban growth during the period.

The economic growth of individual regional cities can be measured in more conventional terms. Memphis and New Orleans qualified as genuine entrepôts, with trade in a large variety of goods and commodities, and other southern port cities followed suit. The value of exports almost doubled in Mobile during the first decade of the century, and rose in Norfolk from $9.5 million in 1914 to more than $137 million in 1926. "The little Norfolk of a few decades before," Wertenbaker

TABLE 5-7.

Rank Order Distribution of Twenty-Five Largest Southern Cities, 1940

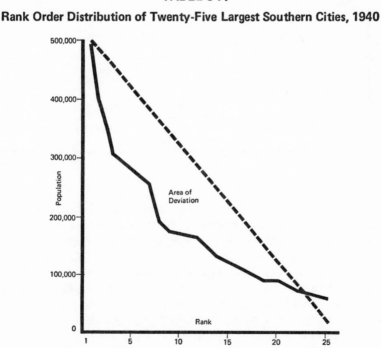

commented, "had become a great prosperous city, with exports equal in value to those of San Francisco, and far in advance of those of Baltimore, Philadelphia, or Boston." The port cities benefited especially from the increased shipping of military goods and troops during World War I. Lumber milling and woodworking were

TABLE 5-8.

Frequency Distribution of Twenty-Five Largest Southern Cities by Population Categories in 1900 and 1940

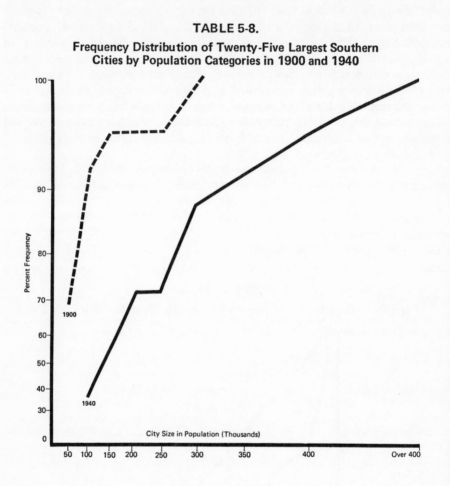

major industries in Memphis, followed closely by the manufacturing of cottonseed products. The city's capital investment in industrial operations rose from about $10 million at the turn of the century to more than $67 million twenty years later. Industrial expansion was especially pronounced in Richmond, Knoxville, and Birmingham, though the efforts of the U. S. Steel Corporation to control its Birmingham subsidiary hampered the major industry of the Alabama metropolis—the Tennessee Coal and Iron Company. Atlanta dominated a vast hinterland through a complex network of railroad connections. Chattanooga drew large numbers of workers from surrounding areas into its burgeoning textile industries, but lost to Birmingham in the race to become the "Pittsburgh of the South."[4]

Fort Worth emerged in the Southwest as a major meat-packing center with a sprinkling of heavy industry, and as the site of nine oil refineries in 1922. Indeed, the petroleum industry financed the city's first skyscrapers and added substantially to the local payroll. Dallas was known for its food-processing and apparel industries (though it never developed into a major textile town). The location of a Federal Reserve bank in Dallas catapulted the city into a commanding position as the financial hub of the Southwest, as was Atlanta (also the site of a Federal Reserve bank) in the Southeast. The completion of the Houston port project during the 1920s enlarged that city's capacity for trade in agricultural goods, especially cotton, and for oil refining and shipment. Throughout the period Houston remained the largest single city in the Southwest.[5]

Major factors behind the national prosperity of the 1920s were new technological innovations—especially electricity, the radio, and the automobile—that exploited new markets and attracted capital investment. And local urban economies were also affected by these innovations. The automobile's impact alone was significant. In addition to the few auto assembly plants located in southern urban areas, motor vehicle manufacturing required large amounts of raw materials—cotton, lumber, petroleum—which were processed in regional cities. The hardwood industry in Memphis, for example, was increasingly geared to processing materials for the automobile. And the growth of businesses that were directly or indirectly related to the motor vehicle were especially important in the wholesale and retail sectors of local economies. Automobile dealerships alone accounted for significant portions of urban retail trade, ranging from 9.3 percent in New Orleans in 1929 to 14.4 percent in Birmingham. Accessory stores, repair shops, filling stations, roadside restaurants, and roadhouses all depended in various ways on the motor vehicle. The retail businesses listed in the automotive category by the U. S. Census in 1929 accounted for more than 20.7 percent of the total retail trade in Birmingham, 20.5 percent of that in Nashville, 18.5 percent of that in Memphis, 16.5 percent of that in Atlanta, and 14.2 percent in New Orleans. In Birmingham the automobile business was the largest single category of retail trade, and the expenditures for autos and related goods and services in Nashville were exceeded only by those for food. In addition, the automobile was at least partly responsible for the economic fortunes of real estate developers and speculators, financial institutions, insurance brokers, and suburban businesses—and led to a boom in commercial, residential, and public construction.[6]

The industrial takeoff of the 1920s was aborted in the subsequent decade. Like a creeping paralysis, economic depression spread from the collapse of the Florida land boom and rising rates of urban unemployment in the mid-1920s to the massive national trauma of the 1930s. While one would never sense, from reading the major southern urban dailies, that the stock market crash in 1929 was anything more than an errant gesture or passing readjustment of the prospering economy, by 1932 a number of banks had failed or were on the brink of failure, and a variety of other signs pointed to the harsh reality of the crisis: unemployment and relief rolls mounted, construction permits plummeted, tax revenues dropped off, school systems and other public services were cut back or eliminated, and heavy declines in retail sales quickly registered layoffs in manufacturing plants, warehouses, and stores. The unemployment figures are dreary generalizations of personal tragedy. In some regional cities at least a quarter of the work force was unemployed by 1932, and the depression reached into all types of work, dragging businessmen and even professional people into the relief lines. As usual, however, unskilled workers—whether black or white—were the first fired, as they were the last hired. Only, this time they faced considerably more competition for the limited stores of public relief and private charity that were available.

The Roosevelt administration identified the South as the nation's "number one economic problem," and Birmingham—with its heavy dependence on the steel industry—was often labeled the country's "hardest hit city." Some municipalities, like Norfolk, managed to escape the full impact of the depression until 1932 and 1933, while soup kitchens were familiar sights in other urban areas several years earlier. Some Texas cities, like Dallas and Houston, were buoyed up by discoveries in the east Texas oil fields, and actually increased their local payrolls during these years in certain categories. Nearly every southern city government could point to northeastern and midwestern industrial centers where the rates of unemployment were comparatively much worse. Indeed, the South's rate of agricultural unemployment was significantly higher than its rate of industrial unemployment, and on the whole the South suffered less severely in its basic industries *relative to 1929* than did other sections of the country. The number of production workers in the region actually increased slightly during the 1930s.

URBAN CONFIGURATIONS

Between 1900 and 1940 a metropolitan configuration became evident in the largest southern cities. Growing suburbs surrounded a relatively dense central core, and urban patterns of trade and influence extended over a large area, perhaps even several counties. Central cities themselves expanded at the same time, through annexation and an increasing proliferation of retail and wholesale businesses, and downtown business districts were more and more differentiated by function. It was altogether like the urban configuration which appeared earlier in the North's largest cities, except that southern metropolises experienced decentralization at earlier stages of their development. The southern metropolitan configuration also tended to reflect greater irregularities; a strict pattern of concentric zones, determined by differences in land use, social class, and ethnic composition, rarely prevailed except in the most general sense. At the beginning of the century, in fact, some regional cities manifested arrangements that seemed almost preindustrial in character: a heavy concentration of business activity and upper class residences near the city core, but with outlying shantytowns and a general mixture of populations and land uses throughout the central city.

The streetcar and the motor vehicle made their appearances before most southern urban areas had achieved the population densities characteristic of the largest nineteenth-century industrial cities. And these two technological innovations were largely responsible for the emerging metropolitan configuration in the twentieth century. The first practical electric railway system, devised by Frank J.

Sprague, was initiated in Richmond in 1888. By 1890 more than fifty cities across the country had installed electric trolley lines, and during the subsequent decade every large city in the South boasted a functioning streetcar system. Exclusive residential areas were generally the first streetcar suburbs to appear in the South, like Ghent in Norfolk and Annesdale Park in Memphis. Atlanta developer Joel Hurt pioneered the city's first residential suburb, Inman Park, in 1887 and also built the city's first electric street railway in 1889. Thomas J. Wertenbaker concluded that the streetcar "tripled the area of Norfolk" even before the advent of the automobile.[7] Aside from connecting existing urban neighborhoods with more efficient transportation, streetcar lines radiated outward to newer subdivisions and, in cities like Birmingham, to industrial suburbs. Streetcars constituted the foundation of the urban transportation system until about 1920, when they were challenged by the private passenger automobile and the motor bus; but they continued to transport the majority of passengers in and out of central business districts through the 1930s.

The transportation revolution initiated by the trolley was completed by the automobile. In 1920 motor vehicle registrations totaled approximately 20,000 in the Atlanta, New Orleans, and Memphis metropolitan areas, 16,000 in Birmingham, and 12,000 in Nashville. During the decade the increase in registrations ranged from about 192 percent in Memphis to 337 percent in Birmingham.[8] Atlanta accounted for almost 20 percent of all the automobiles and motor trucks in Georgia in 1930, New Orleans contained a quarter of the registered vehicles in Louisiana, and Memphis and Nashville together accounted for almost a third of Tennessee's vehicle registration in 1920 and for more than a quarter by the end of the decade.

Increased reliance on the motorcar cut into street railway patronage. The total of trolley patrons reached a peak in New Orleans in 1921 and in Atlanta in 1923, and southern streetcar systems were destined to follow the path of their counterparts in most other American cities. One observer computed that out of a total expenditure of almost $23 million for passenger transportation in Atlanta in 1923, the automobile accounted for more than $16 million.[9] Traffic congestion and problems of parking and auto safety loomed larger as auto registrations mounted, and some local leaders and businessmen began to question the motor vehicle's usefulness in the city even at this early date.

The automobile provided additional impetus for outward population movement, and suburban development was no longer dependent on streetcar connections. Beginning in the 1920s, residential communities appeared which relied completely on automotive transportation. Automobility brought with it, in the words of one authority, "a new kind of horizontal city," in which racial and income groups were more effectively segregated, the former regularity of urban expansion along streetcar lines was destroyed, and commuting zones were enlarged. In most southern cities, in fact, the automobile—rather than the streetcar—provided the technological means for expansion in the stages of most rapid urban growth.[10]

As elsewhere in the country, the principal means of increasing city size was annexation of surrounding communities and territory. Significant population growth on the urban fringes was a major impetus for annexation in southern cities.

Between 1900 and 1920 Birmingham increased its land area by almost seven times through the "Greater Birmingham" annexation of 1910. In 1909 Fort Worth doubled its land area by acquiring North Fort Worth, and doubled it again in 1922 with the addition of Arlington Heights, Riverside, and other outlying settlements. Atlanta more than doubled its geographic size in the first two decades of the century, and added even more territory during the 1920s. (Atlanta's efforts to boost its size by joining outlying towns—including Decatur, College Park, and Hapeville—to the city in a loose system of borough administration was not accepted by the Census Bureau as a basis for enumeration.) Annexations in Memphis more than doubled the city's area in 1899, and this was followed by additional territorial acquisitions in 1909, 1913, 1917, and 1919 that increased the city's area another 56 percent. Knoxville's geographical size in 1920 was more than five and a half times what it had been twenty years earlier.

The centripetal-centrifugal tension characteristic of American urbanization through most of the nineteenth century was especially discernible in the South after 1900. As the streetcar began to disperse segments of the population, and bring outlying communities within effective commuting distance of the center, the city core was also developing. Taller buildings, the addition of new downtown businesses, and the expansion of existing retail outlets increased inner-city densities and pushed out the boundaries of the central business district. The first few years of the century witnessed a significant and growing differentiation between places of work and residence. Certainly, the skylines of 1940 bore little resemblance to those at the turn of the century. New office buildings—reverently identified as "skyscrapers"—hovered over major downtown intersections in the larger southern cities, and cast their shadows over the two- and three-story structures which characterized an earlier time. Together, these monuments to commercial and civic success formed impressive corridors in the heart of downtown, conveying a sense of both permanence and dynamism.

Like other American cities, southern urban centers were becoming more complex and specialized in other ways—in terms of their economies, labor forces, and patterns of land use. Central business districts that were relatively undifferentiated agglomerations of activity in the 1870s and 1880s were gradually arranged into districts and subdistricts on the basis of specialized functions—finance, retail, wholesale, storage, industry, etc. This process was underway in the larger northern cities by the 1870s. One Atlanta historian has suggested that the "period of significant change" in that city was the 1890s.[11] Furthermore, residential areas became increasingly identifiable according to race and socioeconomic rank. Blacks were found more and more toward the inner city, while white working class groups moved further out.

Larger southern cities reflected, certainly by 1940, an urban configuration more or less typical of that of American cities generally. But there were some significant differences in the composition of the southern urban population, and regional cities began to "come of age" after significant population decentralization was already underway—a fact that doubtless accounts for continued differences in their shape and character.

POPULATION AND SOCIAL STRUCTURE

The first half of the twentieth century was a period of geographic mobility for many southerners—a fact often ignored by sole attention to those stranded in farm tenancy. Southern cities grew largely by migration from rural areas and small towns within the region, and there was apparently a good deal of interurban movement as well. A 1918 survey revealed that only about 2 percent of the white parents of Memphis school children had been born in the city,[12] and it was often remarked that few local luminaries in the larger centers were descended from local families. Many prominent businessmen in Atlanta, Birmingham, and Memphis, for example, had migrated to those cities from elsewhere in the South while they were in their twenties and in search of promising career opportunities. One Atlanta publication lamented the absence of any "real aristocracy" in the Gate City: "...you can go down the list and find dozens of houses now prominent in social life, the family trees of which sprouted out of a whitewash bucket, a second-hand furniture shop, or a grist mill, and in one well-known case, out of a peddler's pack."[13]

Within the region principal demographic movements were toward the southern half of Florida, to the Gulf coast between New Orleans and Mobile, to the Tennessee valley, to the mining areas of north Alabama, and to the Carolina Piedmont. In many cases, the movements were in the direction of towns and cities in these developing subregions.

The proportion of foreign born citizens declined in all major southern cities during the period, including urban centers in the Southwest. Even early in the century foreign immigrants rarely accounted for as much as 10 percent of the urban population, and they were found mainly in the port cities. Between 1900 and 1940 the proportion of foreign residents in the populations of New Orleans and Norfolk dropped from 10.6 to 3 percent, and from 3.7 to 1.8 percent, respectively, and San Antonio (17.5 to 11), Houston (9.9 to 4), and Fort Worth (6.7 to 2) reflected a similar trend. In the Southwest, of course, a considerable number of foreign born citizens were Mexican-Americans, while in New Orleans the influence of Italian immigrants was especially notable. The small immigrant populations of other southern cities were composed of a variety of nationalities. On the other hand, the actual numbers of foreign born citizens declined in only three of the dozen largest regional cities during the period (Memphis, Nashville, and New Orleans), and the impact of foreign born groups was often greater than their numbers suggested.

But millions of southern blacks were in motion—to southern cities and then to northern urban centers in a migration that reached flood proportions around World War I and into the 1920s. Between 1910 and 1920 Alabama, Louisiana, Mississippi, and Tennessee suffered net losses of black population, as did Georgia, South Carolina, and Virginia during the 1920s. The increases registered in black populations in southern states after 1910 were generally below the black rate of natural increase, indicating a continuing and significant out-migration.

The numbers of blacks in southern cities rose rapidly throughout the twentieth century, while their proportions of the total urban population declined slightly between 1900 and 1940—a reflection of the large white migration to southern urban areas as well as of the pronounced movement of blacks out of the region. (See table 5-9.)

In cities like New York and Chicago blacks crowded into dense central sections recently occupied by foreign born immigrants. The Great Migration swelled populations in these areas, and spilled over into contiguous districts in a wave of necessity usually accompanied by the rearguard violence of retreating whites. In southern cities, however, black settlements were scattered at the beginning of the century— huddled next to railroad tracks, warehouses, and factories, along the rivers in Nashville and Memphis, and in alleyways, low-lying places, and even wooded areas along the city's fringe. The prevailing type of housing more closely resembled the small sharecroppers' cabins of the rural South—some divided into duplexes—than the

TABLE 5-9.

Black Population in Twelve Largest Southern Cities, 1900 and 1940

	% Black Population of Total		% Increase in Black Population
	1900	1940	1900–1940
Atlanta	39	34	192
Birmingham	43	40	557
Dallas	21	17	457
Ft. Worth	15	14	494
Houston	32	22	490
Jacksonville	57	35	280
Memphis	48	41	143
Nashville	37	28	56
New Orleans	27	30	91
Norfolk	43	31	126
Richmond	37	31	90
San Antonio	14	7	155

Source: U. S. Census, 1900 and 1940.

congested tenements and older single-family homes that predominated in northern ghettos. In most southern cities, especially New Orleans and Charleston, few census tracts contained populations that were less than 10 or 20 percent white or black.

The racial heterogeneity in census districts was, however, misleading. Many blacks living in predominantly white areas were servants who occupied quarters behind their employers' homes, and clusters of black residences contiguous to white sections were like islands set apart. The pattern in all southern cities during the twentieth century was one of advancing racial segregation, the increasing concentration of blacks in fewer, larger residential areas nearer the urban core. Available evidence indicates that the majority of Birmingham's blacks were found immediately around the city's downtown area quite early in the century. As white workers moved to industrial and residential suburbs, according to Paul B. Worthman, "black workers in Birmingham by 1909 showed the classic twentieth-century pattern of concentration in poor quality, racially segregated housing in the core city."[14] In Nashville a rapid racial changeover in residential patterns was especially pronounced during the 1920s, though significant numbers of blacks and whites were found in almost half of the city's census tracts early in the century.[15] Whites searching for housing in New Orleans invaded and fragmented black communities, leaving behind a number of scattered black residential pockets. As late as 1920 only 6 of the 272 census districts in the city were completely white, and none was solidly black.[16]

Municipal streetcar systems facilitated the sorting-out process along racial lines. The trolley enabled whites to live in outlying areas and still be accessible to their work and downtown shopping, while black servants could commute from the city core to white areas. The automobile encouraged even more distant residential sites, but blacks—largely because of economic factors—were forced to rely on deteriorating public transit systems in most regional cities.

Changes in black residential patterns were accompanied by shifts in the economies and leadership of black communities. In the late nineteenth century southern urban blacks dominated, or were well represented in, certain skilled trades and occupations and regularly served a white clientele. This was particularly true of the building trades and of services like barbering. Increasingly in the twentieth century, however, whites displaced blacks in many skilled occupations, and as patrons abandoned black businesses and services. Among other things, these developments acted to further restrict blacks to the lowest rungs of the socioeconomic ladder, to the unskilled, low-paying jobs characterized by frequent layoffs and poor working conditions. But blacks remained a crucial component of the work forces in southern cities, providing much of that manual labor which laid the foundations for regional industry. Blacks comprised 65 percent of all iron and steel workers in Birmingham in 1900, for example, and 75 percent in 1910. "Concentrated in poorly paid, low status jobs, blacks continued to form the base of the southern labor force as they had under slavery."[17]

The increasing racial segregation in the urban South also opened the way for a new group of ambitious black entrepreneurs, who pursued the main chance with the vigor of their white counterparts and directed their efforts toward the black market. The old elite of clergymen, barbers, contractors, and house servants gave way to a newer elite of skilled laborers, larger merchants, doctors, lawyers, and other professional and business types. As W. E. B. Du Bois wrote around the turn of the century:

The old leaders of Negro opinion, in the little groups where there is a Negro social consciousness, are being replaced by new; neither the black preacher nor the black teacher leads as he did two decades ago. Into their places are pushing the farmers and gardeners, the well-paid porters and artisans, the business-men—all those with property and money.[18]

The new black elite advocated—as had most of their forebears—a philosophy of thrift, hard work, property ownership, material advancement, and even urban boosterism. Though oriented toward the city rather than the farm, these business-men supported the goals of Booker T. Washington—especially as they were ex-pressed by the National Negro Business League—and called for an end to ideological conflicts among national black spokesmen and organizations "to permit those of us, who are dying to do business in a business way, [to] live in peace."[19] They were not, however, passive accommodationists. Throughout the period black business and civic leaders protested the economic restrictions and legal sanctions applied to their race and lamented the conditions in their communities.

Indeed, most black residential areas were marked by poor housing, horrendous sanitation facilities, inadequate schools, police harassment rather than protection, and unpaved streets that turned to an impenetrable mire in heavy rains. But south-ern urban blacks contributed forcefully to the improvement of their communities in a number of ways, and their accomplishments are all the more impressive con-sidering the obstacles cast in their way. As the twentieth century advanced, black communities became larger and more complex, economically diverse, and socially organized. Black civic and service organizations proliferated, along with existing religious and fraternal groups, especially in those cities with a significant black middle class.

One outstanding example of community service work in the black community is Atlanta's Neighborhood Union, organized in 1908 by women in the vicinity of Spelman and Morehouse colleges. The Union eventually became involved in a wide variety of projects, from providing recreation to black children to establishing a health center and inspecting black schools throughout the city. Neighborhood clean-up campaigns were launched to encourage community pride, and a program of home visits and literature distribution constituted a very early, and effective, effort at disseminating available health information and resources. Though unusual in several respects, the Neighborhood Union has been categorized by one writer as "a representative prototype" of black women's organizations. Like other such groups, the Union was composed of realtively well-educated, and usually middle class, women who were concerned with the plight of their less fortunate brethren and who encouraged self-help and race pride in their communities.[20]

Black protest against racial injustice was often both vocal and resourceful in the urban South. Just after the turn of the century, for example, blacks boycotted streetcar lines in more than twenty-five southern cities to protest new state and local Jim Crow laws. The boycotts ultimately failed; but they lasted at least ten months in Atlanta and eight months in New Orleans and Nashville, and as long as three years in Augusta. In Nashville boycott leaders organized an ambitious, though ill-fated, black-owned car line as an alternative to segregated transportation. Sig-nificantly, prominent black business and professional men were at the head of these protests against racial oppression, even at the height of accommodationism.[21]

The impact of Afro-Americans on southern culture has been, of course, both substantial and abiding, and almost impossible to measure with precision. The large black districts in the cities, with their distinct yet related subcultures, are a pro-found historical fact, comparable to and perhaps even greater than the cultural influence of massive foreign immigration on northern urban centers. The culture of the urban South is thus a biracial product, though whites have not been inclined to admit it. The relatively greater penchant among southerners for the institutions of family and church, for example, is certainly a shared cultural tendency.

The class structure in the urban South was not generally so elaborate or clearly stratified as that in the heavily industrialized North (with the exception, of course, of the relationship between whites and blacks, which approached the rigidity of a racial caste system). Generally, the lowest rungs on the socioeconomic ladder were occupied by unskilled black and white laborers, many of whom moved from place to place in search of work and on and off the meager public and private assistance rolls. Semiskilled workers were a little better off, and were sometimes able to move into skilled occupations. Skilled artisans, white collar employees, and smaller businessmen constituted the bulk of the white middle class—and of the black upper class—while the largest white businessmen and professional people comprised the city's upper crust. Available evidence suggests that most white workers achieved a modicum of success, at least until the Depression, and that population movement within and among regional cities was quite pronounced.

Many white workers were able to rise in occupational status from unskilled to semiskilled work and even from blue collar to white collar jobs. And they were also able to amass real property holdings.[22] As was the case in many other American cities, those who held property and a higher place on the social rank scale tended to remain longer—were more geographically stable—than those who did not, because property holding was an important measure of local "success" and property owners found it more difficult and less desirable to pull up stakes and move away. Undoubtedly, some movement was to better jobs in other towns, but the evidence suggests that the less successful workers were in terms of occupational status and property ownership, the more likely they were to move out of the city.

Rates of geographical mobility were pronounced in the urban South. In the late nineteenth and early twentieth centuries, for example, less than half the young men in Atlanta and Birmingham remained in those cities for as long as ten years. And mobility within southern cities was also quite high. Many renters changed their places of residence annually, indicating a very volatile rate of residential turnover. Cities throughout the country contained populations that were on the move—searching for better jobs, better housing, a better life. If mobility was an important facet of American culture, it was nowhere more prevalent than in the cities. And this was true for the South as it was for the rest of the country.

Southern urban blacks experienced far less upward occupational mobility than did whites, and were much less successful in accumulating real property in the early twentieth century. Black workers were generally more geographically stable than blue collar whites in Birmingham in the late nineteenth century—perhaps because they were able to find work in the area's mines and factories, or because their prospects of improving their status in other cities was not very good. After the turn of the century, however, the rate of black geographic mobility increased significantly, at least in Birmingham, as black workers were pushed out of certain skilled trades and the siren call of opportunity in the urban North beckoned.

The greatest influence over economic and political affairs in the urban South rested with a *commercial-civic elite* composed of larger merchants, real estate agents, insurance brokers, bankers, contractors, and a variety of other people—attorneys, journalists, doctors, teachers, clergymen, and city officials—who were associated directly or indirectly with the business middle class. The social and economic interests of this elite group were wide ranging, but were concentrated primarily in the local area and specifically in the downtown business district. Their influence was expressed in a variety of ways, and manifested in an array of voluntary civic clubs and organizations that proliferated during the early twentieth century.

Perhaps the most important local associations were the chambers of commerce that took upon themselves the burdens of urban problems and posed as representative groups to fashion solutions for those problems. Besides their function as meeting places and discussion groups for the local elite, chambers usually maintained a lobby in the state legislature, dispatched members into surrounding counties and states to drum up business for the city, raised funds for national advertising drives, promoted more "efficient" forms of government, and advocated comprehensive city planning. In the opinion of some observers, local chambers actually served as quasigovernments. The editors of the *Memphis Commercial-Appeal* wondered what the city would be like without a chamber of commerce: "What body would then take up propositions that daily come before the city in its business, in its efforts for better transportation, in its efforts for road improvements and a thousand and one other things that go to make up the economic and social life of a great modern city?"[23]

The commercial-civic elite was the most influential group in the southern city, but it did not preside over a monolithic community power structure. Its members did not agree on all matters of public policy, and they did not have anything resembling absolute control over public opinion and the electorate. Competing interest groups often forced commercial and civic organizations to back away from controversial issues, and many municipal governments were not powerful enough to impose specific business goals. Southern cities experienced the type of leadership generally associated with predominantly commercial cities—with merchants, bankers, and real estate brokers wielding the most influence in the direction of expanding local trade, promoting urban loyalties, and encouraging urban growth.

A recent study of Birmingham's leadership demonstrates a general relationship between economic power and political influence. The "upper-ranking" and "middle-ranking" economic interest groups were clearly more powerful than the "lower-ranking" groups when it came to the allocation of public services, or to almost any other aspect of public policy. The bulk of the city's elected officials were associated with the "middle-ranking" interest groups (real estate firms, contractors, larger merchants, and professional men), and most of the members of the leading commercial and civic associations also hailed from this group.[24]

Clearly, the commercial-civic elite reigned supreme throughout the early twentieth century, reaching their heyday in the business decade of the 1920s when their leadership was virtually unquestioned. The Depression was a genuine crisis for this group: the economy did not respond to any of the old, safe remedies, and enlightened free enterprise was unable to stem the tide of unemployment or even care successfully for its victims. But while the initiative may have passed to the national government in 1932 and 1933, the commercial-civic elite did not fade away. On the contrary, some of its members presided over the administration of government programs and actively solicited federal funds for civic projects. While most of them disapproved of public housing, the encouragement of private home ownership in burgeoning new suburbs through the Federal Housing Administration was eagerly accepted as one additional means of promoting metropolitan growth. Certainly, by the early 1940s the commercial-civic elite was as much in evidence as it had ever been.

URBAN CONSCIOUSNESS

A significant degree of urban consciousness existed in the cities of the nation's most rural region. Southern urban spokesmen—drawn largely from the commercial-civic elite—understood the unique problems and opportunities of cities and identified their own city with other urban areas throughout the country. Based on a fervent local loyalty—a sort-of urban patriotism—urban consciousness became the general context within which public policy was developed and problems perceived. It was, in other words, a distinctly urban frame of reference with both social and spatial dimensions.

Southern cities were regarded, first of all, as different from the rural areas which surrounded them. The city belonged, in this view, to an entirely different category of human settlement, and was likely to take a similar shape and character no matter what its regional location. It was inherently dynamic and expansive, reaching out to new markets with growing populations and economic capacity. The healthy, growing city—not the stable and somnolent town—was the model for the southern commercial-civic elite. Rural areas were judged according to their contributions to the city and the character of urban life; small towns were often condemned for their provinciality and praised for their aping of big city ways; and suburbs were regarded neither as rural retreats nor as social safety valves, but as outposts along an expanding urban frontier.

Agriculture and the rural way of life were often praised in the southern urban media, though the periodic expression of such sentiments was apparently more obligatory, in response to accepted and noncontroversial American ideals, than deeply sincere or convincing. This view, like so many others, was couched in an urban frame of reference. When the city was experiencing hard times (during the recession of the early 1920s and the depression of the 1930s), urban migration was discouraged. Unskilled farm families only added to the housing and unemployment problems of the city and threatened to become charges on the local community. Also, low urban food prices were dependent on sufficient supplies, and the technology in this period was not available to replace large numbers of regional farm workers and maintain a high level of agricultural production. When times were good, however, homage to the family farm was paid less often. And urban spokesmen rarely questioned, at any time, the obvious attractions of the city for rural folk, especially young people. The excitement of the city was perhaps second only to the greater prospects for success that could be found there—and who could blame an ambitious country youth for wanting to make his or her way in the world? The farm-to-city movement had a certain inevitability about it. "As long as the reward for labor in the towns and cities is greater than it is in the country," the *Nashville Tennessean* observed in 1927, "we need not expect this movement to be checked. Nor for business reasons should we be anxious to check it."[25]

The small town was regarded by spokesmen in the larger cities with considerable ambiguity and condescension, for it was poised most precariously between city and country. Denounced on the one hand for its dullness and lack of opportunity and progress, the small town was also criticized for its pretention and snobbiness. Atlanta novelist Ward Greene described small town society as composed of "either a lot of busted old Joes pretending they're aristocrats when they haven't a dime's worth of culture left, or a lot of howling god-hoppers running the town for purity and pep." His fictional Corinth "was snobbish as only a city can be that has outgrown the friendly country town stage and not yet attained the variegation of the cosmopolis. . . ." Or, as the *Tennessean* put it in 1925, "It isn't a hick town unless there's no place to go where you shouldn't be."[26] The significant point is that, whether favorable or not, attitudes toward the small town were fashioned within an urban crucible, in the awareness that a "real" city was a very different and basically preferable sort of environment.

The residential suburb represented a very real way of escaping the congestion and soot of inner-city life, but the prevailing image in the urban South was not of a static marriage between country and city. Commercial-civic spokesmen waxed romantic about new population centers carved out of earth, rock, and trees on the urban periphery. They seemed less impressed by bubbling brooks than by the streams of population that penetrated the surrounding hinterland and thus increased the city's size and extent. If this was not urbanism, strictly defined, it was certainly metropolitanism—hailed as the wave of the future and the signal of progress. Thus, suburbs were not seen as distinct units, but as extensions of the growing city. Southern urban businessmen, like academic urbanists, were well aware that the municipal limits which separated the central city from its suburbs were but an "imaginary line."

Urban consciousness was also built on the constant reminders that certain sorts of problems distinguished cities as singular environments. The difficulties of governing a large and relatively heterogeneous population; providing streets, transportation, recreation, and housing; and dealing with the possibilities for disease and disorder, assumed massive proportions in the cities. Southern urban dwellers were well aware of these problems, and the most articulate among them readily and frequently noted their existence in cities across the country. Southern urban areas looked to New York and Los Angeles for positive examples in city planning and transportation, and to Chicago for examples to be avoided, especially in problems of government. The crime, political corruption, and foreign born influence in the Illinois metropolis provided southern writers with an endless source of horror stories and a platform for self-righteousness. Commercial-civic spokesmen tended to see their cities as part of an emerging southern urban network—distinguished by a higher rate of growth and by the supposed absence of some severe big city problems. But they also perceived that cities were cities, and that the urban South was very much a part of a larger national urban community and was becoming more so with each passing decade. As the *Birmingham Age-Herald* remarked in a discussion of regional cities in 1920, "We are part and parcel of the same destiny."[27] The eyes of southern urban leaders were focused on other cities, within and without the region, and not on the surrounding rural districts from which they drew much of their population and economic sustenance.

Clearly, the leaders in southern cities did not share the emotional proclivity for the soil or the ideological justifications of agriculture that have often been attributed in blanket fashion to the region. The southern Agrarians of the 1920s were identified with Nashville, to be sure, but theirs was an almost unique voice virtually drowned out by the din of urban boosterism. Commercial-civic groups avidly cultivated an intense urban patriotism among local citizens, sang the praises of city life—where great success was possible with ambition and a little luck—and fashioned an ideal of a healthy, prosperous metropolis that was quite compelling when compared with its rural counterpart.

SOUTHERN CULTURE AND URBAN LIFE

Southern cities were often characterized in this period by violence, extreme conservatism on social and racial issues, religious frenzy, and moral absolutism. These tendencies have been labeled manifestations of traditional southern rural values as they responded to the diversity and unpredictability of change. Some observers have even gone so far as to describe the great majority of the southern urban population as essentially rural, ignorant, and prejudiced. Surely this is an overstatement. Aside from the fact that we have probably accepted far too readily the assertions of urban evils and rural virtues, we are discovering that moral righteousness, unbending mores, violence, and sin are not confined to either an urban or a rural environment. Ethnic neighborhoods in the North, for example, were known for the strength of their religious institutions and the prevalence of their violence and disorder. The same generalization could apply to many sections of the urban South and, for that matter, even to small towns and rural areas. Southern cities were known for their proscriptions against various patterns of behavior and entertainments during the period; but such policies are more readily associated with Boston than with Atlanta. The point is that there were few problems or attitudes present in southern cities that were *generically* different from those in cities elsewhere in the country.

Having said this, however, we must also recognize that cities have always been repositories of regional culture. The process of urbanization doubtless heightened the contrasts between older customs and newer habits, and the inconsistencies that always existed in the South—hospitality and violence, racism and tolerance, ingenuity and fatalism—were apparent in the region's cities. Whether southern cultural patterns were inherently rural or not, or distinct from those of other regions, it is almost certainly true that most southern urban policies and attitudes in this period were efforts to cope in various ways with the phenomenon of the city—to render the city comprehensible and to carve out some relatively secure and meaningful roles in the urban arena for a number of different groups.

The proclivity to violence among southern urban dwellers seemed very much a part of the regional heritage. The ancient doctrines of personal honor, once held high by a plantation aristocracy, somehow persisted among the lower classes of urban whites and blacks. If we can believe local newspaper reports, large numbers of men in both races and of all social classes habitually packed sidearms in city streets, and a profusion of weapons would appear on the slightest pretext. Reporters working the downtown sections considered a pencil, a bottle of whiskey, and a revolver as standard equipment.

Such reports appear to be confirmed by the relatively high murder rates in southern cities in the early twentieth century. Memphis was titled the "murder capital of the world" in 1916, when 89 homicides per 100,000 people were recorded. Murder rates in Atlanta, Nashville, and New Orleans rose in the 1920s by 32 percent, 183 percent, and 44 percent, respectively. On the whole, homicide rates in major southern cities substantially exceeded those in the North and Midwest. As William D. Miller concluded, murder was a "prominent feature of the life of southern cities at the time they were achieving a metropolitan character, that is, between 1890 and 1920." The unsettled patterns of urban social life doubtless contributed to a rate of personal violence that reached a peak during the 1920s and 1930s (though it still remains comparatively high to this day). Violence was particularly pronounced in black sections, where population mobility was volatile, living conditions poor, and opportunities limited. The most articulate and persuasive explanation for this phenomenon focuses on the southern "world view" or on a "feudal agrarian myth" that demanded violence as a perverse cement of community.[28]

Urban whites were just as committed to the maintenance of the southern racial system as their rural counterparts. True, lynchings rarely occurred in the larger cities, and blacks were able to develop institutions in the urban centers, establish an infrastructure of social and economic leadership, and attain a measure of autonomy, or at least anonymity. But white methods of social control were, if anything, more complex and reticulated in the urban setting—less harsh in some ways, perhaps, but just as oppressive and certainly more formal.[29] Blacks were pushed toward the lower rungs on the occupational ladder, as we have seen, and the reign of Jim Crow was firmly established in the statute books by the first decade of the twentieth century. Blacks attended segregated schools, lived in mostly segregated housing, were relegated to separate seating in theaters and streetcars, and were either segregated in parks and other public places or denied admittance altogether. Continual police harassment was periodically punctuated by drives to arrest "vagrants" (usually blacks without regular employment), and those arrested might well find themselves acting as conscripted city laborers—repairing the streets or leased by city and county officials to work in private mines and factories. Black freedoms were further circumscribed by curfews instituted in black sections and by outbreaks of white vigilantism.[30] Because of their size and diversity, cities posed a number of difficulties for the strict maintenance of the racial system; but urban whites responded to the challenge by an even greater dedication to the task.

The religious prejudices so characteristic of the rural South were also found in the cities, though here again we cannot designate this as an inherently rural tendency. Overwhelmingly Protestant in religious affiliation, rural migrants to the cities often lashed out at Roman Catholics, Jews, and "nonbelievers" in general. Baptists and Methodists were the leading denominations in most southern cities. But Catholics were the fourth largest single religious group in Birmingham and the third largest group in Dallas in the 1920s, and were exceptionally significant in New Orleans and Mobile. The presence of Catholics and Jews in the cities stimulated some Protestant leaders and followers to fits of religious bigotry, often manifested in the frequent revivals that swept the urban South throughout the period, and in secret nativist organizations like the True Americans which flourished in Birmingham around World War I. For many urban southerners, black and white, the Pope represented the very personification of evil.

The largest and most notorious of all the urban groups dedicated to white Protestant supremacy and moral purity was the Ku Klux Klan. Revived in Atlanta in 1915 after showings of the racially inflammatory motion picture *The Birth of a Nation,* the new organization expanded rapidly after 1920 under the promotional talents of Edward Young Clarke and Mrs. Elizabeth Tyler. Racist, anti-Catholic, anti-Semitic, nativist, and obsessively patriotic, the Klan espoused a fervent Protestant fundamentalism. As Kenneth T. Jackson has demonstrated, the Klan was predominantly an *urban,* rather than a rural, organization—with activities directed primarily at Roman Catholics, who were more organized than blacks, and at "moral transgressors" who violated the Klansmens' sense of traditional values. Most of all, the Klan resisted "modernism" in its variety of guises. The Klan was particularly strong in Atlanta (the "Imperial City"), Memphis, Knoxville, and Dallas. Birmingham's Robert E. Lee Klan No. 1, with some 10,000 members, was perhaps "the most powerful klavern in the Southeast. . . ."[31]

Klan violence seemed to focus most on chastising (which meant, in many cases, whipping and bludgeoning) philanderers, prostitutes, and other moral transgressors. But the secret fraternal order was not merely a group of thugs and mindless vigilantes. In the cities it became a sort of voluntary civic organization that numbered attorneys, politicians, police officers, and white collar employees among its members and that participated in politics and spoke the phrases of urban boosterism. Large initiation ceremonies were sometimes held in public parks after elaborate parades through the downtown sections. A mayor of Atlanta during the 1920s was an acknowledged Klansman, as were large numbers of police officers in Birmingham. The only major Deep South city successfully to resist Klan influence was New Orleans, with its large and influential Roman Catholic population.

The strength of the Klan waned considerably after the mid-1920s, though it was quite active in Birmingham as late as 1932. Reasons behind the Klan's rise and fall number in the dozens, but it seems apparent that it was a response to the threats inherent in twentieth-century urban life to older moral values and social habits. It was one additional tool for coping with the realities of the city. And it was not a uniquely southern phenomenon: the two American cities with the largest Klan membership were Chicago and Indianapolis.

The Klan was but one manifestation of concern for traditional values. Throughout the early twentieth century moral issues flared with unusual intensity across the urban South, occasionally dominating local politics and paralleling the rise in urban boosterism. In the South as in the North, efforts to regulate behavior constituted a powerful undercurrent of the progressive impulse—perhaps best symbolized by the Prohibition movement. A wide variety of urban groups—from the socially concerned to the reactionary, from chambers of commerce to the Ku Klux Klan—seemed intent on proscribing dangerous or unwanted activities, and encouraging "proper" standards of behavior.

Birmingham provides an interesting, and not atypical, example. An effort to open a public dance pavilion in a city park in 1921 aroused the ire of many local ministers—especially Baptists—who opposed dancing as an immoral act. A city-wide vote in 1922 resulted in the defeat of the proposal, and local business leaders shook their heads in dismay at the national reputation such policies fixed upon the city. The most controversial public issue in the city during the first few decades of the twentieth century, however, was the showing of motion pictures on the Sabbath. The City Commission approved the showing of Sunday movies in 1915, in response to the demands of theater owners and local labor unions. The Birmingham Pastors' Union responded vigorously in a campaign which vilified Catholics and Jews and virtually declared war on "Sabbath breakers." The city's voters, especially those in the heavily Protestant, newly annexed suburbs, reversed the municipal government's ruling in 1918. Ten years later another referendum on the issue was proposed. Again the Pastors' Union quickly organized the opposition, and branded Sunday movies a threat to "American Chrisitian civilization." Voters upheld the ban in the largest total vote ever polled in a municipal election up to that time.[32]

Birmingham's commercial-civic elite tended to oppose these regulations of personal conduct. They preferred the existence of well-regulated public amusements for the city's workers, especially on the Sabbath when most laborers were idle. But their influence proved to be insufficient in the face of aroused opposition to the lowering of moral standards.

Sabbatarian legislation existed throughout the urban South, and was about as enthusiastically proclaimed and widely violated as in other American cities—and perhaps more so. In most southern urban areas amusements were prohibited on Sundays, and virtually all business activity was banned. Druggists and newsdealers were usually allowed to operate, and in some cases "high grade" musical shows, gasoline filling stations, and auto repair shops were permitted to open their doors. New Orleans citizens who desired a few beers in their favorite tavern during or after church could have them if they used the back door and kept the blinds pulled. And the enforcement of Sabbath restrictions in other regional cities varied with different municipal administrations and the periodic outrage at violations voiced by ministerial associations.

According to an Atlanta minister in 1920, the city contained "no Bible, but lots of bunny hug; no Jesus, but plenty of jazz; no God, but gambling a-plenty."[33] In a complex society, some argued, the unsuspecting and confused public required protection from the indecency purveyed by unscrupulous men and women and encouraged by new innovations like the motion picture and the automobile. The result was a number of efforts at official censorship of public amusements, especially movies. Nashville instituted a five member board of censorship in 1914, with authority to investigate all complaints of immoral or obscene motion pictures, dance halls, or places of amusement where admission was charged, and to *enforce its rulings.* As an afterthought, a separate Negro board of censorship was established in 1921.[34] In New Orleans the first ordinance prohibiting the showing of "indecent" motion pictures dated back to 1909, and a local board of movie censors was appointed in Fort Worth in 1911.

The Memphis city government unanimously created a three member board of censors in 1920 and prohibited immoral activities in the public dance halls. A year later ordinances were passed to regulate movies and other public exhibitions. The chairman of the new board identified vaudeville productions as "the greatest problem for solution, as the Memphis standard seems to be higher than that obtaining in any other city that I know of." In 1921 the board eliminated 57 motion pictures, disallowed 9, prohibited 3 from returning, and struck 175 pieces from spoken lines and songs in stage shows, modified 11 dances, altered 7 costumes, and removed one act entirely. A dozen movies were condemned on Beale Street, the main thoroughfare of the city's black entertainment and business district. "We of course apply a somewhat different standard to the negro shows from that applied to white shows," the chairman explained without elaboration.[35]

Crusades against vice—especially prostitution—absorbed the attention of some civic-minded groups. Between 1911 and 1915 local ministers and women's societies waged a war against saloons, gambling, and prostitution in Charleston. When Mayor John P. Grace demonstrated little enthusiasm in this task, the governor of South Carolina ordered the county sheriff to close down the vice dens.[36] New Orleans's famous Storyville, a district set apart for prostitution and gambling in a practical effort to keep such activities out of other parts of the city (a policy widely followed in many American cities, though usually unofficially), was shut down in 1917 at the insistence of the U. S. War Department. The district was within five miles of a naval station! Mayor Martin Behrman, leader of the Choctaw machine, was defeated in 1920, in part because of his efforts to save the old official district. But within a few years prostitution was very much in evidence in the Crescent City. An investigator discovered in 1927 that the unofficial segregated district contained upwards of 250 places of prostitution, ranging from the pitiful to the ornate, with women of virtually every nationality, race, age, shape, and size. This section of New Orleans, he wrote, was "still honeycombed with parlor houses, cribs, disorderly saloons, cabarets (colored), etc., in which prositution and sexual perversion are practiced flagrantly and upon a large scale by both white and colored prostitutes."[37]

Prohibition was *the* perennial moral issue, especially in the rural South. Though many urban dwellers seemed as determined to block the path of modernization and easy virtue as their country cousins, they could not summon nearly as much enthusiasm for Prohibition. Saloons were very much a part of the southern urban landscape in the early twentieth century, especially in "recreation" cities like Memphis and New Orleans. They were havens for workingmen and a component of the ethnic cultures in the seaport cities. Memphis recorded 504 saloons in 1903, which was more than its share. As William D. Miller wrote, "Whiskey was sold in such quantities that on the sidewalks of Front Street bottles were piled in bushel baskets and sold on the spot."[38]

While rural southerners staggered to the polls to vote for Prohibition, the urban electorate generally opposed this "reform"—soberly or otherwise. Birmingham cast heavy majorities against a state Prohibition law in 1907, though a heavy vote in the rural areas carried Jefferson County for the measure. Charleston voted against a similar statute in 1915 by more than a 7 to 1 margin, while it passed in the state as a whole. By all indications, strict Prohibition was a failure in the urban South, even during the days of the national Volstead Act. And while it was usually justified on moral grounds, its proponents were perhaps more interested in it as a tool for the control of blacks than as a curb on white drinking habits. Almost any hotel bellboy, if we can believe contemporary accounts, was a ready source of moonshine; and middle and upper class cocktail parties did not go without hard spirits at any time during the early twentieth century. Illicit liquor was so available in Atlanta, for example, that one newspaper regularly printed the prevailing prices for whiskey on the black market during the 1920s.

Southern cities were thus a strange composition of evangelists and worldly businessmen, moral purists and ardent vaudeville fans, strict blue laws and lax enforcement. As in cities throughout the country, the patterns of social life were diverse, and the efforts to direct and regulate behavior according to varying standards were pronounced. It was in the urban South that the regional culture came into contact with the opportunities and demands of a modern era and where the largely static and homogeneous social life of the countryside broke into a welter of heterogeneity.

POLITICS AND PUBLIC POLICY

Members of the commercial-civic elite hardly controlled all aspects of public policy—as demonstrated by their failure to counteract periodic outbursts of moral fervor over some issues, or to convince taxpayers on all occasions that new municipal bond issues were necessary. But their power and influence cannot be denied. Until the Depression of the 1930s their leadership was virtually unquestioned. Most major urban decisions in the early twentieth century, and the conceptual context within which these decisions were made, can be traced directly to this socio-economic elite group.

Commercial-civic spokesmen ennuciated a brand of business progressivism that called for expanded public services, increased industrial development, and a reliance upon trained experts and experienced leaders in government and business. A growing economy promised to spread its benefits to greater and greater numbers of people, precluding the necessity for government welfare programs. Members of this group were the philosophical descendants of the New South spokesmen of the late nineteenth century, who looked to industry for economic growth and to cities as arenas of opportunities—and to an urban-industrial society as the South's salvation.[39] As the statesmen of a developing region, they adopted most of the elements of the northern urban-industrial model.

Throughout the early twentieth century, and especially during the 1920s, commercial-civic groups concentrated on two major themes: urban growth and urban order. The "good" city, in their view, was "corporate-expansive"—that is, stable and orderly as well as growing and prosperous. Experience increasingly suggested that these goals might be contradictory, that growth always threatened to get out of hand. The addition of new populations and industries was a fundamental measure of urban "success"; yet it also posed severe difficulties for municipal administration and encouraged social fragmentation and economic confusion. Needless to say, commercial-civic spokesmen never confronted this dilemma directly, for this would have undermined their entire vision of society and "progress."

The public policies and private decisions which emerged from this conception of the city and from the values of business progressivism were utterly predictable. Prior to the Depression southern urban leaders promoted annexations of surrounding territory, the recruitment of new populations and business enterprises, and the improvement of city facilities and services—especially streets, streetcar lines, and public utilities and amusements—that would presumably attract new citizens and raise the standard of urban living. They looked to police and fire departments for the protection of property, and to parks and public schools as additional bulwarks of social order, serving ever-increasing populations and fostering the "healthy" use of leisure time and the cultivation of "responsible citizenship." Since the prevailing economic system was thought to be the central engine for social progress, the principal challenge was to provide adequate facilities for growing populations and to achieve the most efficient and economical municipal administration possible. Like their counterparts in other sections of the country, southern commercial-civic leaders drew frequently on the model of the business corporation for specific public policy recommendations.

One of the most heralded commercial-civic policies in the early twentieth century was the creation of city commissioner and city manager forms of municipal government.[40] The larger cities of the North were often unable or unwilling to abandon the mayor-council form of government, with its ward-based systems of voting and representation. But the smaller and medium-sized cities of the country—including many in the South—were far more susceptible to such changes. Southern cities, in fact, were pioneers in these new developments.

Galveston, Texas, was the first city in the United States to adopt the city commission form, in 1900, after a hurricane left the area in a shambles. A group of elected commissioners, each with a designated administrative responsibility, seemed a very efficient way of dealing with the consequences of crisis. Voters in Fort Worth approved a commission government by a wide margin in 1907, and a city commission appeared in Memphis in 1909 under an act of the Tennessee legislature, after the new government had been discussed and recommended by local commercial-civic groups. Other regional cities followed suit: Chattanooga (1910), Birmingham and Mobile (1911), and Nashville (1913). Commission governments were usually accompanied by the adoption of city-wide, "at large" voting provisions—rather than representation by wards or districts—which had the effect of diluting black political influence and increasing that of the white elite. In Birmingham the commission form increased the power of the newly annexed suburbs and small suburban businessmen. New Orleans adopted a mixed commission-council form in 1912, though the ward-based voting system was retained. Norfolk voters approved a commission-manager government in 1917 by a 3 to 1 margin.

The first city manager in the United States was appointed in Staunton, Virginia, in 1908. The city manager promised maximum efficiency in public administration because he was a professional "expert" dedicated to principles of good management and budgetary restraint, and presumably free from everyday political pressures. He was, indeed, an official at least one step removed from the electorate. Knoxville shifted from a commission to a manager government a year later. Dallas became in 1931 one of the largest southern cities to adopt the manager form. Some cities, like Atlanta, persisted with their older forms of government—though the administrative structure was somewhat simplified during the period—and Nashville experienced a rapid sequence of changes, from the establishment of a city commission in 1913 to a city manager in 1921 and to a mayor-council government in 1923.

One observer of the urban South in the 1920s, William J. Robertson, wrote that in

practically every Southern city is to be found a central political clique which rules the destinies of the city. . . . In these matters Southern communities are not unlike those of the North. I dare say that in every city in the South of 75,000 population or more there is a political organization as formidable as Tammany Hall in its machine rule, and in its ability to take care of its political friends.

He found that the "average Southern mayor is a weak vessel, subject to the beck and call of the unscrupulous politicians."[41] Robertson's observations are demonstrably inaccurate. Certainly, the South had its share of politicians; but the major political influence in southern cities was not traceable to a mysterious group of professional politicians, but to the white business-oriented elite.

Some notable political personalities did emerge in the early twentieth century, like George Ward, the "reform" mayor of Birmingham who advocated expanded services, the commission form of government, and efficient administration of city affairs. But only two major southern cities were dominated by political organizations resembling the northern big-city machine. "Boss" Edward H. Crump was elected mayor of Memphis in 1909 by a coalition of business groups, recent rural newcomers, and several ethnic minorities. Crump cast himself in the role of a "reformer," though in most respects he represented the business progressivism of the time. His platform included a pledge to clean up the vice in one of the most notorious watering holes in the South, and he did make some ritual efforts in this direction. But Memphis remained throughout his tenure a prominent recreation center. Crump's influence continued, behind the scenes, into the 1920s and beyond; and by 1940 he was perhaps the most powerful single political leader in the state of Tennessee.[42]

New Orleans politics was dominated by a faction of the local Democratic party called the Choctaw Club, which contained bankers and merchants as well as professional politicians. Funded by contributions from businesses and the gambling, racing, liquor, and prostitution interests, the Choctaws tolerated much open vice, provided jobs for constituents, and fulfilled most of the roles generally expected of urban machines. A major figure in city politics was Martin Behrman, a New York Jew who judiciously converted to Roman Catholicism after his arrival in New Orleans. Working his way up through the Choctaw ward organization, he was elected mayor in 1904. Ousted from office in 1921, Behrman regained the mayoralty in 1925—though he died in office a year later.

The New Orleans Choctaw organization was the closest urban counterpart in the South to Tammany Hall. No major southern political figure can be accurately described as a "reform boss" in the category with Hazen Pingree of Detroit or Samuel "Golden Rule" Jones of Toledo. Even in Memphis and New Orleans, the commercial-civic elite maintained considerable influence in the dominant political organizations, and no significant attempts were made to alter the prevailing economic structure or to make businesses more responsible and accountable to the public. Urban boosterism, in fact, emerged as a principal activity of the political organizations, just as it was of the chambers of commerce. Since even the largest southern cities lacked the liberal-immigrant-labor union coalitions that prevailed in many northern centers, the political arena was largely left to the commercial-civic elite and sympathetic politicians.

Black political power was muted in southern cities, but it was considerably more potent than in the rural areas of the region after disfranchisement. Blacks continued to hold public office in many cities into the twentieth century. In Chattanooga, for example, blacks regularly served as councilmen or aldermen until 1910, as well as deputy sheriffs and police officers. Adoption of at-large representation in that year diluted black voting strength, and blacks consequently disappeared from elected municipal offices. The Crump machine in Memphis cultivated certain black politicians and sought black votes, and in some instances blacks were able to extract benefits in other cities in return for their support of policies and bond issues sponsored by commercial-civic leaders. But southern blacks, whether on farms or in the cities, would not be a significant political force until the voting rights legislation of the 1960s.

The list of problems facing larger southern urban areas as they entered the twentieth century was large and familiar: public health and safety, housing, education, recreation, law enforcement, relief, transportation, government, and—in a broad sense—how to control future urban development. The policies proposed and adopted to deal with these difficulties reflected, of course, the significant influence of the local commercial-civic elite as well as the state of the theory and art of urban administration.

One of the most severe urban problems was a pattern of recurrent epidemics that stemmed from the South's largely subtropical climate and the lack of expertise for coping with communicable disease before the late nineteenth century. The Memphis yellow fever epidemic of 1878 virtually wiped out the city's population—through death and migration to escape the disease—and this was only one example of public health crises that afflicted southern cities. The advent of modern sanitation methods and public health services, based on the germ theory of disease, found ready acceptance in the region. Even so, Mobile was stricken by a yellow fever epidemic as late as 1905, and most southern urban areas contained inadequate sewer systems and large numbers of outdoor toilets in their poorer neighborhoods. Most cities suffered flooding in their low-lying sections during heavy rains, which caused health problems as well as property damage. The first two decades of the century witnessed concerted efforts throughout the urban South to eliminate the worst public health hazards by running fresh water and sewer lines into peripheral areas and previously deprived inner-city neighborhoods. In New Orleans problems of flooding were especially acute. It was not until the early twentieth century that a system of pumps and sewers opened up swampy areas of the city to settlement and offset the constant threats posed by the unpredictable Mississippi River and the extremely high water table. In Birmingham the elimination of some eight thousand outdoor privies was credited, in part, with a reduction of the city's typhoid rate by about 80 percent.

Air pollution was a noticeable problem quite early in the century, especially in cities with components of heavy industry, like Birmingham. But most pollution was attributable to coal-fired residential and commercial heating plants. Dense accumulations of particulates in the air of Nashville blocked out the sun on some days in January and February of virtually every year, and the atmosphere around railroad sheds, roundhouses, and industrial operations was predictably grimy and unpleasant. The usual commercial-civic explanation was that smoke was a sign of progress, almost to be welcomed as an indication of economic growth. But this policy did little to alleviate the problem. Nashville and Birmingham had elaborate smoke ordinances on the books by 1920, and Atlanta and Memphis added similar statutes in the subsequent decade. They were, to say the least, quite ineffective. Regulatory commissions and appointed smoke inspectors faced an impossible task, but they did attempt to reprimand the worst offenders and keep heating plants relatively clean. The contributions of gasoline-powered vehicles to air pollution was noticed by the 1920s, but most people found their motorcar infinitely cleaner in operation and far less dangerous to public health than horses and mules.

Though plagued by housing shortages and rent gouging at various times during the period—especially in the years just after World War I—southern city governments never seriously contemplated public housing. Rather, increased supplies of home mortgage capital as a support for private home ownership was the only acceptable means of dealing with the problem. The prevailing attitude among the commercial-civic elite was that public housing ventures would undermine the housing market, deter individual initiative, and set a frightening precedent for public policy. And the same spirit underlay public welfare. Most relief for the urban poor was provided by private agencies like churches, benevolent associations, and united charity campaigns like the Community Chest. Public welfare was generally centered on almshouses operated by cities and counties for the most destitute of the population, rather than through a system of outright financial grants. In at least one case—Nashville—the city charter specifically prohibited the local government from awarding more than $10,000 annually to the local Charities Commission. The efforts of private charity were often sincere and concerted, and benefits were extended to poor whites and blacks alike. But thousands of needy citizens—the precise number is incalculable—went without help, even during the boom years of the 1920s. And the depression of the 1930s revealed these sources of relief to be totally inadequate.

The pattern of municipal expenditures provides one means of assessing the priorities of urban policy. Though budgets differed from city to city and from year to year, the general emphasis was on public education, police forces, and fire departments. These outlays usually accounted for more than half of available municipal funds in most cities. Local bond issues supported new school construction, and many southern cities erected their first all-black high schools in this period. Rising populations of school-age children demanded considerable resources and more teachers and classrooms. Nevertheless, southern school systems suffered through periods of financial stringency, and expenditures per pupil lagged behind the average rates in the urban education systems of the North. The South still had a long way to go in making up the regional deficiency in public education, and educational opportunities for blacks were especially limited. Police forces and fire departments were considered priority items because of their role in maintaining order and protecting property; yet here too improvements seemed to lag behind the increased demands posed by rapidly increasing populations, additions of new territory, new traffic control problems brought about by the automobile, and the metamorphosis of southern business districts into relatively dense concentrations of high property values.

While proportions of municipal budgets were often increased for streets, health, and sanitation, outlays for recreation and charities tended to increase only slightly and even decline in their percentage of the overall budgets. Though no one has yet attempted a detailed analysis of southern city budgets, and compared them with those of nonregional cities, it would appear that the range of priorities did not differ much from city to city across the country. The South simply had less money to allocate to public services and facilities. Regional cities tended to rank fairly low among American cities of similar size in their rates of bonded indebtedness and taxation. Obviously, in the nation's poorest region city governments had a less lucrative tax base to draw upon. But the statistics suggest a moderate, and increasing, effort to solve urban ills through the early twentieth century.

Streets and transportation accounted for most of the attention of municipal governments during the period. In 1900 most regional urban areas were traversed by dirt roads and poorly surfaced streets. Downtown merchants were in the forefront of those demanding street paving programs, the laying of new thoroughfares, and the widening and connection of existing roads. As southern cities annexed outlying areas and extended their influence further into their hinterlands, ready access to the city core became crucial to exploiting the economic advantages of this expansion. Principal streets were paved very rapidly, though dirt roads prevailed in black sections until much later in the century. Since those residing or owning property on a specific street usually had to foot a portion of the bill for any improvements, the allocation of decent streets throughout the community was especially inequitable.

Closely following demands for better streets were cries from the commercial-civic elite for efficient traffic regulation and the protection and extension of streetcar lines. The street systems of the South were ill-prepared for the onslaught of the motor vehicle, and automobiles and trucks quickly led to considerable traffic problems after 1920. The dilemma for downtown merchants was that the motor vehicle rendered the central business district potentially more accessible to outlying populations, while the glut of motor vehicles routinely encountered in the 1920s threatened to counteract this advantage substantially. On-street parking deterred traffic flow, yet the elimination of convenient parking made it more difficult for potential customers to stop; in either case, the volume of downtown retail business was threatened. The result was a good deal of confusion in urban transportation poli-cies: municipal governments acted to protect franchised streetcar lines from auto competition while encouraging, and indeed subsidizing, motor vehicle travel through street construction and improvements, and surveys of transportation needs by outside consultants resulted in new systems of parking and traffic control that were readily modified at the insistence of competing interest groups. The compara-tive lack of financial resources in the urban South, and the reluctance to interfere with the prerogatives of private enterprise, resulted in an increasing reliance on the individual motor vehicle as the bulwark of urban transportation—a story repeated across the country in these years.

By 1920 all major cities in the South had enacted detailed and comprehensive traffic codes to regulate the operation of motor vehicles. By 1930 one-way streets, automated traffic signals, no-turn intersections, variable-time parking areas, and driver's license examinations were fairly common throughout the urban South. And increasing numbers of police personnel were being assigned to traffic duties and traffic courts.

An overriding concern of the period was to devise means of contending with all these specific problems. Thus, new forms of government were created to provide more efficient and professional administration, to bring community resources to bear on particular ills, at least in theory. Annexation was promoted as an expansion of the municipal tax base. Growing out of these efforts, and perhaps most clearly reflective of the outlines of the commercial-civic conception of the city, was the movement toward comprehensive city planning that began in some regional urban areas in the second decade of the century.

Unofficial planning committees, appointed by local chambers of commerce and other civic groups, existed prior to World War I in some cities, and official munici-pal commissions were appointed in Atlanta and Memphis in 1920, in Knoxville and New Orleans in 1923, and in Nashville in 1925. In all cases, these agencies were originally promoted by commercial-civic bodies, which also supplied most of the members of the new commissions. In most cases, outside consultants were called in to prepare surveys or plans, but the commissions themselves exercised considerable authority in setting the parameters and purposes of planning. Atlanta did not achieve a comprehensive city plan until after 1940, but Memphis, New Orleans, and Knoxville boasted plans during the 1920s—all of them drawn by consultant Harland Bartholomew of St. Louis.

The underlying philosophy of these plans was the corporate-expansive ideal. The major street plans sought to link the center of the city with the expanding periphery, to vitalize the central business district and balance the centripetal/ centrifugal forces so much in evidence during the period. Zoning plans were calcu-lated to preserve the land use functions of designated districts, protect property values, insure adequate land for industrial and commercial use, segregate the races, and—to the extent possible—control development along the urban outskirts. Parks and recreation received some attention in most plans, and matters of "civic art" were also discussed; but these paled in significance beside the emphases on trans-portation and zoning.

City plans were not rigorously followed in the South, and exceptions to zoning ordinances were apparently easy enough to obtain. Bartholomew's grandiose Greek design for the entire Memphis waterfront remained a paper fantasy, and the plans to relocate and centralize railroad stations and rail connections usually met with the opposition of the railroads affected. But these plans did have a general impact on the city, charting the principal paths of urban growth into outlying districts and, in any case, underlining the joint focus on the central core and the burgeoning periphery that was the model of the twentieth-century metropolis.

The Great Depression was a phenomenon without a place in the commercial-civic scheme of things. Gradually, as 1930 approached and passed, the notions and social policies which rested on faith in an ever-expanding economy were cast adrift in a sea of stagnation and uncertainty. Urban dailies and business publications were loath to admit that real crisis was at hand, and persisted in looking at the brighter side of things even down to 1932—desperately attempting to instill a sense of public confidence that would turn events around. The Atlanta Chamber of Commerce magazine remarked in 1932, for example:

Atlanta has not lost its sense of humor—we are still here—the stores are open and the trains are running. You can get your number on the telephone, we have a traffic problem, seats are hard to get in the theaters, doctors and dentists make appointments weeks ahead, lawyers' briefs are just as long, prohibition and politics are live topics. Amos and Andy are still in the taxicab business.[43]

But the taxicab business was not so good after all, and rising unemployment was not very humorous. Private charity made heroic efforts to stem the crisis: some Community Chests doubled and even tripled their stated goals, only to see their resources exhausted within the space of a few months, while other charity drives discovered that no amount of beseeching could increase their number of contributions. When such voluntary measures failed, local governments often became involved. Some of the first steps were meager: setting up a few soup kitchens, an employment agency to fill all locally available jobs, and perhaps even initiation of a limited amount of public service employment. But as tax revenues fell and the demand for municipal bonds dwindled, cities found it impossible to maintain even normal services: schoolteachers and other city employees were fired or laid off, wages were cut, and services trimmed. Some cities, like Houston, were the literal prisoners of local banks, which refused to continue credit unless municipal budgets were balanced.[44]

The New Deal made large amounts of federal funds directly available to local communities for the first time. Most city, county, and state governments quickly applied for such assistance, not only for direct relief of the unemployed but for the construction of public buildings, roads, airports, and civic centers. In Fort Worth alone, for example, about $15 million in federal funds were spent during the depression, compared with $5 million drawn from local sources. Aside from providing crucial financial aid to nearly destitute cities and towns, the New Deal inaugurated a new era in federal-urban relations in the South and in the nation as a whole. After World War II federal expenditures constituted a significant part of the economic foundations of southern urbanization.

The most notable changes in local policies occurred in the areas of public relief and housing. The private, voluntaristic philosophy of the commercial-civic elite was displaced—though by no means destroyed, as postdepression policies reveal— by new federal legislation. Relief efforts ran the gamut from the distribution of food to public works projects. But public welfare was administered and distributed on an unprecedented scale by southern municipalities and urban agencies. Even with the influx of outside resources, local communities attempted to distribute relief, as much as possible, only to local citizens. Migrant laborers moving about in search of work were sometimes refused assistance entirely, and usually advised to take themselves elsewhere. In this sense, economic crisis reaffirmed the provincial character of local attitudes and policy. In addition, some cities apparently discriminated against blacks, Mexican-Americans, and other minority groups in the allocation of relief, though this is an area which needs much more detailed investigation.

Commercial-civic prejudices against public housing continued through the depression, but local policies were altered by the climate and opportunities of the 1930s. In fact, the first federally subsidized low-income housing project to be executed by the Public Works Administration was the Techwood Homes development in Atlanta, dedicated by President Roosevelt in November 1935.[45] Government programs to encourage private home ownership were, of course, much more popular among southern urban leaders, and the impact of such policies was especially noticeable as veterans of World War II returned to establish families and buy houses. As was the case after the first World War, it was hard to keep young men in the country once they had seen Memphis or Atlanta, much less Paree.

World War II brought high levels of activity to southern seaports and created a sizable demand for regional raw materials and manufactured goods. As processing plants and factories cranked up to full production and large numbers of marginal workers were drawn into the forced employment of military service, the depression's economic pall began to lift and disappear. Government stimulation of the market economy marked the end of the depression, but it did nothing to change established patterns of race relations, social structure, and local leadership and social control.

The first forty years of the twentieth century laid the social and economic foundations for regional urbanization after World War II. At the end of this period southern cities were more industrial and considerably greater in population size than they had been before, and they began to reflect the configuration and characteristics of the twentieth-century metropolis. If there had ever been any question about it, cities in the South were by mid-century very much within the national urban mainstream. And they were in an excellent position to reap the benefits of a decentralizing economy and the rising consumer capacity of a regional population traditionally shackled with low per capita incomes and limited economic opportunities. The rigid system of white supremacy and racial oppression had, however, continued intact through these years and had even been strengthened in some respects. This fundamental debility in the southern urban social structure would set the stage for dramatic change in the years to follow.

6

EDWARD F. HAAS

THE SOUTHERN METROPOLIS, 1940-1976

In 1940 the South looked toward an urban future. During the early decades of the twentieth century, southern cities had experienced tremendous growth. Population increases, economic diversification, and transportation and communication advances had contributed directly to urban maturation in the South. Migrations and annexations enlarged the populations and sizes of southern cities, and industrialization provided greater commercial and financial opportunities as well as more jobs. The electric trolley and the automobile gave new dimensions to urban mobility and altered the spatial configurations of southern cities. These transportation innovations permitted southern urban areas to develop the metropolitan pattern of central cores and connecting suburbs that characterized the major American cities. The motor vehicle and later the airplane also provided flexible links between the various southern cities that the railroads and water traffic could never match. By 1940 interlocking urban networks were evident in the Southeast and in the Southwest. The radio was an additional boon to interurban communication and cultural development, although the measure of its influence was less discernible. During the 1930s urban expansion in the region admittedly faltered under the weight of the depression, but it did not cease. In 1940 the South had a firm base for continued urban growth.[1]

Urban development, however, was relative. Despite significant industrial progress and the unmistakable urbanizing trend of the early twentieth century, the South was still a predominantly rural and agricultural region. The theory of a fifty-year lag that many sociologists, urban geographers, and other scholars have simplistically attached to the urbanization process in the South belied the regional influence of cities that ranged beyond the limits of population and geographical area, but it did correctly acknowledge the disparity between southern urban and rural areas that existed before World War II. The 1940 census figures clearly exhibited rural preeminence in the South. In that year no southern state equaled the average urban population of the country, and only Florida had an urban majority. The largest southern city was New Orleans, with a population of 494,537, hardly a rival for the hulking megalopolises of the North and the West.[2]

Politics reflected the dominance of the rural South. Despite the growth of southern cities, malapportionment characterized state legislatures in Dixie. In Georgia the county unit system insured a majority vote that was both rural and white. During the 1930s Huey Long, the "Kingfish" of Louisiana, had used his rural power base and a state constitution that did not recognize home rule to defeat the Regular Democratic Organization of New Orleans, the strongest urban political machine in the South.[3]

Population increases, furthermore, did not mean the automatic creation of an urban mentality. Many of the people who migrated to southern cities during the early twentieth century came from a distinctly rural background. For these southerners, who often retained their rural values, the urbanization process was a difficult cultural struggle that frequently ended in disorientation and defeat.[4]

In 1940, nonetheless, southern cities held the potential for sustained future expansion, and World War II provided the impetus. The American mobilization effort revitalized trends that were operative in southern urban areas before the depression. In the South the construction of military training camps and war industries that produced ships, aircraft, ordinance, chemicals, aluminum, and oil fostered extensive urban development. The major seaports—New Orleans, Galveston-Houston, Mobile, Charleston, Norfolk-Portsmouth, and Savannah—benefited tremendously from their strategic locations with increased commerce and the rise of shipyards. In New Orleans, for example, A. J. Higgins Industries had been a small manufacturer of shallow-draft plywood boats with a production force of only 400 people before the war. In 1944 the Higgins corporation employed 20,000 workers who constructed twenty-five landing craft and PT boats daily for the use of the United States and its overseas allies. In Houston, another city that was noted for shipbuilding, investments in the local chemical industry totaled approximately $600 million during World War II. Inland cities also benefited from the war and experienced dramatic economic expansion and rapid population growth. In Huntsville, Alabama, the construction of the Redstone Arsenal quickly reversed the economic fate of a community that had been deeply mired in the depression.[5]

In most southern cities growth was welcomed, but it was often uncontrolled and chaotic. Mobile, a city with two major shipyards and an aluminum factory, provided a classic case of the wartime boom and the strain that it placed upon public services. In 1940 the population of Mobile was 114,906; four years later the figure stood at 201,369. Growing pains were severe. A flood of new inhabitants, many from nearby rural areas, swiftly rendered housing facilities inadequate and overwhelmed municipal services. In 1943 John Dos Passos wrote that Mobile looked "trampled and battered like a city that's been taken by storm. Sidewalks are overcrowded. Gutters are stacked with litter. . . . Garbage cans are overflowing. Frame houses on treeshaded streets bulge with men in shirtsleeves." Public education deteriorated in the face of expanded enrollments, and the understaffed police force could not cope with the higher incidence of juvenile delinquency, robbery, racial conflict, and labor unrest that accompanied rapid and unbridled urban development.

Similar problems befell other southern cities. In New Orleans the heavy influx of transient servicemen raised the level of vice to new highs and reinforced the local reputation for immoral diversions. Norfolk also won national prominence for its licentiousness. Author Marvin Schlegal observed that many local "V-girls" became "VD-girls" in their efforts to improve wartime morale. At one Norfolk trailer park that specialized in prostitution, a well-placed sign proclaimed "All That Money Can Buy." More than a few servicemen and workers came and bought. With federal aid and increased municipal efforts, however, Norfolk and other southern towns began to deal successfully with their problems of housing, crime, and overtaxed public services before the end of the war.

The global conflict certainly had a traumatic effect upon several southern towns, but its impact upon urban growth was definite. Thirty-nine of the forty-eight urban areas in the South increased in population. During the decade of the 1940s the urban population of the region increased 35.9 percent. This rate of expansion was more than 50 percent greater than the national average. Population growth, moreover, was only one indication of the enhanced economic opportunities, greater confidence in the industrial potential of the region, new trends of thought, and awareness of the need for improved public services that were becoming evident in the South.[6]

For many southern urbanites such as Andrew Jackson Higgins of Higgins Industries, World War II had brought great economic prosperity that they did not wish to see erode with the coming of peace. These leaders believed that military shipping, airplane factories, and munitions plants were only temporary products of the war and sought viable peacetime substitutes. This search took a variety of forms in different southern cities.

In New Orleans one solution was an international trade movement. Before Pearl Harbor local businessmen had toyed with the concept of a permanent international trade organization that would encourage foreign commerce with the city, but the idea dimmed after the outbreak of war. The plan, however, did not die. In 1942 William G. Zetzmann, a soft drink bottler, Rudolph S. Hecht of the Hibernia National Bank, and Theodore Brent, president of the Mississippi Shipping Company, revived the idea. One year later these men supported the official incorporation of International House. In 1945 the trade organization opened its doors to visitors from all parts of the world.

International House was eminently successful. In 1947 New Orleans became second among the nation's ports in dollar value of trade, and fourth in tonnage. In 1948 the estimated total business of the port was $1.3 billion, a significant increase over the yearly trade value of the prewar period. That same year the International Trade Mart, an exhibition hall and office building that supplemented the promotional program of International House, began operation. During the 1950s trade activity in the port of New Orleans continued to rise. In 1962 business leaders in Houston, the Crescent City's major commercial rival, paid the supreme compliment when they followed the example of International House and established their own international facility, the World Trade Center.[7]

The international trade movement provided a tremendous lift to the economy of New Orleans, but it resolved only one of the complex problems that faced the city in the postwar years. In 1945 New Orleans was in the grasp of Mayor Robert S. Maestri, once the main financial backer of Huey Long, and the Regular Democratic Organization (RDO). A decade earlier the Long organization had used its statewide power to subjugate the Crescent City and to coerce the incumbent mayor into resignation. Maestri was his carefully chosen successor. An earthy, direct man who was ill at ease during public appearances and often made embarrassing remarks to the press, Maestri used his local patronage and the strength of his close association with the Long machine to whip the Old Regulars into line. During his regime favoritism, payroll padding, and corruption characterized city politics. Gambling and prostitution were equally prevalent in New Orleans. The "brown envelope" system, a sophisticated network of graft collections that included criminals, law enforcement officials, and politicians, insured protection to those vice operators who cooperated with the police and made their payoffs regularly. Although Maestri did not initiate this scheme of organized graft, he certainly condoned its continued existence.[8]

During his first years in office Maestri balanced the negative features of his regime with sound administration. He made good use of funds from the Works Progress Administration and pursued an impressive program of public construction. The mayor also reduced the municipal debt, introduced economy measures, and responded to the public needs. After his reelection in 1942, however, Maestri changed. He devoted more attention to political concerns and neglected city affairs. Municipal administration stagnated. Building stopped, and the mayor became increasingly inaccessible to the people. With this decline in governmental activity, the seamier side of machine rule grew more obvious to the public. Maestri, moreover, looked and acted like a backroom politico. His presence in City Hall repeatedly cast the Crescent City in a bad light.

In March 1945 civic and business leaders—including many participants in the international trade movement—formed a citizens committee to oppose Maestri and the Old Regulars in the forthcoming municipal elections. Political observers, however, had seen reform groups come and go in New Orleans. Few realists believed that this new set of reformers had a chance. For that reason, willing candidates were hard to find. After much consideration and more debate the citizens group finally settled upon J. O. Fernandez, a former associate of Huey Long, to head the reform ticket. He proved to be a poor choice. In December 1945 Fernandez campaigned briefly and then defected to the Maestri camp. The reformers were suddenly without a candidate, and the election was fast approaching.

In an act of desperation the reformers prevailed upon Colonel de Lesseps Story "Chep" Morrison, a returning veteran, to run for mayor. The decision was a stroke of blind genius. Morrison, an incumbent state representative from New Orleans and an eager young politician, agreed. Despite his relative inexperience and wartime absence from the city, the handsome new candidate proved to be a dynamic campaigner. He sought personal contact with the people and stressed a platform of progress for New Orleans. His presence in the race immediately provided a rallying point for a growing reform coalition of civic leaders, women's organizations and veterans. Throughout the campaign the returning servicemen played an important role. In their minds the coming of peace meant the advent of a new era of prosperity and growth, and they were ready to do their part. Among other southern urbanites of the postwar era, such attitudes were also common. In New Orleans they manifested themselves in strong support for de Lesseps Morrison.

During the campaign Maestri and his cohorts were complacent. They casually engaged in minor disputes among themselves with the firm belief that the old techniques of payroll padding and political coercion would again be successful. This time, however, they underestimated the opposition. In January 1946 Morrison won a narrow victory over Maestri.

Morrison, then thirty-four years old, introduced a spirit of youthful exuberance to municipal government that contrasted sharply with the lethargy of the previous administration. After surrounding himself with able advisors, he embarked upon the reform program that the voters had demanded. Morrison began with a reorganization of city government that eliminated some positions, consolidated others, and reduced operating costs. The mayor also joined with the commissioner of finance, a member of his election ticket, to promote budgetary reform. For veterans he created a municipal department to help with peacetime readjustment and sought federal aid to remedy the postwar housing shortage. In the interest of municipal transportation and public safety, he endorsed the establishment of a regulatory bureau for the supervision of taxicab drivers. Morrison was also responsible for the creation of the New Orleans Recreation Department (NORD), an imaginative agency that sponsored athletic leagues for youngsters and cultural activities for people of all ages. Within two years NORD won national praise for the diversity and depth of its program and its successful influence upon juvenile delinquency.

Mayor Morrison took special care to include outlying areas in his municipal improvement plans. During the previous adminstration city officials had neglected to extend streets and drainage lines into the suburbs, and their decision had been costly in the election of 1946. Morrison did not intend to make the same mistake.

Blacks, like suburbanites, also participated in the Morrison program. Under the Old Regulars they had endured overt racial discrimination. Morrison, however, quickly recognized the growing potential of the black vote and repeatedly announced that he was "mayor of all the people." Although he personally believed in the correctness of racial segregation, his plans provided new streets, improved sanitation, and better recreational facilities for black neighborhoods. The mayor also submitted to court orders that integrated the police department, municipal parks, and public transportation. He did, however, take steps to minimize the social effects of these changes and to preserve racial separation in New Orleans.

The major construction projects of the Morrison years were closely interrelated. At the heart of the overall plan was the clearance of a slum-infested section in downtown New Orleans. On this site the mayor planned to build a new railroad station and a civic center complex. The railway terminal project was actually an extensive multifaceted enterprise that drew financing from the city, the state government, and the railroads that serviced New Orleans. It involved the construction of a union passenger terminal, the consolidation of most railroad tracks within the city limits, the elimination of 144 dangerous grade crossings, and the erection of an expressway that would link the downtown area with the suburbs northwest of the city and the residential neighborhoods near Lake Pontchartrain. In May 1954 this project reached completion. The civic center plan also had several components. It called for the construction of a new city hall, main library branch, municipal court building, and a pedestrian mall, as well as a state office building and a facility for the Louisiana State Supreme Court. In May 1957 the mayor dedicated the new city hall, the capstone of the entire downtown renovation project.

During his administration Morrison developed an excellent public image for his city and for himself. It was the result of a conscious effort. From the beginning the Crescent City mayor was a politician, astute and ambitious; he knew the worth of good public relations. In 1946 Morrison established the first municipal department of public relations under the direction of David R. McGuire, Jr., a brainy former newspaperman. The new department rendered invaluable service, and McGuire quickly became a major cog in the Morrison organization. His deft news releases continually kept the achievements of the Morrison administration in the public eye and lured to the Crescent City national journalists who sought fresh material for their articles. McGuire was also a trusted advisor who often saved the hard-driving and sometimes impetuous mayor from serious mistakes.

Observers in New Orleans readily acknowledged that Morrison would not be content with only a local reputation. Throughout his administration he played an active role in the international trade movement. He created a municipal department of international relations, learned Spanish, and made numerous promotional junkets to Latin America and to Europe. Morrison also sought new industry for the Crescent City. His biggest catch was a Kaiser Aluminum factory; Henry Kaiser decided to locate the plant in the New Orleans suburb of Chalmette after a telephone conversation with the mayor.

Urban cooperation was another Morrison forte. He regularly attended meetings of the American Municipal Association and in 1949 became its president. At these annual conferences Morrison discussed mutual problems and exchanged ideas with other outstanding postwar mayors, including Hubert Humphrey of Minneapolis, Raymond Tucker of St. Louis, and Richard J. Daley of Chicago. A similarity of style among these urban chief executives was quite apparent. They, like Morrison, pursued a municipal program of physical construction, good public relations, and economic development.

The national prominence that Morrison sought was soon forthcoming. Numerous organizations ranked him among the top young leaders in the country, and national journals recorded his triumphs in laudatory terms. In November 1947 *Time* magazine stated that "Chep Morrison, symbol of the bright new day which had come to the city of charming ruins, also symbolized as well as anyone or anything the postwar energy of the nation's cities."

One year later Morrison faced his most formidable challenge, a conflict with the state government. In 1948 Governor Earl K. Long, the younger brother of Huey, defeated Sam Houston Jones, the Morrison candidate, in a runoff election. His victory meant sure trouble for the New Orleans chief executive. Uncle Earl, eager to emulate the Kingfish, joined with remnants of the Old Regulars to fashion a statewide political machine. De Lesseps Morrison, the most promising member of the opposition and hence the most dangerous rival, became a prime target for destruction. Shortly after the election Long took a leaf from his brother's ledger and turned the extraordinary powers of the rural-dominated state legislature against the city of New Orleans and its mayor. The obedient legislators reduced the tax revenue of the city, increased its budget, disrupted municipal civil service, and reorganized the commission council, the governing body of the city, to favor the election of Old Regular candidates in the upcoming city primaries. The legislature also endorsed a series of constitutional amendments that proposed to take more municipal powers away from the city and place them in the hands of state agencies.

Morrison responded to this challenge with a vengeance. He and David McGuire immediately labeled the new state legislation as the "punitive acts" and the "power-grab" amendments. On several occasions the mayor and Crescent City business leaders mounted motor cavalcades to the state capitol in Baton Rouge to protest the actions of the state legislature and to endorse home rule. Morrison then widened his appeal in a series of radio speeches which warned other Louisiana municipalities that they could be the next targets of debilitating state legislation. When the "power-grab" amendments came to a statewide vote in the fall of 1948, Morrison concentrated his campaign efforts in the expanding secondary cities of Louisiana and soundly defeated the Long-supported amendment package. In New Orleans the mayor repeatedly declared that those Old Regulars who had backed the governor's legislative program were traitors to the city. In the municipal elections of 1950 these tactics proved fruitful; Morrison and his ticket won a convincing victory over the Old Regulars despite the gerrymandering of the commission council and extensive opposition from the governor. Morrison's reelection marked the first successful effort of a New Orleans mayor to overcome the concerted opposition of a Louisiana governor during the twentieth century. His victory was prophetic of the growing power of New Orleans and other southern cities in state politics.

City-state relations improved after 1950. Although Long and Morrison remained bitter enemies throughout their lives, the governor began to reassess his attitude toward New Orleans. The impact of World War II and the early Morrison years upon the city was clear. In 1950 New Orleans had a population of 570,445, an increase of nearly 20 percent over the previous decade. Long readily perceived the political implications of these statistics and changed his strategy. He first instructed the state legislature to restore administrative and fiscal power to the city. The governor then backed a proposal for a home rule charter in New Orleans. In later years Long backed social welfare and public education programs for the Crescent City. In 1957, for example, he endorsed the establishment of Louisiana State University in New Orleans (now the University of New Orleans) and Southern University in New Orleans.

The new charter was one of the monumental achievements of the Morrison years. In 1952 municipal officials created a charter committee with representatives from business, labor, education, civic and legal organizations, and city government. After extensive study of municipal administration the committee drafted a home rule charter that replaced the commission council with a new strong mayor-council form of government. Under the old system commissioners performed both executive and legislative duties, and overlapping authority repeatedly caused confusion and a lack of accountability. The new charter solved these difficulties. It vested all executive power and responsibility in the mayor and a chief administrative officer, who recommended appointments, planned for future projects, and managed the budget. The city council became strictly a legislative body. After the city elections of 1954 the new charter went into effect. Morrison became the first mayor under the new system, and David McGuire became his chief administrative officer. Morrison supporters won a heavy majority of the council seats.

Growth marked the Morrison years in New Orleans. In 1950 the population of the city was 570,445, and the metropolitan area held 712,393. Ten years later the city had 627,525 inhabitants. Commercial and industrial development accompanied the population increases. Morrison, moreover, had transformed the public image of the city. During his tenure New Orleans attained a new reputation for respectability, good leadership, and civic pride.

Beneath this public image of reform, however, the Morrison administration had a soft underbelly. Although Morrison periodically chastised the machine tactics of the Old Regulars, he established his own political organization, the Crescent City Democratic Association (CCDA), before he took office. At first the leaders of the CCDA were members of the reform coalition of 1946, but Morrison systematically replaced the idealists with professional politicians. Many of the newcomers to the reform ranks were former Old Regular bosses and their followers whom Morrison lured into the CCDA with promises of choice positions and future advancement. For these men the shift in allegiance represented a change in organizational labels rather than an alteration of political tactics. Within two years after Morrison's election the payrolls of several municipal departments exceeded the highest levels of the Maestri regime.

Law enforcement also languished during the Morrison years. In 1946 the mayor appointed A. Adair Watters, a former Marine Corps colonel, to the post of superintendent of police. Watters was an honest man who sought departmental reorganization, took steps to eliminate the "brown envelope" system, and enforced the law. This forthright policy, however, grated upon the sensibilities of police officials and politicos who profited financially from graft and bar owners who walked the razor edge of legality. These individuals took their grievances to Morrison who prevailed upon Watters to relent. After several sharp confrontations with the mayor, the superintendent of police resigned in 1949. Morrison immediately replaced him with Chief of Detectives Joseph Scheuering, a veteran police officer. Scheuering lost no time in allowing the force to revert to the old ways of corruption.

Under Scheuering conditions deteriorated rapidly. Muggings of French Quarter tourists became frequent. Upon one noted occasion a prominent engineer from Nashville died in a French Quarter lounge after someone had slipped him a "Mickey

Finn." Newsmen investigated these unsavory conditions and uncovered ample evidence of widespread gambling and prostitution, police corruption, and even a clever robbery gang that employed police officers as lookouts. Each day the New Orleans press printed a new article on crime in the Crescent City.

In 1952 Richard Foster and other outstanding citizens—including several members of the reform coalition of 1946—organized the Metropolitan Crime Commission of New Orleans, Inc., a surveillance agency that would detect and expose illegal activities in the city. The sponsors of the new crime commission then pressed for a thorough investigation of the police department and law enforcement operations in New Orleans. In 1953 their pleas and a growing public discontent with crime forced municipal authorities to form a special citizens investigating committee. This three-man body and its chief investigator, Aaron M. Kohn, worked for six months and discovered overwhelming evidence of crime and corruption in New Orleans that extended from the man on the beat to the mayor's office. When the committee tried to reveal its findings, however, Mayor Morrison maintained that the disclosures were vicious political smears and tried to suppress the completion and publication of the committee's final report. The mayor grudgingly made several personnel changes in the police force to quell the public outcry, but the scandals dragged on for several years. In 1960 Morrison finally took firm action when he named Joseph I. Giarrusso to the top position in the police department. Giarrusso, a young veteran of the force, brought professionalism to local law enforcement, improved the reputation of the police department, and ended the lingering controversy.

The lengthy police scandals, however, undermined Morrison's image of reform. In July 1956 Ralph M. Pons, a local businessman, wrote Morrison:

I am afraid that in the process of politics you may have lost your soul and your intellectual honesty about some things. . . . Chep, on the face of the record, and the facts that are known to date, I don't think that you can convince me or anyone else that the citizens have gotten a square deal, insofar as a house cleaning of the Police Department is concerned.

One year later Scott Wilson, a trusted Morrison advisor, observed that "whatever comes of it [the police scandals] cannot fail to be damaging to some degree."

Other flaws in the Morrison administration were more subtle and perhaps more damaging. Cities have endured—and even thrived—under the weight of machine rule and police corruption, but municipal extravagance and poor planning were heavier, less manageable civic burdens. The Morrison building program unfortunately often included both deficiencies. In his quest for a strong reform reputation, the Crescent City mayor stressed the construction of gymnasiums, streets, and overpasses—"the visible evidence of my achievements." Frequently these projects proceeded in a slipshod fashion that caused long-term problems. Morrison, for example, once diverted $1 million in municipal bond revenue to finance a street improvement program that used oyster shells and gravel for road surfacing. These repairs provided a quick solution to the problem of muddy streets, but in the marshy subsoil and rainy climate of New Orleans the rocky new surfaces lasted only six months.

The bonds that funded the project, however, had a longevity of forty years. Upon another occasion the mayor informed the commission council that municipal construction crews could use war surplus materials to build a badly needed municipal court building at a cost of $50,000. The project began without the benefit of blueprints and soon encountered a series of recurring snags that required additional fiscal outlays. When the structure eventually reached completion, its final cost exceeded $600,000. Five years later local officials reported that the building was inadequate for current needs.

The union terminal project and the civic center complex also exhibited evidence of improper planning. The leveling of a squalid area in downtown New Orleans created a suitable site for the new facilities, but it simultaneously destroyed the homes of many people, mainly blacks. Because the city government did not provide these refugees from urban renewal with adequate housing, many had to crowd into existing neighborhoods. The resultant concentration contributed to greater racial segregation in the city and caused the decay of several residential sections that had previously been healthy. The union passenger terminal, furthermore, became outmoded with the rising importance of air travel and the decline of the railroads. Fifteen years after its completion the terminal functioned primarily as a bus station.

Improvident spending and the needs of a growing metropolitan area caused financial difficulties for the municipal government of New Orleans. So did the flight to the suburbs. Although the exodus from the city did not receive much publicity until the 1960s, the trend was already in high gear during the Morrison years. The attractiveness of suburban living, the completion of connecting highways, and the construction of new industrial plants on cheap land sites beyond the city limits combined to lure predominantly white, middle class citizens and their tax dollars into new residential subdivisions in outlying areas. Mayor Morrison compounded these fiscal problems with a stubborn tax policy. The mayor maintained that new taxes were political liabilities because they alienated the voting public. He preferred to finance municipal improvement projects with revenue bonds, a fiscal approach that created a dual dilemma. It undermined the future bonding capacity of the city, and it did not provide adequate funds to meet expanding municipal needs. Financial matters therefore often dominated communications between the mayor and his chief administrative officer. In February 1957 David McGuire stated, "I cannot support expanding our spending level by $1 until we have a review with the Council members on our budget situation." In July 1958 Councilman Glenn P. Clasen said, "We have requests facing us now that we can't meet."

Executive neglect constituted another problem for New Orleans. In 1956 Mayor Morrison ran for governor against Earl Long and lost. Afterward the ambitious Crescent City chief executive devoted more and more time to state politics. He organized his legislative supporters against the governor's men in Baton Rouge and at times opposed legislative measures that were beneficial to New Orleans because Long supported them. This intense involvement in state politics continually drew Morrison's attention away from urban affairs and thus deprived New Orleans of vital leadership at a critical time.

During this period in Morrison's career race relations became a hotly contested issue. For the New Orleans mayor this change in Louisiana politics had serious ramifications. Throughout his years in office Morrison had always presented a moderate attitude toward black citizens that commonly won the Negro vote and retained the endorsement of the white majority. The mayor, however, did not falter in his support of segregation. City services operated on the basis of racial separation, and integration in municipal government rested firmly within the realm of tokenism. The CCDA, furthermore, remained a white man's organization. Morrison, nonetheless, bore the taint of moderation in an era of racial turmoil. Despite his obvious unwillingness to breach the color line, his temperate appeal to black voters antagonized reactionary whites who claimed that the New Orleans mayor had betrayed his race.

These extremist attitudes pervaded the Louisiana gubernatorial campaign of 1959-1960. Morrison again ran for governor on a platform of economic progress for the state and won a first primary plurality. In the runoff election the New Orleans mayor faced Jimmie H. Davis, a former governor and country-western singer. In the first primary Davis had stressed peace and harmony in his campaign, but in the runoff he became the darling of radical segregationists. Leander Perez of Plaquemines Parish and William M. "Willie" Rainach of Claiborne Parish, leaders in the Citizens' Councils movement, endorsed his candidacy and stumped the state for him. Their support set the tenor of the entire campaign. Davis backers unleashed a stunning assault against Morrison that criticized his urban background, his Catholicism, and his close association with such glamourous national figures as movie star Zsa Zsa Gabor and Senator John F. Kennedy. The key argument, however, was Morrison's racial stance. Davis leaders claimed that the New Orleans mayor was soft on integration, produced photographs of Morrison with Negro dignitaries, and charged that the restrooms at the union passenger terminal and the new City Hall were integrated—they were not. With each passing day the campaign sank to a new low for viciousness. Morrison protested that he was a segregationist and cited his municipal record, but Louisiana voters were in no mood to listen to reason. Davis won the election, and Morrison, a victim of irrational emotionalism, emerged from the contest with a new cautiousness toward the race issue.

This cautiousness continued into the school desegregation crisis of 1960. After eight years of litigation Judge J. Skelly Wright ordered New Orleans public schools to desegregate in November 1960. Mayor Morrison and local civic leaders had not prepared for the fateful decision. Over the years they had deluded themselves into thinking that public silence would preserve segregation in the city schools. After the court order the mayor and local leaders refused to take a strong stand. Morrison believed that any definite public statement would risk the political support of either his reliable black voting bloc or the white majority. Both were necessary for his future political plans. Businessmen also were reticent because they feared economic boycotts. The ultimate result of these attitudes was a leadership void in the Crescent City.

Into this vacuum rushed the racial extremists of Louisiana: Governor Davis and the state legislature, a group of raving New Orleans housewives who became known as the "cheerleaders," and members of the Greater New Orleans Citizens' Councils (GNOCC) and related organizations. While Mayor Morrison and the Crescent City's leading citizens tarried, Governor Davis called a special session of the state legislature and introduced a legislative package to obstruct the integration of New Orleans public schools. This package included bills to place city schools under the supervision of a state-appointed board, to restrict the powers of the mayor and the police superintendent, to deny pay to public school teachers, and to close the schools completely. In an act of brazen defiance, the legislature suspended its rules and hurriedly enacted these various bills into law; only Representative Maurice "Moon" Landrieu of New Orleans consistently spoke out against the measures. Although federal judges methodically overruled these state laws, actions of the legislature paved the way for the ensuing events.

When federal marshals escorted four little black girls into two elementary schools in the Ninth Ward of New Orleans on November 14, 1960, racial hatred flared. White mothers immediately withdrew their children from the schools and began a boycott. Each day the "cheerleaders" arrived to curse, spit, and hurl rocks at the black children and those whites who violated the boycott. After school the "cheerleaders" followed the white children and their parents home, slashed their automobile tires, and made threatening telephone calls. The fathers of several of the white children who continued to attend school lost their jobs. Although police were present at the schools to prevent overt violence, they permitted the "cheerleaders" to crowd near the black children and their parents and to heap verbal abuse upon them. During the crisis the novelist John Steinbeck visited the schools to observe the scene, but he retreated in dismay when he heard the profanity of the "cheerleaders." In a television address Mayor Morrison asked the people to stay in their homes and spoke against violence. He then added incongruously that peaceful vocal demonstration was the American way. Morrison later called for a news moratorium on school integration because, in his opinion, many of the news films were fraudulent and the "cheerleaders" demonstrated only to see themselves on television.

During the early days of the conflict, Leander Perez and William Rainach entered New Orleans to lead the segregationists. One evening they addressed a large gathering at the Municipal Auditorium; in the past Mayor Morrison had refused to allow Thurgood Marshall to use the public facility because the black leader might precipitate racial unrest. In their presentations Rainach and Perez spoke heatedly against racial mixing and urged the audience to take a firm stand against integration. Perez specifically denounced Morrison and Judge Wright. He told the audience:

Don't wait for your daughter to be raped by these Congolese. Don't wait until the burr-heads are forced into your schools. Do something about it now.

One bystander compared the gathering to a rally in Nazi Germany. The next morning a mob of white teenagers marched on City Hall, assaulted blacks in downtown New Orleans, and committed various acts of vandalism. Firemen had to use high-pressure hoses to disperse the crowd. After sunset blacks retaliated in kind. The police arrested over two hundred persons, mostly blacks.

Racial strife permeated life in New Orleans throughout the school year. The "cheerleaders" remained on hand to enforce the boycott. In September and later in April 1961, civil rights workers staged sit-in demonstrations in downtown department stores. Upon both occasions Mayor Morrison ordered the arrest of the demonstrators because, in his words, "the effect of such demonstrations is not in the public interest of this community." In May 1961 American Nazi party leader George Lincoln Rockwell and his "hate bus" arrived in New Orleans. Police arrested Rockwell and his followers when they created a disturbance at a downtown theater. The mayor stated that "the 'Nazi' stormtroopers and the Freedom Riders are not welcome in our City."

During the desegregation crisis Mayor Morrison received criticism from all sides. Civil rights advocates blasted the mayor for his reluctance to take a firm stand on school integration, and segregationists argued that he favored racial mixing. Morrison's attempt to ply a moderate course between groups ended in dismal failure. Although the mayor tried to regain widespread support with a bevy of conciliatory letters and television appearances, the damage to his reputation was already done.

The city also suffered. The tourist trade, a key element of the local economy, declined sharply. Many potential visitors feared violence. Others vowed never to patronize a city that allowed racial discrimination. On December 21, 1960, Scott Wilson wrote, "I am fearful that by March there will be more good weather than business in New Orleans—the school situation is that bad." Several local merchants compared conditions with the days of the depression. This economic squeeze, however, produced beneficial results. It convinced many businessmen to put aside their silence and to call for open schools and an end to violence. Their public statements eventually restored rational leadership to the community and helped to ease racial tension, but they came too late. The early reticence of governmental and business spokesmen had permitted the "cheerleaders" and other uncompromising advocates of segregation to hold the public eye and to turn popular opinion against New Orleans. In the end Mayor Morrison and his city emerged from the controversy with badly bruised public images.

In 1961 Morrison faced a precarious political future. He had fully expected to win the governorship in 1960, but Jimmie Davis and the racial issue had foiled his attempt. The mayor, furthermore, was serving his second term under the new city charter. He could not succeed himself. For several months Morrison considered the election of a caretaker mayor, but there were few available candidates who were sufficiently loyal. David McGuire, the most likely prospect, had died suddenly in November 1960. After much deliberation Morrison decided to seek a change in the charter that would permit him to succeed himself. The mayor and Scott Wilson launched the campaign to modify the charter with the slogan, "Change Charter, Keep Chep." This plan encountered immediate opposition from a host of antagonists, including good government supporters who believed that the charter should be inviolable, members of the Morrison camp who sought independent political advancement, and several Old Regulars who since 1946 had managed to hold power on the ward and precinct levels and now hoped to regain control of city government. These Old Regulars responded imaginatively to the Morrison slogan with one of their own, "Keep Charter, Change Chep." At the polls the public agreed with the Regulars and voted down the proposed charter change. Morrison remained a lame duck.

An offer from President Kennedy salvaged Morrison's public career. In July 1961 the mayor resigned to become United States ambassador to the Organization of American States. For two years Morrison toured Latin America, promoted the Alliance for Progress, and periodically visited New Orleans to sniff the political winds. In 1963 he returned to Louisiana to run for governor once more. This campaign unfortunately resembled his previous effort. After winning a plurality in the first primary, Morrison lost the runoff. In early 1964 he entered private life and sought time to plot his political future. His plans, however, went untested. On May 22, 1964, de Lesseps Morrison died in an airplane crash in Mexico.

His death ended a colorful era in New Orleans politics. Although Morrison was unable to pull completely free of the local heritage of corrupt practices and machine rule and his reform programs often misfirred, he enhanced the national image of New Orleans and brought a respectable measure of progress to the city. His vibrant personality, concern for good public relations, and flair for the dramatic, moreover, changed the fabric of local politics. Victor H. Schiro and "Moon" Landrieu, Morrison's successors in City Hall, were veterans of the Crescent City Democratic Association. District Attorney James Garrison—whom many New Orleanians would prefer to forget—was another Morrison disciple. So was Councilman (and later Lieutenant Governor) James E. Fitzmorris, Jr. Although many of his reform programs were less than successful, Morrison left a deep imprint upon the city of New Orleans, its politics, and its politicians.

In other southern cities the urbanization process paralleled developments in New Orleans during the Morrison heyday. Although few municipal chief executives combined guile and dynamic achievement with the charisma of Mayor Morrison, other urban centers in the South possessed their own powerful postwar heroes. In Atlanta William B. Hartsfield and Ivan Allen, Jr. were dominant figures. In Miami Robert King High provided urban leadership. In Houston Judge Roy M. Hofheinz, father of the Astrodome, was a vital force in the community.

Each of these men mirrored the spirit of urban boosterism that permeated the twentieth-century South. They were members of the southern white commercial-civic elite, a powerful coalition of old families and business leaders that commonly controlled local affairs. In New Orleans representatives of this group backed the initial candidacy of de Lesseps Morrison because he would improve the national image and the business prospects of the city. Later these individuals formed the nucleus of the Cold Water Committee that advised and financed the Crescent City mayor during his entire administration. In 1960 the Atlanta white commercial-civic elite supported a three-year, $1.5 million "Forward Atlanta" program that sought new industry and trade for the city. In each case these municipal leaders endorsed moderate government that stressed economic progress.[9]

After World War II growth was the prime characteristic of the urban South. In 1950 Houston boasted a population of 596,163 and surpassed New Orleans to become the largest city in the South. Two decades later the Bayou City retained its leadership with a population of 1,232,802. Throughout the region annexations, migrations from rural areas, and the baby boom caused unprecedented urban expansion. Within three decades several cities more than doubled their populations. (See table 6-1.) In 1940, for example, San Antonio had 253,854 inhabitants; thirty years later the figure was 654,153. Annexations helped Jacksonville grow from a city of 173,065 in 1940 to a sprawling metropolis of 528,865 in 1970. During the same period Dallas showed a population increase of approximately 550,000. Secondary cities exhibited similar—and sometimes greater—population growth. El Paso tripled in population. In 1940 Tampa had 108,391 residents; three decades later the total was 277,767. During the 1940s Baton Rouge mushroomed from a small town of 34,719 into a respectable city of 125,629. In 1970 165,963 people lived in the Louisiana capital.[10]

TABLE 6-1.

Population Changes in Leading Southern Cities, 1940-1970

City	1940	1950	1960	1970
New Orleans	494,537	570,445	627,525	593,471
Houston	384,514	596,163	938,219	1,232,802
Atlanta	302,288	331,314	487,455	496,973
Dallas	294,734	434,462	679,684	844,401
Memphis	292,942	396,000	497,524	623,540
Birmingham	267,583	326,037	340,887	300,910
San Antonio	253,854	408,442	587,718	654,153
Richmond	193,042	230,310	219,958	249,621
Fort Worth	177,662	278,778	356,268	393,476
Jacksonville	173,065	204,517	201,030	528,865
Miami	172,172	249,276	291,688	334,859
Nashville	167,402	174,307	170,874	448,003
Norfolk	144,332	213,513	305,872	307,951
El Paso	96,810	130,485	276,687	322,261

The migration of returning servicemen contributed to the urbanization process in the South. During World War II numerous rural southerners had traveled to cities in other sections of the United States and abroad. For many of them, the thoughts and experiences that these new environments invoked changed their lives. After the war they could no longer accept the traditional perspectives of their rural past and sought a fresh beginning in southern urban areas. Military service also exposed numerous nonsoutherners to the prospects of Dixie. To the minds of many, the South was the land of opportunity, the new frontier. After the war they returned to the region to build their future. In the following decades it was a rare southern city that did not have at least one president of the chamber of commerce or businessman of the year who was a transplanted Yankee.[11] This migration into the South continued during the entire postwar period and in the 1960s substantially offset the constant flow of people away from the region that had dominated southern demographic charts throughout the century.[12]

Economic progress provided the essential underpinning for urban expansion in the South. Much of the economic improvement in the region was due to industrialization. During the 1960s the annual capital investment in southern industry tripled. The number of industrial workers increased steadily from approximately 2.4 million in 1950 to 4.4 million in 1972. Between 1962 and 1972 the average income in the South doubled. Although these statistics often masked the continuing lag in southern income and failed to account for exploitative industries that robbed the region of its natural resources, they did indicate that the South was becoming more self-sufficient and was developing greater economic diversity.[13]

One reason for the economic surge of the South was the retention of military installations. The uneasy peace of the Cold War, the Korean conflict, and the Vietnam debacle prevented the sharp decline in military expenditures that many southerners had anticipated after World War II. During the postwar period military bases and defense industries remained an integral segment of the southern economy. Barksdale Air Force Base, Fort Benning, Eglin Field, Fort Bragg, and England Air Force Base, to cite some examples, were vital to the economic prosperity of their respective communities.

The importance of military spending was especially evident in the secondary cities of Georgia. In 1969, at the height of the Vietnam war, Fort Benning, the largest military installment in the state, had an annual payroll and supply budget of approximately $300 million that flowed mainly into the economy of nearby Columbus. New construction on the post with an estimated value of $43 million further bolstered local business. In Savannah, Hunter Army Airfield, the helicopter training center for Vietnamese, and Fort Stewart, an armor facility, pumped millions of dollars in payrolls and procurement into the surrounding economy. In Augusta, Fort Gordon, headquarters for Signal Corps training and the site of the Dwight D. Eisenhower Army Hospital, brought approximately $150 million each year into the economy. Between 1964 and 1974, moreover, the Department of Defense awarded nearly $8 billion in defense contracts to state industries.

An added economic supplement was the national space program and related enterprises. During the 1950s and 1960s southern politicians, urban and rural, used their formidable power within the legislative seniority system in Washington to obtain numerous aerospace industries for their region. The subsequent construction of new factories, testing facilities, and communications centers wrought an enormous economic and technological revolution in the South. The sudden infusion of large amounts of federal and private funds into southern urban areas significantly bolstered their economic foundations. Cape Canaveral and Oak Ridge were two obvious beneficiaries. In Marietta, Georgia, an Atlanta suburb, the Lockheed-Georgia Company became an economic mainstay that for two decades was the largest private employer in the state. In New Orleans the renovation of the Michoud

Assembly Facility to produce Saturn S-1 booster rockets for the Apollo missions brought Boeing and Chrysler corporations into the community and led directly to the expansion of the eastern section of the city. In Huntsville the construction of the Marshall Space Flight Center, a major facility of the National Aeronautics and Space Administration (NASA), combined with the Redstone Arsenal, headquarters of the United States Army Missile Command, to create 27,000 jobs and a yearly payroll of approximately $350 million. Houston, however, won the biggest prize, the Johnson Manned Spacecraft Center, a $60 million complex that also promoted additional private and public development in the surrounding area. In 1964 spokesmen for Humble Oil, one of the participants in the project, presented a master plan for the expansion of industry, commerce, and residential neighborhoods near the spacecraft center that predicted an ultimate investment of $900 million and the creation of 25,000 jobs over a twenty-year period. During the postwar years these and similar programs initiated a broad spectrum of promising economic opportunities and a greater need for technological skills in the region, primary reasons for accelerated migration to southern cities.[14]

Increased mobility also influenced economic development in the urban South. The postwar expansion of the automobile industry, the construction of the interstate highway system, and the rise of commercial air transportation permitted major corporations to locate large factories on cheaper southern land sites outside the great manufacturing regions of the North and the Midwest. Service industries in the South also profited from decentralization. After World War II several national firms established important branch offices and sometimes their main headquarters in key southern cities such as Atlanta, Miami, Dallas, Houston, and New Orleans. Improved transportation also allowed many prospective investors and settlers, especially retired people, to investigate sparsely populated areas in the South and eventually to make their homes in the region. Tourists constituted another group that welcomed the chance to travel in the South, to enjoy the climate, and to spend money. Many of them also returned later to stay. The growing presence of these diverse groups created bigger markets for southern products and services that in turn attracted more businesses and more people to the region.[15]

The expansion of commercial aviation and the construction of interstate highways also had an important effect upon the relationship of southern cities to each other and to the rest of the country. After 1945 air travel drew southern cities closer together and at the same time brought them into more direct contact with urban centers in other parts of the United States and the world. In the South the growth of commercial flying and the development of urban areas proved to be mutually beneficial. Braniff International and Delta airlines indicated their faith in regional urban centers when they located their national headquarters in Dallas and Atlanta, respectively. Southern cities, furthermore, have worked conscientiously to make the most of their potential for air travel. Within the past decade Houston, Dallas, Tampa, and Shreveport constructed modern air terminals. New Orleans is currently expanding its international airport to cope with increasing commercial air traffic.[16]

The modern highway network and the growing numbers of automobiles had a similar effect upon the South. Because more southerners owned automobiles after World War II, the average person became increasingly mobile. For the first time many southern urbanites could visit other cities in the region and travel throughout the country. Rural southerners, moreover, had the same opportunities. Together the automobile and the superhighway literally broadened the horizons of the region. These innovations—plus the communications revolution that motion pictures, radio, and later television introduced—exposed untold millions of rural southerners to urban culture, intensified the relationships between regional cities, and moved the South into the main currents of American urban life.[17]

The transportation revolution also affected the spatial configurations of southern cities. After 1945 the automobile and the wheel pattern of highway construction contributed to urban decentralization in the South. Millions of southerners left congested central cities for the presumably greener pastures of the suburbs. The

TABLE 6-2.

Metropolitan Growth of Leading Southern Cities, 1950-1970

City	1950	1970
Houston	935,539	1,985,031
Dallas	780,827	1,555,950
Atlanta	726,989	1,390,164
New Orleans	712,393	1,045,809
Birmingham	653,059	739,274
Memphis	529,577	770,120
San Antonio	525,852	864,014
Miami	495,084	1,267,792
Jacksonville	304,029	528,865
Richmond	266,185	518,319

trend in the South, as in the nation, was clearly toward metropolitan expansion, suburban sprawl. In 1945 Houston became the first southern city to have a metropolitan population of one million. Six years later Houston, Dallas, and Atlanta were respectively the sixteenth, twentieth, and twenty-fourth largest Standard Metropolitan Statistical Areas (SMSA) in the country. By 1970 five southern SMSAs— Houston, Dallas, Atlanta, Miami, and New Orleans—exceeded one million in population. (See table 6-2.)

In several southern central cities a population decline accompanied the growth of the suburbs. During the 1960s New Orleans and Birmingham suffered population declines in their urban cores—11.7 percent and 5.7 percent, respectively. In Atlanta the core increase was a nominal 2 percent. Southern suburbia, nonetheless, continued to expand. Between 1960 and 1970 the suburban areas around Dallas,

Atlanta, and New Orleans experienced population growth rates of 60 percent or more, and the Houston suburbs approximated that figure. (See table 6-3.) During the 1960s the rate of population increase in the fringe areas that surrounded southern cities was higher than the national average.[18]

After World War II the persistence of metropolitan growth in the South convinced many social scientists that future urban development in the region will proceed along the lines of the conurbation, "an almost continuous urban sprawl spreading out from one or more metropolitan centers." In 1965 the sociologist Leonard Reissman suggested that in the South there were five major conurbations—Gulf Coast, Atlantic Coast, Eastern Inner Core, Western Inner Core, and Carolinas—and two lesser ones—the Nashville-Memphis and the Shreveport chains. Houston and New Orleans were the key metropolises in the Gulf Coast Conurbation, largest in the region. The various urban places in Florida formed the heart of the Atlantic

TABLE 6-3.

Percentage of Population Change
in Leading Southern Metropolitan Areas, 1960–1970

City	Central City	Outside Central City
Houston	31.2	57.0
Dallas	24.2	61.8
Atlanta	2.0	68.6
New Orleans	-5.7	62.5
Birmingham	-11.7	15.3
Memphis	25.3	-17.2
Miami	14.8	45.0
Richmond	13.5	24.3

Coast Conurbation that extended from Miami to Charleston. Atlanta and Dallas were the respective centers of the Eastern Inner Core and the Western Inner Core Conurbations. The fifth major urban complex, the Carolinas Conurbation, was unusual because it included several small metropolitan areas, not one or two large ones. In the opinion of Reissman, the status of the two lesser metropolitan groups was tenuous. He believed that the Shreveport and Memphis-Nashville chains could either continue to exist separately or perhaps meld into one of the nearby major conurbations. Reissman purposely excluded Newport News, Portsmouth-Norfolk, and other Virginia cities from his seven southern conurbations because they belonged to the giant Boston–New York–Washington megalopolis that dominated the northeastern portion of the United States.[19]

Since 1965 metropolitanization has been a continuing process in the South. In Louisiana, for example, a population shift from the northern part of the state to the southern portion that falls within the Gulf Coast Conurbation has accompanied the traditional movement from country to city. Industrial expansions in Lake Charles, Lafayette, and Baton Rouge as well as in New Orleans precipitated this southward movement, and the proposed construction of a superport off the Louisiana coast to accommodate deep-draft oceangoing oil tankers promises only to intensify this trend.[20] A similar port is planned for the Texas coast. Metropolitan development in the South also benefited from the recent growth of several independent suburban towns that bordered major urban cities. Population increases in Richardson and Arlington, for example, contributed directly to the tremendous expansion of the Dallas–Fort Worth metroplex.[21] Extensive use of Interstate 20, moreover, has drawn the Shreveport metropolitan chain into a closer relationship with Dallas and the Western Inner Core Conurbation.

Metropolitan growth also promoted significant social, economic, and cultural changes in the South. Innumerable shopping malls, apartment complexes, subdivisions, and traffic loops have been merely the obvious manifestations of suburban sprawl, but other transformations have been equally important. In southeastern Louisiana developers recently unveiled the Plaza, a massive regional shopping center that will, it is hoped, attract customers from the Mississippi Gulf Coast and New Orleans East. On the other side of the Crescent City in suburban Jefferson Parish, a garish series of restaurants, discotheques, coffee houses, and boutiques with the bizarre collective name of Fat City opened to entertain nearby apartment dwellers. Promoters confidently predicted that Fat City would eventually draw patrons away from the more famous bistros and shops of the historic French Quarter. In 1975 the spread of Mardi Gras celebrations into suburbia only reinforced this faith. On February 11, 1975, Mardi Gras day, Fat Tuesday came to Fat City with the first annual parade of the Krewe of Argus, replete with fourteen floats, motorcycle escorts, and cheering crowds. David Levy of the Fat City Businessmen's Association declared, "You can't stop progress—Mardi Gras is destined to come here." One exuberant participant in the festivities agreed, "It's safe to say that Mardi Gras will become bigger and better out here. Fat City is starting a tradition that's bound to catch on for one simple reason. There's money here. Money to be made." Although no one promised to make metropolitan New Orleans into the SMSA that care forgot, that intent was quite clear.[22]

The monetary spirit that burned in Fat City also attracted outside investors to the South. During the 1960s rapid population increases and the development of a substantial urban middle class convinced the barons of American professional athletics that the region was ripe for major league sports. With an eye toward civic pride, many southern cities responded to this sudden interest and constructed new stadiums and arenas to lure professional teams and major athletic events into their areas. Throughout the decade and into the 1970s, established teams moved to the South, and several expansion franchises began operation in the region. At present major league baseball clubs play in Houston, Atlanta, and Arlington, Texas. The National Football League currently has teams in Miami, Dallas, Houston, Atlanta, New Orleans, and Tampa. The Tampa team's first season was 1976. In 1974, its first shaky year of competition, the World Football League had a distinctly southern flavor with teams in Memphis, Birmingham, Orlando, Charlotte, and Shreveport and briefly in Jacksonville and Houston, In 1975 San Antonio joined the ill-fated league. Professional basketball teams currently rebound and fast break in Houston, New Orleans, San Antonio, Atlanta, and Norfolk-Hampton Roads. In Atlanta and Houston the cold weather sport of hockey attracts southern audiences, and Dallas is the headquarters of World Championship Tennis and a new soccer league. Throughout the region cities host prestigious professional golf tournaments and auto races.[23]

The arts also received their due. Cities of varying sizes built theaters, concert halls, and exhibition centers. Within the past decade, for example, New Orleans completed both the Rivergate International Exhibition Facility and the Theater for the Performing Arts, and renovated the ancient Municipal Auditorium. In 1965 Shreveport completed a new convention center. In 1966 the impressive Jesse H. Jones Hall for the Performing Arts opened in Houston. Two years later the new Alley Theater opened in the same city with a performance of Bertolt Brecht's *Galileo*.[24]

The rush of people into southern cities and their environs and the technological needs of the post-Sputnik age created strong demands for higher education in all parts of the region. Several southern state universities answered this challenge with the construction of branch campuses in major urban centers. Often the beginnings of these subsidiary schools were inauspicious. In 1958 the University of New Orleans (then Louisiana State University in New Orleans) welcomed new students to its lakefront campus, once the home of a naval air station. During the early days of the school, students and faculty used abandoned barracks and storage huts for classrooms. In 1967 Louisiana State University in Shreveport began classes on the site of an erstwhile cotton field. One year earlier the University of Alabama officially added a branch campus to the state medical school in Birmingham. Since its inception the $100 million university complex has been a driving force for urban renewal in the slum neighborhood that surrounds the campus and now rivals United States Steel as the largest employer in metropolitan Birmingham. In recent years the University of Texas has continued the expansionist trend with the establishment of branches in Arlington, San Antonio, and Dallas.

Another form of educational growth in the urban South was the upgrading of small state colleges to university status. During the 1960s Georgia State College in Atlanta, once a branch of Georgia Tech's evening program that maintained its headquarters in a local garage, became Georgia State University, a thriving institution with 18,000 students, that competed with the main campus in Athens.[25] In Louisiana, Southeastern College in Hammond became Southeastern Louisiana University, and McNeese State College in Lake Charles became McNeese State University. If education and cultural enrichment indeed were key elements for urban assimilation in the South, the process reached a high-water mark in the postwar years.

After World War II the civil rights revolution constituted the greatest social change in the South, and much of its focus was in the cities. The main impetus for the movement came from outside the region. Its leaders were the National

Association for the Advancement of Colored People (NAACP) and the federal courts. After several years of chipping away at the edges of segregation, on May 17, 1954, the United States Supreme Court declared that the doctrine of "separate but equal" was unconstitutional. This decision prompted a bitter struggle between civil rights advocates and protectors of traditional southern social institutions. Often the southern city was the battleground.[26]

After 1954 blacks and cooperative white liberals launched a concerted assault upon Jim Crow. In 1955 Rosa Parks's refusal to move to the back of the bus sparked a boycott to protest racial segregation in public transit in Montgomery, Alabama, and pushed Martin Luther King, Jr., a young black clergyman, into the national limelight. Other boycotts followed. In 1957 King founded the Southern Christian Leadership Conference (SCLC) to establish a regional base for his nonviolent approach to civil rights and to coordinate protest activities in southern urban areas. The SCLC and other civil rights groups including the Congress for Racial Equality (CORE) and the Student Nonviolent Coordinating Committee (SNCC) participated in a multitude of nonviolent protests throughout the South. In 1960 sit-in demonstrations began in Greensboro and spread to New Orleans, Atlanta, and other large southern cities. In 1961 civil rights workers made freedom rides into the South to publicize discriminatory practices in public accommodations and interstate commerce.

White conservatives responded to these activities with a wave of massive resistance. State legislatures created committees to investigate the membership and practices of the NAACP and other protest organizations. Lawmakers also enacted measures that authorized state control over the operation of local schools, pupil placement, teacher salaries and tenure, and law enforcement agencies in communities that faced the prospect of desegregation. Other laws harassed civil rights groups and generally undermined their civil liberties. At the same time white middle class conservatives formed Citizens' Councils to promote the doctrine of white supremacy, to influence state legislators, and to intimidate blacks and civil rights advocates. Often legislative leaders were also top officials in the Citizens' Councils. In Louisiana, for instance, State Senator William Rainach and Representative John Sidney Garrett of the Joint Legislative Committee to Maintain Segregation, and Leander Perez, the reputed "third house of the Louisiana legislature" who drafted the bulk of state segregation statutes, were prominent members of the Association of Citizens' Councils of Louisiana (ACCL). The resurgence of the Ku Klux Klan added a lower class and sometimes violent element to this conglomerate of repression and intimidation.

The roots of massive resistance in the South were rural. Although Citizens' Council chapters appeared in southern cities and many urban representatives endorsed restrictive legislation, the main thrust of the movement came from the outlying parishes and counties, especially the Black Belt. In Louisiana, Rainach and Garrett were from Claiborne Parish in the northern portion of the state, and Perez was the perennial political boss of Plaquemines Parish in the south. In Virginia the Harry Byrd machine used its rural strength to mount the drive for massive resistance. For this reason the battle to preserve segregation frequently had sharp overtones of an urban-rural conflict. When the Louisiana legislature in November 1960 overrode moderate opposition from the Orleans Parish delegation and named a state committee to take control over New Orleans public schools in an attempt to prevent racial integration, Mayor Morrison became outraged. In his mind, the primary issue was home rule. On November 8, 1960, the New Orleans chief executive declared publicly:

I have been shocked to learn that the House . . . rejected a proposed amendment by Orleans legislators seeking local control of its own affairs. . . . It is just as wrong for Mr. Garrett [of Claiborne Parish] to try to run our Orleans school affairs as it is wrong for the U. S. Supreme Court to dictate to the people of Louisiana. . . . It looks like home rule is taking another licking.

Four days later Morrison requested that state lawmakers "take no action to violate the principles of Home Rule in connection with any proposed removal of any public official of this community who is duly elected by the people. . . ."[27] The mayor's refusal to come to grips with the issue of integration indicated another problem. Many urban representatives privately opposed legislative incursions into their cities, but they refused to speak out because they feared political reprisals from diehard segregationists that could destroy their public careers.

Southern cities met the reality of desegregation in a variety of ways that often changed over time. In New Orleans, for instance, local officials and citizens peacefully accepted the integration of public transportation and recreational facilities, but they rejected sit-in demonstrations at lunch counters. In September 1960 and again in the spring of 1961, New Orleans police arrested CORE demonstrators. In both the Crescent City and Little Rock, the refusal of local leaders to take a firm stand on school desegregation permitted members of the Citizens' Councils and other reactionary segregationists to gain the upper hand and to create civil disorder. In many southern communities municipal officials jailed freedom riders, and outraged citizens burned their buses. In May 1963 Birmingham Police Commissioner Eugene "Bull" Connor directed his officers to use fire hoses, cattle prods, police dogs, clubs, and wholesale arrests to break up the peaceful demonstrations of Martin Luther King, Jr., and his followers. News photographs of helpless black demonstrators dodging vicious dogs and enraged policemen reached a national audience and caused the federal government to push for important civil rights legislation.

Urban leaders paid a stiff price for their inability to keep the peace. The economic decline that accompanied school desegregation in New Orleans reappeared again and again in other southern cities that experienced racial unrest. These business losses, however, fell heaviest upon the members of the white commercial-civic elite, the economic leaders of their respective cities, and forced them to reevaluate their public stance on race relations. Although white business leaders were hardly racial egalitarians, they came to realize the importance of racial harmony and civil rights to economics. In New Orleans community leaders publicly endorsed open schools and promoted civil order. In Birmingham Charles Morgan, Jr., a young attorney, and other members of the white commercial-civic elite worked to rid local law enforcement of the "Bull" Connor mentality and City Hall acquiescence. In 1967 business leaders, with vital black aid, supported the election of George G. Seibels, one of their number and a respected member of the city council, to the office of mayor. Although Seibels displayed administrative deficiencies and also had some serious health problems, he conscientiously strove to bring racial peace to the community. In 1969, two years after the election of Seibels, Operation New Birmingham, a program to enhance the physical development of the city, gave rise to the Community Affairs Council, a biracial group that focused attention on the social and economic problems of the southern steel metropolis. In 1971 George Seibels easily won reelection.[28] Atlanta civic leaders, unlike their counterparts in other southern urban centers, averted racial unrest and its attendant injury to local commerce and prestige when they acceded to several of the early demands that black spokesmen advanced.[29]

The pragmatism of white leaders, the firm resolve of civil rights workers and federal judges, and the enactment of important federal civil rights legislation in 1964, 1965, and 1968 shook the foundations of Jim Crow and racial discrimination in the urban South. So did the rise of professional sports in the region. White youths who worshiped the athletic triumphs of the black superstars Henry Aaron, Paul Warfield, Lou Hudson, and Arthur Ashe often reassessed their harsh views on race relations. The greater exposure of blacks on television and in motion pictures had a similar influence. By 1970 the color line in the South was a shambles. Historian Blaine A. Brownell correctly noted that "residential segregation persisted (and compounded the difficulties of desegregating public schools), and white racism still existed behind the bulwarks of private social clubs and academies," but few observers would deny that the civil rights struggles of the postwar years had brought tangible victories to southern blacks.[30]

The decline of racial segregation and discriminatory practices afforded southern blacks greater opportunities for social and economic advancement, but these improvements did not mark the end of racial problems in the metropolitan South. During the 1960s many whites who patronized the "private social clubs and academies"—and many who did not—voted on the question of civil rights with their feet—or more correctly with their automobiles. Numerous middle class white southerners who sought to evade racial unrest, integrated schools, and heavy municipal taxes moved from the central cities to rapidly expanding suburban areas. Although many southern blacks exhibited their new affluence and followed the whites into suburbia, most stayed in the core cities. The discriminatory lending policies of governmental agencies such as the Federal Housing Administration (FHA), furthermore, subsidized this trend with federal funds. Historian Kenneth T. Jackson observed that because urban areas with slums and "inharmonious racial and nationality groups" did not merit federal aid, "only 1 percent of the government insured homes constructed between 1945 and 1965 went to blacks." Applicants from white suburban neighborhoods received most of the federal loans. The consequences of these unfair FHA fiscal practices became readily apparent in southern residential patterns. After 1950 the percentage of blacks in the urban population of the South rose at the same time that the overall population in the core cities declined. (See tables 6-3 and 6-4.) In 1974 the Southern Regional Council reported that blacks constituted more than 30 percent of the total population in many southern cities. In nine cities including New Orleans, Birmingham, and Memphis, blacks accounted for 40 percent or more of the total, and in Atlanta blacks had a definite majority.[31]

In many southern metropolitan areas the members of other ethnic minorities also concentrated in the core cities. In Texas census reports indicated that 46 percent of the state's Chicano population resided in San Antonio, Houston, Dallas, Fort Worth, and El Paso. In Miami Cuban refugees from the Castro revolution numbered over 350,000. During the 1960s Cuban immigrants also established sizable communities in New Orleans and Houston.[32]

This rising concentration of blacks and other minority groups in the inner cities of the South often caused resentment among white urbanites. Although many

TABLE 6-4.
Black Percentage of Population in Major Southern Cities

City	1930	1950	1970
Atlanta	33.3	36.6	51.3
Birmingham	38.2	39.9	42.0
Dallas	14.9	13.2	24.9
Houston	21.7	21.1	25.7
Jacksonville	37.2	35.5	22.3
Memphis	38.1	37.2	38.9
Miami	22.7	16.3	22.7
New Orleans	28.3	32.0	45.0
San Antonio	7.8	—	7.6

southern whites fled to the suburbs, members of the white commercial-civic elite generally retained their positions of power within southern cities. A disproportionate number of whites continued to be mayors, city councilmen, police officers, firemen, and municipal department heads in the urban South. Often the racial views of these leaders were less than enlightened. The intense controversy that erupted over school busing represented one manifestation of these attitudes. The failure of the civil rights revolution to deal adequately with the economic problems of blacks was another. Despite the legal fall of the color line during the decade of the 1960s, blacks remained on the lower economic and social levels in southern society. An added problem was the persistence of the "Bull" Connor mentality among white police officers. Throughout the South innocent blacks were commonly the targets of police brutality. One unfortunate incident involved Rico Carty, a dark-skinned Latin outfielder with the Atlanta Braves baseball team, who received an unmerciful and unwarranted beating at the hands of local police.

During the late 1960s the spread of militant black nationalism and a subsequent white backlash further aggravated the already tense relations between police and the black communities within southern cities. In New Orleans these simmering feelings flared upon two unhappy occasions. In early 1970 members of the Black Panthers established a headquarters in Desire, a deteriorating black housing project in downtown New Orleans. Desire was best known for its high incidence of rapes and muggings, piles of uncollected refuse, and poor recreational facilities. An official report stated that the housing project was "an ideal incubator for crime, social disintegration and disease." Many Desire residents were afraid to leave their homes, and the presence of the Panthers only contributed to their fear. When the black nationalists began to fortify their location and to intimidate local businessmen, Clarence Giarrusso, the new superintendent of police and the former superintendent's younger brother, ordered an assault with automatic weapons and tear gas upon the Panther headquarters. The ensuing gunfight left one young black dead and twenty-one other persons wounded. The battle destroyed the Panthers' power in New Orleans, but several of the injured claimed that they were not Black Panthers and did nothing to provoke gunfire from the police. A jury later acquitted twelve Panthers who stood trial for the attempted murder of policemen.

The second incident occurred in January 1973 when Mark Essex, a young black whose hatred for whites drove him to insanity, took a position atop the Howard Johnson motel in downtown New Orleans and started sniping at passersby below. Essex chose his location well. Although he had no path of retreat, his field of fire commanded "Chep" Morrison's civic center complex as well as several busy downtown thoroughfares. For several hours the mentally unbalanced sniper terrorized the business district of the Crescent City. Superintendent Giarrusso once more responded zealously. Believing that Essex's shots signaled the beginning of a full-fledged urban race war, the superintendent decided against a waiting game with the isolated young black and directed an impulsive frontal assault upon the roof of the hotel. Local viewers and later a national audience watched spellbound on television as New Orleans police and military helicopters stalked the sniper. Several police officers were exposed to gunfire and died in the hazardous operation that ended ultimately in the death of Essex. One of the tragic victims was Louis Sirgo, the deputy superintendent of police. In a case of bitter irony, Sirgo was one ranking police official who recognized the problems of the black community and strongly advocated more understanding between police and local blacks. He had stated earlier that "we must be prepared to deal with the greatest sin of American society, and that is the status of the Negro." In his opinion, until the conditions of blacks improved, the police would be continuously "putting out the fires which erupt in society."

Superintendent Giarrusso's views on race, however, offered a better representation of the attitudes of white New Orleanians. In the early 1970s a poll of 644 civic leaders revealed that they believed improvements in nine specific areas of municipal affairs including transportation and education were more essential to the community than changes in race relations. Such thoughts helped to explain the municipal paranoia on the race question that surfaced periodically in the police department.[33]

In the 1970s, however, the rise of black politicos rattled the white power structure in the urban South. The Voting Rights Act of 1965 and sheer numbers were the prime determinants in the growth of black political power. The decision of several civil rights organizations to shift from protest demonstrations to voter education was also important. By the 1970s an expanding black electorate began to use the ballot to express political desires and to elect dependable candidates. Throughout the South an increasing number of blacks won election to the bench, city councils, and school boards; served on police and fire departments; and held ranking posts in key governmental agencies. A few advanced to City Hall. In 1973 Maynard Jackson defeated ten other candidates to become the first black mayor of Atlanta. Several smaller southern cities copied the Atlanta example and also elected black chief executives. White politicians, moreover, came to understand that the black vote was essential to future political successes in the region. In Birmingham Mayor George G. Seibels relied upon strong black support to win election. In New Orleans "Moon" Landrieu adopted the organizational methods of his predecessors, but he added a vital difference. Under the young mayor, blacks received a fair share of the patronage plums. Landrieu openly courted the black vote and purposely appointed leaders from the Southern Organization for United Leadership (SOUL), the Orleans Parish Progressive Voters League (OPPVL), and other black political groups to responsible positions in his administration. The sum total of these political innovations marked the foremost achievement of the civil rights movement in the South.[34]

The legitimate entry of blacks into the electoral process undeniably constituted an important shift in regional politics, but it did not resolve the problems that the flight to the suburbs created. The movement of middle class whites to the suburbs deprived the cities of major revenue sources at the same time that the number of lower class urban dwellers—ethnic minorities and poor whites—who needed greater municipal assistance and contributed relatively little revenue to their respective cities was increasing. For southern cities the net result of these demographic changes was a sharp revenue loss with a coinciding demand for more public services. In many metropolitan areas suburban exploitation was an additional burden. Several suburban counties and parishes consciously neglected to provide adequate schools, recreational facilities, and general services for their citizens because these commodities were readily available in nearby cities. Although they constantly used municipal facilities, the suburbanites' payment for these services remained minimal. One New Orleanian, commenting on the residents of adjacent Jefferson Parish, noted cogently: "They don't pay a cent of taxes to us. They don't want to pay no taxes and ain't going to pay no taxes." In a more grammatical statement Mayor Landrieu explained that during the 1960s the city of New Orleans "lost 125,000 people—mostly white and affluent—moving out to the suburbs, and in their place, 90,000, mostly poor and black, moved in." Although the taxpayers of New Orleans financed "the transportation facilities, the parks, the zoo, the airport, the cultural facilities for a metropolitan area of 1.1 million [more than twice New Orleans's own population]," the mayor observed, ". . . we get nothing back from the suburbs. We don't even get the sales tax, because they have their own shopping centers."

Although no southern city approached the deplorable financial condition of New York, during the 1970s the need for municipal revenue was indeed a pervasive problem in the urban South. In March 1975 the *Atlanta Constitution* argued that the golden days of the Gate City had ended and the widely acclaimed capital of the New South was "a city in crisis." At various times urban officials in the South suggested hikes in sales and property taxes to ease their financial woes, but these solutions only alienated inner city residents and business leaders. The poor repeatedly argued that the tax load was already too heavy, and business contended that higher property taxes would only drive more middle-class citizens to the suburbs. The financial problems therefore continued to linger. Without revenue, southern cities could not provide necessary public services or cope adequately with urban problems. Mayor Landrieu of New Orleans declared, "We don't have enough money even to put a coat of paint on our problems."[35]

One obvious malady that the urban South faced after World War II was an ascending crime rate. In 1958 *Time* magazine tagged Houston with the unwelcome epithet of "Murdertown, USA." During the following decade two of the most infamous political assassinations of the twentieth century took place in Dallas and Memphis, respectively. In 1970 Ramsey Clark, the former attorney general, announced that the homicide rate in the South was double the national average. During the early 1970s this trend continued. In several sociological analyses, Atlanta, Houston, and New Orleans vied with Cleveland, Detroit, and other major American cities for the dubious title of murder capital of the United States. Throughout the region few weekends passed in urban areas without a killing or a serious shooting. The occurrence of rape, aggravated assault, robbery, narcotics use, gambling, and prostitution also displayed a sharp upswing that population increases only compounded.[36]

This rapidly climbing crime rate, however, seemingly did not disturb the majority of southern urbanites. The depleted ranks of municipal police departments vividly reflected the almost lackadaisical attitude toward acts of violence that existed in the urban South. In 1966, for example, the International Association of Chiefs of Police recommended 2,600 police officers for a city of Houston's size. The Bayou City force, however, numbered only 1,342. In 1961 sociologist Henry Allen Bullock attributed the casual southern view of crime partially to "a frontiersman's reliance upon himself for survival." Historian William D. Miller later pointed to "the agrarian feudal myth of the Old South" and "a homicidal sensitivity about 'honor,' 'bravery,' and, above all, white womanhood. . . ." The heavy involvement of blacks in violent and nonviolent crimes also contributed to the southern outlook. A study of homicides in Houston indicated that 62 percent of the assailants and 61 percent of the victims were black. A similar examination of Atlanta census tracts revealed that the heaviest concentrations of murders, aggravated assaults, robberies, and burglaries occurred in predominantly black neighborhoods. Because blacks were the primary sufferers from crime, many whites, particularly suburban residents who had fled the cities' troubles, remained unaffected and chose to ignore the problem. This viewpoint changed only when whites were the victims of black violence as in the cases of the Black Panthers and Mark Essex in New Orleans.

Throughout the post-World War II period social scientists continually recommended extensive improvements in the social and economic status of blacks to alleviate the problem of urban crime, but these plans commonly met fierce opposition from southern leaders who summarily rejected any proposed alterations to the existing social order. Most southern cities, furthermore, did not have the funds to finance these changes, regardless of public opinion.[37]

The rapid metropolitan expansion that overextended municipal treasuries and law enforcement agencies also produced other urban problems in the South. During the three decades after World War II, deteriorating school systems, inadequate fire protection, poor housing and medical facilities, corruption, overcrowded transit lines and municipal thoroughfares, labor disputes, air pollution, and faulty water supplies became characteristic of southern cities and urban centers throughout the country. The case of New Orleans demonstrated the commonality of urban problems in the United States. During the 1970s the Louisiana port, despite civic efforts to boast its uniqueness, experienced typical urban crises and repeatedly affirmed its kinship with other major American cities. In 1970 the police raid on the Desire project highlighted housing problems in New Orleans. In Desire small black children regularly swam in sewers and played among uncollected heaps of garbage. Other housing projects in the city were equally dismal. Educational problems also evinced racial overtones. After school integration in 1960 many white parents moved their families to the suburbs and enrolled their children in private and parochial schools. By 1970 these shifts had caused a frightening resegregation in New Orleans public schools. In 1972 most city schools were either predominantly black or predominantly white, and blacks numbered 70 percent of the total enrollment. (In Atlanta the figure was 85 percent.) One Crescent City liberal stated: "Nobody cares about the school system. There's violence in the school corridors, and policemen have to be assigned to keep order in the heavily black schools."[38]

The race question, however, was not primary to all municipal problems in New Orleans. On November 29, 1972, a flash fire on the top floors of the Rault Center in the downtown business district turned the sixteen-story structure into a towering inferno and exposed the frailty of fire protection in an era of high-rise office buildings and apartments. Firemen and a stunned television audience watched helplessly as three entrapped secretaries leaped to their deaths from the fifteenth floor. The desperate women panicked and jumped because city fire equipment could not reach them. Fire Chief Louis San Salvador lamented, "We were three stories too short." Helicopters rescued those who fought their way to the roof.

Two years later Crescent City residents received another jolt when the Environmental Protection Agency reported that the water supplies of New Orleans, Cincinnati, and several other cities contained potentially cancer-causing chemicals. The following month, December 1974, a city-wide transit strike virtually paralyzed the entire metropolitan area. Commuters flooded the access highways into New Orleans with private vehicles, and downtown business district took a severe economic beating. The strike lasted until early 1975. On February 28, 1975, a white sniper in the famous French Quarter proved that all urban violence did not have racial origins when he killed two people and shot several others before police fatally wounded him. To citizens of Atlanta, Houston, and Memphis as well as those in New York and Los Angeles, the news releases from New Orleans undoubtedly seemed sickeningly familiar.[39]

In 1962 and again in 1964 the United States Supreme Court offered new hope to the urban South for the solution of these problems when it advanced the principle of one-man-one-vote in the cases of *Baker* v. *Carr* and *Reynolds* v. *Sims,* respectively. These decisions legally ended malapportionment in the South and promised to give southern cities greater representation in state and national politics. The early effects of the two rulings were encouraging. In Georgia the county-unit system became an anachronism. In Virginia growing urban representation undermined the power of Harry Byrd's rural-based political organization. A corollary to reapportionment was the rise of urban blacks in southern politics. In Georgia Julian Bond of Atlanta stormed his way into the state legislature. In Louisiana Dorothy Mae Taylor of New Orleans became the first black woman to enter the state House of Representatives. On the national scene Congress responded to increased urban pressure with the enactment of the first general revenue sharing bill in 1972. Crescent City Mayor Landrieu, chairman of the Legislative Action Committee of the United States Conference of Mayors, was an important leader in several legislative confrontations that preceded passage of the law.[40]

Reapportionment certainly increased urban representation in regional and national legislatures, but it did not fulfill its great expectations. The addition of blacks to urban delegations frequently destroyed much of the unity that had previously existed. Urban legislators suddenly discovered that the differences between themselves and their suburbanite colleagues were as great as the traditional urban-rural cleavages. Representatives of the white suburbs, furthermore, learned that rural conservatives were ready and willing allies in any legislative debates with urbanites, particularly blacks. These new alignments often precipitated the accurate comment that reapportionment did little to alter legislative policy in the South.[41]

Another reason for the disappointing consequences of legislative reapportionment was the dissimilarity of southern cities. Although all American cities to some degree shared expectations and difficulties, major urban centers and secondary cities in the South were not alike. Big cities in the region were often closely in tune with their counterparts in other sections of the nation. Throughout the United States the spatial configurations, architecture, urban problems, and racial compositions of major cities were usually much the same. In the South the heavy influx of national corporations, outside capital, and new residents further blurred regional distinctions. Travelers who roamed the country soon discovered that a Holiday Inn in Atlanta was not much different from the franchise representative in Los Angeles, and that a McDonald's hamburger tasted remarkably alike in both places. After World War II the proliferation of these homogeneous characteristics on a nationwide basis served only to thrust large southern cities into the mainstream of American urban civilization. By 1970 evidence of a regional heritage in the metropolitan South survived mainly in souvenir shops, museums, and political oratory.

Secondary southern cities exhibited more diversity. Many reflected national urban trends. In 1973 a black man became mayor of Raleigh. In Huntsville the expansion of aerospace industries created an economic resurgence and altered the complexion of the community. In 1970 James G. Haney of PPG Industries contended: "Huntsville had everything we were looking for. It was completely integrated. It had an excellent school system, and the city, though not large, had a cosmopolitan atmosphere."[42]

Other secondary cities retained a definite southern flavor that featured overt racial segregation and prejudice, religious orthodoxy, close ties with agriculture, and reverence for womanhood. In October 1974 the Council of Municipal Performance reported that six southern cities—Shreveport, Winston-Salem, Charlotte, Augusta, Montgomery, and Dallas—had the most racially segregated housing in the country. All except Dallas were secondary southern cities. Shreveport, the second largest city in Louisiana, with a population of 182,064, ranked first among the most segregated urban areas in the country and presented a good example of a secondary southern city that maintained a traditional regional outlook. In the 1970s the ruling commission council of Shreveport displayed a white dominance that mirrored local attitudes. On June 12, 1975, twenty years after the censure of Senator Joseph McCarthy and six years after the death of Leander Perez, the *Shreveport Journal* printed a reader's letter on school busing which declared that federal judges "have done more to help the Communist cause than all the Communists in the United States." In the north Louisiana city the appointment of new ministers, especially Baptists and Methodists, commonly merited extensive coverage in the local press, and in several suburban neighborhoods modern apartment complexes and cotton fields coexisted on adjacent lots. On June 11, 1975, Shreveport representatives to the state legislature voiced their opinions on the role of women in American society when they voted unanimously against the Equal Rights Amendment (ERA). The leading proponent of the ERA in Louisiana was Dorothy Mae Taylor.[43]

The disparate nature of southern cities frequently frustrated legislative attempts to solve urban problems and forced the great metropolitan centers of the region to seek their own solutions. In Houston annexation of surrounding suburbs provided one answer to decreasing municipal revenues. In 1930 the city had an area of 72 square miles. Thirty-seven years later the figure was almost 447 square miles.[44] In early 1975 Mayor Maynard Jackson of Altanta also suggested annexation as a means of easing his city's financial difficulties, but he immediately encountered opposition from his strongest black supporters. Although the incorporation of nearby communities into the city of Atlanta would increase the municipal tax base, the addition of predominantly white suburbs would also reduce black voting power.

Mayor Jackson proposed other solutions to Atlanta's fiscal troubles. In April 1975 he and representatives of the Atlanta Chamber of Commerce toured Europe to attract new industry to the Georgia metropolis. The mayor also advocated an increase in property taxes.[45] Many Atlanta residents, however, have focused their hopes on the Metropolitan Atlanta Rapid Transit Authority (MARTA), a new agency that has developed an integrated mass transit plan for the metropolitan counties of De Kalb and Fulton. This new system will provide 90 percent of the residents in the two counties with access to rapid, inexpensive mass transit facilities. Advocates of the proposal believe that mass rapid transit will ease the burdens of heavy vehicular traffic, encourage suburbanites to shop in the city, and permit inner city residents to seek better jobs in the urban fringe. Many foresee that MARTA will rejuvenate downtown Atlanta.[46]

In Miami the answer to suburban sprawl and administrative confusion was metropolitan government. In 1959 Dade County used its extensive home-rule powers to unite its twenty-seven individual municipalities under a federal form of government. The separate municipalities retained control over police and fire protection, parks, garbage collection, and zoning, but the metro government acquired power over the water supply, sewers, transportation, and central planning. In 1963 several of the municipalities joined in an unsuccessful attempt to destroy the federal system, but their failure only strengthened the unique government. Under the metro plan, the voters elect a councilman from each of nine separate districts. One of these council members becomes mayor, but a professional city manager actually supervises metropolitan administration. Although the system has encountered problems with tax equalization and the water supply, in 1969 a University of Miami study stated that the new plan "transformed an obsolete and anachronous commission form of government into a first-rate, high caliber administration. . . ."[47]

In New Orleans the keys to the regeneration of the business district have been the tourist and a gigantic domed stadium–convention center complex called the Louisiana Superdome. Scheduled for completion in 1975 after a long series of labor disputes, delays, and charges of malfeasance, the $163 million stadium with plush penthouse suites, six interior wide-angle television screens, and an artificial playing surface will ultimately house major sporting events, national conventions, and Mardi Gras celebrations. The dome and a controversial renovation of the old French Market have already triggered a flurry of new hotel construction in the downtown business district. Although the razing of several famous old buildings and the construction of modern multistoried hotels have encountered vocal opposition from television personality Dick Cavett and local preservationists, Mayor Landrieu and the Crescent City progressives will undoubtedly hold sway. In June 1975 government officials predicted that the domed stadium will lose $5 million during its first year of operation, but they quickly added that it will also attract $150 million in tourist revenue to the local economy. Those, needless to say, were figures that Mayor Landrieu and Crescent City businessmen applauded.[48]

In late 1975 the ultimate impact of these diversified projects upon their respective communities remained to be seen, but the construction of the Louisiana Superdome, the organization of MARTA, and the institution of urban federalism, products of civic pride and urban needs, clearly marked the arrival of the southern metropolis. After 1940 the urban South that regional observers had forecast for so many years became a concrete reality. In 1970 census reports indicated that eight of the former Confederate states had urban majorities, and five southern metropolitan areas had over one million inhabitants.[49] Urban growth in the South admittedly fostered inner city decay, racial tension, suburban sprawl, and governmental confusion, but these problems only reaffirmed the South's entry into the national urban pattern. In 1976 southerners, with alternate feelings of achievement and anxiety, realized that the present as well as the future of their region rested in its cities.

NOTES

Chapter One
Blaine A. Brownell and David R. Goldfield
Southern Urban History

1. Richard Hildreth, *Despotism in America: An Inquiry into the Nature, Results, and Legal Basis of the Slave-Holding System in the United States* (Boston, 1854): 139.
2. David L. Smiley, "The Quest for a Central Theme in Southern History," *South Atlantic Quarterly* 62 (summer 1972): 318; Raimondo Luraghi, "The Civil War and the Modernization of American Society," *Civil War History* 18 (September 1972): 236.
3. For a brief summary of recent scholarship, see Blaine A. Brownell, "Urbanization in the South: A Unique Experience?" *Mississippi Quarterly* 26 (spring 1973): 105-20.
4. For some recent attempts, see Sheldon Hackney, "The South as a Counterculture," *American Scholar* 42 (spring 1973): 283-93; Michael C. O'Brien, "C. Vann Woodward and the Burden of Southern Liberalism," *American Historical Review* 78 (June 1973): 589-604; Smiley, 307-25; George Brown Tindall, "Beyond the Mainstream: The Ethnic Southerners," *Journal of Southern History* 40 (February 1974): 3-18.
5. Quoted in Hennig Cohen, review of Grady McWhiney, *Southerners and Other Americans,* in *American Historical Review* 79 (April 1974): 582-83.
6. Ralph Ellison, *Invisible Man* (New York, 1952).
7. Tindall, 3-18.
8. See, for example, George Fitzhugh, *Sociology for the South, or, The Failure of Free Society* (New York, 1854): 136, 158.
9. Quoted in Charles Garofalo, "The Atlanta Spirit: A Study in Urban Ideology," *South Atlantic Quarterly* 74 (winter 1975): 37.
10. Carl N. Degler, *The Other South: Southern Dissenters in the Nineteenth Century* (New York, 1974): 3.
11. Sinclair Lewis, *Babbitt* (New York, 1922): 154.
12. Richard S. Alcorn, "Leadership and Stability in Mid-Nineteenth Century: A Case Study of an Illinois Town," *Journal of American History* 61 (December 1974): 685-702.
13. For an interesting view of the urban reformer in antebellum Virginia, see J. Stephen Knight, Jr., "Discontent, Disunity, and Dissent in the Antebellum South: Virginia as a Test Case, 1844-1846," *Virginia Magazine of History and Biography* 78 (October 1970): 437-50.
14. Quoted in Garofalo, 42.
15. See Robert R. Russel, "Southern Secessionists *Per Se* and the Crisis of 1850," in Russel, *Critical Studies in Antebellum Sectionalism: Essays in American Political and Economic History* (Westport, Conn., 1972): 75-86.
16. Allan R. Pred, *Urban Growth and the Circulation of Information: The United States System of Cities, 1790-1840* (Cambridge, Mass., 1973). Employing various communications

models, Pred identifies three urban subsystems in the United States which were reasonably well articulated and economically integrated by 1840: the northeastern subsystem, the Lake Erie subsystem, and the Ohio and upper Mississippi valley subsystem.

17. See Paul M. Gaston, *The New South Creed: A Study in Southern Mythmaking* (New York, 1970).

18. Robert William Fogel and Stanley L. Engerman, *Time on the Cross: The Economics of American Negro Slavery* (Boston and Toronto, 1974); Gunnar Myrdal, *An American Dilemma*, 2 vols. (New York, 1944).

19. See W. E. B. Du Bois, *The Philadelphia Negro* (Philadelphia, 1899), and the Atlanta University publications. Among the most notable recent studies of northern urban blacks are David M. Katzman, *Before the Ghetto: Black Detroit in the Nineteenth Century* (Urbana, Ill., 1973); Gilbert Osofsky, *Harlem: The Making of a Ghetto: Negro New York, 1890-1930* (New York, 1966); Allan H. Spear, *Black Chicago: The Making of a Negro Ghetto, 1890-1920* (Chicago, 1967).

20. Richard C. Wade, *Slavery in the Cities: The South, 1820-1860* (New York, 1964). For an interesting critique of Wade's interpretation, see Claudia Dale Goldin, "Urbanization and Slavery: The Issue of Compatibility," in Leo F. Schnore (ed.), *The New Urban History: Quantitative Explorations by American Historians* (Princeton, 1975): 231-46.

21. Herbert G. Gutman, "The World Two Cliometricians Made: A Review Essay of F + E + $\frac{T}{C}$," *Journal of Negro History* 60 (January 1975): 53-227.

22. John W. Blassingame, *Black New Orleans, 1860-1880* (Chicago, 1973): Zane L. Miller, "Urban Blacks in the South, 1865-1920: The Richmond, Savannah, New Orleans, Louisville and Birmingham Experience," in Schnore, 184-204. Also see Miller's review essay, "Urban Blacks in the Post-Civil War South," *Journal of Urban History* 1 (February 1975): 247-51.

23. Ira Berlin, *Slaves without Masters: The Free Negro in the Antebellum South* (New York, 1974).

24. See Walter B. Weare's perceptive study, *Black Business in the New South: A Social History of the North Carolina Mutual Life Insurance Company* (Urbana, Ill., 1973).

25. Chandler Davidson, *Biracial Politics: Conflict and Coalition in the Metropolitan South* (Baton Rouge, 1972).

26. Quoted in Robert Coles, *Farewell to the South* (Boston, 1972).

27. Both Lampard and Hobsbawm quoted in Lynn H. Lees, "The Study of Cities and the Study of Social Process: Two Directions in Recent Urban History," *Journal of Social History* 7 (spring 1974): 330.

28. Ibid., 333.

29. See, for example, Pred; Richard D. Brown, "The Emergence of Urban Society in Rural Massachusetts, 1760-1820," *Journal of American History* 61 (June 1974): 29-51; Ronald C. Tobey, "How Urbane is the Urbanite? An Historical Model of the Urban Hierarchy and the Social Motivation of Service Classes," *Historical Methods Newsletter* 7 (September 1974): 259-75.

30. Mark Abrahamson and Michael Dubick, "Historical Patterns of City Dominance: The U. S. in 1890," Occasional Paper no. 18, Metropolitan Studies Program, Syracuse, N. Y., April 1975.

31. Pred.

32. Seymour J. Mandelbaum, *Boss Tweed's New York* (New York, 1965).

33. Richard M. Bernard, "A Portrait of Baltimore in 1800: Economic and Occupational Patterns in an Early American City," *Maryland Historical Magazine* 69 (winter 1974): 341-60.

34. Sam Bass Warner, Jr., *Streetcar Suburbs: The Process of Growth in Boston, 1870-1900* (Cambridge, Mass., 1962).

35. Maygene Daniels, "District of Columbia Building Permits," *American Archivist* 38 (January 1975): 23-30.

36. Tamara K. Hareven, "The Historical Study of the Family in Urban Society," *Journal of Urban History* 1 (May 1975): 262.

37. See, for example, Nathan I. Huggins, *Protestants against Poverty: Boston's Charities, 1870-1900* (Westport, Conn., 1971).

38. See James E. Vance, Jr., "Focus on Downtown," in Larry S. Bourne (ed.), *Internal Structure of the City: Readings on Space and Environment* (New York, 1971): 112-20.

194 / NOTES

39. Warner; Kenneth T. Jackson, "The Crabgrass Frontier: 150 Years of Suburban Growth in America," in Raymond A. Mohl and James F. Richardson (eds.), *The Urban Experience: Themes in American History* (Belmont, Cal., 1973): 162-221.
40. See Timothy J. Crimmins and Dana F. White, "Urban Structure, Atlanta," *Journal of Urban History* 2 (February 1976): Howard L. Preston, "A New Kind of Horizontal City: Automobility in Atlanta, 1900-1930" (Ph.D. dissertation, Emory University, 1974).
41. See Richard J. Hopkins, "Are Southern Cities Unique? Persistence As a Clue," *Mississippi Quarterly* 26 (spring 1973): 121-41; Richard J. Hopkins, "Status, Mobility, and the Dimensions of Change in a Southern City: Atlanta, 1870-1910," in Kenneth T. Jackson and Stanley K. Schultz (eds.), *Cities in American History* (New York, 1972): 216-31.
42. Robert P. Swierenga, "Towards the 'New Rural History': A Review Essay," *Historical Methods Newsletter* 6 (June 1973): 111-22; Michael P. Conzen, *Frontier Farming in an Urban Shadow: The Influence of Madison's Proximity on the Agricultural Development of Blooming Grove, Wisconsin* (Madison, Wis., 1971).
43. Richard P. McCormick, "The Comparative Method: Its Application to American History," *Mid-America* 56 (October 1974): 231-47.

Chapter Two
Carville Earle and Ronald Hoffman
The Urban South: The First Two Centuries

The authors wish to thank Joanne Giza and Sally Mason for their assistance in the preparation of this essay.

1. Maxine Fern Neustadt, "Proprietary Purposes in the Anglo-American Colonies: Problems in the Transplantation of English Patterns of Social Organization" (Ph.D. dissertation, University of Wisconsin, 1968): 526, 543; Converse D. Clowse, *Economic Beginnings in Colonial South Carolina, 1670-1730* (Columbia, 1971): 67.
2. Langdon Cheves (ed.), *The Shaftesbury Papers and Other Records Relating to Carolina, and First Settlement on the Ashley River Prior to the Year 1676*, in Collections of the South Carolina Historical Society (Charleston, 1897): 120.
3. Verner W. Crane, *The Southern Frontier, 1670-1732* (Durham. N. C., 1928): 4.
4. W. L. Saunders (ed.), *Colonial Records of North Carolina* (Raleigh, 1886-90), 1: 1229.
5. Earl of Shaftesbury to Sir John Yeamans, April 10, 1671; September 18, 1671; Cheves, 315, 342-44; see also Shaftesbury to William Sayle, April 10, 1671: 310-12.
6. Peter Clark and Paul Slack (eds.), *Crisis and Order in English Towns, 1500-1700: Essays in Urban History* (London, 1972): 31.
7. W. G. Hoskins, *Provincial England: Essays in Social and Economic History* (London, 1964): 81; Clark and Slack, 146.
8. Neustadt, 571.
9. Ibid.
10. Ibid., 569.
11. Ibid., 585-86; Carl and Roberta Bridenbaugh, *No Peace Beyond the Line: The English in the Caribbean, 1624-1690* (New York, 1972): 11; Agnes Leland Baldwin, *First Settlers of South Carolina, 1670-1680* (Columbia, 1969).
12. Joan Thirsk, "Industries in the Countryside," in F. J. Fisher (ed.), *Essays in the Economic and Social History of Tudor and Stuart England* (Cambridge, 1961): 70-88; Clark and Slack, 11; Hoskins, 132.
13. These instructions, given in 1606, are printed in Alexander Brown, *The Genesis of the United States,* 2 vols. (Boston, 1890) 1: 79-85.
14. Brown, 1: 353-56. The idea of an elaborate division of labor in the New World goes back at least to Richard Hakluyt's "Discourse of Western Planting" written in 1584. E. G. R. Taylor (ed.), *The Original Writings and Correspondence of the Two Richard Hakluyts,* 2nd ser.: 76-77 (London, 1935) 2: 323-34, 327-38.
15. Sigmund Diamond, "From Organization to Society: Virginia in the Seventeenth Century," *American Journal of Sociology* 63 (1958): 457-75; Irene W. D. Hecht, "The Virginia Colony, 1607-1640: A Study in Frontier Growth," (Ph.D. dissertation, University of Washington, 1969): 1-62; Edmund S. Morgan, "The Labor Problem at

Jamestown, 1607-1618," *American Historical Review* 76: (1971): 595-611; Nancy O. Lurie, "Indian Cultural Adjustment to European Civilization," in J. M. Smith (ed.), *Seventeenth-Century America* (Chapel Hill, N. C., 1959): 33-60; Gary B. Nash, "The Image of the Indian in the Southern Colonial Mind," *William and Mary Quarterly*, 3rd ser. 29 (1972): 197-230.

16. Treasurer and Council for Virginia: Letter to Governor and Council in Virginia, August 1, 1622; quoted in John W. Reps, *Tidewater Towns: City Planning in Colonial Virginia and Maryland* (Williamsburg, Va., 1972): 46.

17. John C. Rainbolt, "The Absence of Towns in Seventeenth-Century Virginia," *Journal of Southern History* 35 (1969): 343-60; Reps: 92-116; Edward M. Riley, "The Town Acts of Colonial Virginia," *Journal of Southern History* 16 (1950): 306-23.

18. *Archives of Maryland*, ed. William Hand Brown and others, 72 vols. (Baltimore, 1883 to present), 5: 268. For similar views, see Henry Hartwell, James Blair, and Edward Chilton, *The Present State of Virginia, and the College*, ed. Hunter Dickinson Farish (Charlottesville, Va., 1964): 8-16; Francis Makemie, "A Persuasive to Towns and Cohabitation," *Virginia Magazine of History and Biography* 4 (1897): 252-71; "Report of the Journey of Francis Louis Michel, from Berne, Switzerland, to Virginia, October 2, 1701-December 1, 1702, part 1," *Virginia Magazine of History and Biography* 24 (1916): 30-31.

19. Michael G. Kammen (ed.), "Maryland in 1699: A Letter from the Reverend Hugh Jones," *Journal of Southern History* 29 (1963): 368.

20. On barter between supercargoes and planters, see George Alsop, "A Character of the Province of Maryland, 1666," *Narratives of Early Maryland, 1633-84*, ed. Clayton Colman Hall (New York, 1959): 363. On the extent of the consignment trade in the seventeenth century, see Carville V. Earle, *The Evolution of a Tidewater Settlement System: All Hallows Parish, Maryland, 1650-1783*, Department of Geography Research Paper no. 170 (Chicago, 1975): 164-65, ch. 6; Philip Alexander Bruce, *Economic History of Virginia in the Seventeenth Century*, 2 vols., (New York, 1935), 2: 522-65.

21. Kammen, 371. Hartwell, Blair, and Chilton, 9.

22. See Mildred Campbell, "Social Origins of Some Early Americans," in Smith, 63-89; H. Roy Merrens and Carville V. Earle, *Historical Geography of the Southern Colonies* (forthcoming), ch. 2.

23. Quoted in Joan Thirsk, *The Agrarian History of England and Wales, 1500-1640*, (London, 1967), chap. 3.

24. Within a decade of their founding, Boston contained about 8% of Massachusetts's population, and Philadelphia about 33% of Pennsylvania's. Carl Bridenbaugh, *Cities in the Wilderness: Urban Life in America, 1625-1742* (New York, 1964), 6; Bernard Bailyn, *The New England Merchants in the Seventeenth Century* (New York, 1964): 32-39. Population figures for these two colonies come from U. S. Department of Commerce and Labor, Bureau of the Census, *A Century of Population Growth, from the First Census of the United States to the Twelfth, 1790-1900*, by W. S. Rossiter (Washington, D. C., 1909): 3-15.

25. On the relations between tobacco price fluctuations and the development of plantation self-sufficiency, see Earle, 101-35. Declining opportunities for servants after 1660 are documented in Russell R. Menard, "From Servant to Freeholder: Property Accumulation and Social Mobility in Seventeenth-Century Maryland," *William and Mary Quarterly*, 3rd ser., 30 (1973): 37-64.

26. Rainbolt, 343-60; Reps, 65-116.

27. Governor Nicholson to Council of Trade and Plantations, March 27, 1697, *Calendar of State Papers, Colonial Series*, 44 vols. (London, 1860-) 15: 421.

28. Lois Green Carr, "The Metropolis of Maryland: A Comment on Town Development along the Tobacco Coast," *Maryland Historical Magazine* 69 (1974): 124-45.

29. Evarts B. Greene and Virginia D. Harrington, *American Population before the Federal Census of 1790* (Gloucester, Mass., 1966): 127, 148-49; Carr, 124-45.

30. Hugh Jones, *The Present State of Virginia*, ed. Richard L. Morton (Chapel Hill, N. C., 1956): 66.

31. Kammen, 372.

32. "Report of the Journey of Francis Louis Michel," 26.

33. Reps, 65-116.

34. For evidence of this decentralized settlement system, see Earle, 78-91.

35. Herbert R. Paschal, Jr., "Proprietary North Carolina: A Study in Colonial Government" (Ph.D. dissertation, University of North Carolina, 1961): 591-92; Mattie Erma Edwards Parker (ed.), *North Carolina Charters and Constitutions* (Raleigh, 1963).

36. Robert K. Ackerman, "South Carolina Colonial Land Policies" (Ph.D. dissertation, University of South Carolina, 1965): 29, 34; Clowse, 47-49.

37. Council in the Carolinas to Lords Proprietors, March 27, 1670, Cheves, 284.

38. Joseph Dalton to Earl of Shaftesbury January 20, 1671, ibid., 380.

39. Earl of Shaftesbury to Governor William Sayle, April 10, 1671, ibid., 311.

40. Earl of Shaftesbury to Sir John Yeamans, December 15, 1671, ibid., 360.

41. The Proprietors to the Governor and Council at the Ashley River, May 18, 1674, ibid., 438.

42. Clowse, 67.

43. Proprietors to Governor and Council, June 31, 1684, *Records in the British Public Records Relating to South Carolina, 1663-1710* (Atlanta and Columbia, 1928-1947) 1: 291-92.

44. Baldwin.

45. Thomas Newe to Father, August 23, 1682, "Letters of Thomas Newe," *American Historical Review* 12 (1907): 324.

46. H. Roy Merrens, *Colonial North Carolina in the Eighteenth Century: A Study in Historical Geography* (Chapel Hill, N. C., 1964): 147-54.

47. Merrens, 147-54; Lawrence Lee, *The Lower Cape Fear in Colonial Days* (Chapel Hill, N. C., 1965): 117-32, 141; Duane Gilbert Meyer, *The Highland Scots of North Carolina*, (Raleigh, N. C., 1963): 71, 72.

48. J. F. D. Smyth, *Tour of the United States of America*, 2 vols. (London, 1785) 2: 98-99; Charles Crittenden, *The Commerce of North Carolina, 1763-1789* (New York, 1936): 75.

49. Thomas Newe to Father, May 29, 1682, 322.

50. Carl Bridenbaugh, *Cities in the Wilderness; Urban Life in America, 1625-1742* (New York, 1938): 6, 143, 204; Greene and Harrington, 172; Clowse, 251.

51. John Oldmixon, *The British Empire in America* . . . , 2 vols. (2nd ed., 1741): 1:512.

52. Johann David Shoepf, *Travels in the Confederation*, 2 vols. (Baltimore, 1911), 2: 172.

53. John Duffy, "Eighteenth-Century Carolina Health Conditions," *Journal of Southern History* 18 (1952): 289-302; see also St. Julien R. Childs, *Malaria and Colonization in the Carolina Low Country* (Baltimore, 1940).

54. Alexander Hewatt, *An Historical Account of the Rise and Progress of the Colonies of South Carolina and Georgia*, (London: A. Donaldson, 1779) 2: 289.

55. Crane, 22, 29, 65-67.

56. Clowse, 139, 159, 227, 243.

57. Report of Governor Nathaniel Johnson and Council, 1708, quoted in William J. Rivers, *A Sketch of the History of South Carolina, from Its First Settlement in 1670, to the Year 1808,* 2 vols. (Charleston, 1856), 1: 233-38.

58. Chapman J. Milling (ed.), "A Description of South Carolina by James Glen," in *Colonial South Carolina: Two Contemporary Descriptions* (Columbia, 1951): 56-58.

59. Ibid., 36.

60. Charles Joseph Gayle, "The Nature and Volume of Exports from Charleston 1724-1774," in Robert L. Meriwether (ed.), *Proceedings of the South Carolina Historical Association* (1937), 25.

61. Quoted in Hewatt, 2: 294.

62. Merrens, 156.

63. Robert L. Meriwether, *The Expansion of South Carolina, 1729-1765* (Kingsport, Tenn., 1940): 19, 36, 51, 84, 87-89; M. Eugene Sirmans, *Colonial South Carolina: A Political History, 1663-1763* (Chapel Hill, N. C., 1966): 32, 161-62; Ackerman, 135, 140, 142-43.

64. Meriwether, *The Expansion of South Carolina*, 89.

65. Joseph A. Ernst and H. Roy Merrens, "Camden's Turrets Pierce the Skies! The Urban Process in the Southern Colonies during the Eighteenth Century," *William and Mary Quarterly*, 3rd ser., 30 (1973): 559.

66. U. S. Bureau of the Census, *Historical Statistics of the United States, Colonial Times to 1957* (Washington, D. C., 1960): 766.

67. Earle, 77-100.

68. Jacob M. Price, *France and the Chesapeake: A History of the French Tobacco Monopoly*,

1674-1791, and of its Relationship to the British and American Tobacco Trades, 2 vols. (Ann Arbor, Mich., 1973), 1: 178-85, 509-30; and the same author's "The Rise of Glasgow in the Chesapeake Tobacco Trade, 1707-1775," *William and Mary Quarterly,* 3rd ser., 9 (1954): 179-99.

69. Price, "Rise of Glasgow," 179-99; Robert Polk Thomson, "The Merchant in Virginia, 1700-1775," (Ph.D. dissertation, University of Wisconsin, 1955): 157-99; Paul G. E. Clemens, "From Tobacco to Grain: Economic Development on Maryland's Eastern Shore, 1660-1750," (Ph.D. dissertation, University of Wisconsin, 1974).

70. Earle, 77-100.

71. *Archives of Maryland,* 7: 609-19.

72. Kammen, 371.

73. *Archives of Maryland,* 7: 554, 601; 38: 23-25.

74. Earle, 89-91.

75. Higginson and Bird to Patrick Sympson, December 2, 1718, *Bird Letterbook,* no. 1727.

76. Annapolis, Hall of Records MSS, Anne Arundel County Deeds, WC #1, ff. 33-36, hereafter cited as AACo Deeds; Annapolis, Hall of Records MSS, Inventories, 79, ff. 34-38.

77. AACo Deeds, RD #2, f. 76; SY #1, ff. 297, 321; CW #1, ff. 5, 227, 499-505; RCW #2, ff. 223-24; RD #1, ff. 16-19; Annapolis, Hall of Records MSS, Judgments, G, f. 646; *Maryland Gazette,* March 10, 1730.

78. Arthur E. Karinen, "Numerical and Distributional Aspects of Maryland Population, 1631-1840" (Ph.D. dissertation, University of Maryland, 1958): 195.

79. Earle, 157-69.

80. Ibid., 92-95.

81. "Journal of a French Traveller in the Colonies, 1765, II," *American Historical Review* 27 (1921): 71; Lord Adam Gordon, "Journal of an Officer Who Travelled in America and the West Indies in 1764 and 1765," *Travels in the American Colonies,* ed. Newton D. Mereness (New York, 1916), 409; J. F. D. Smyth, *A Tour in the United States of America,* 2 vols. (London, 1784): 2: 211.

82. Earle, 14-18.

83. Vertrees J. Wyckoff, *Tobacco Regulation in Colonial Maryland,* Johns Hopkins University Studies in Historical and Political Science, no. 22 (1936); Arthur Pierce Middleton, *Tobacco Coast: A Maritime History of Chesapeake Bay in the Colonial Era* (Newport News, Va., 1953): 120-26.

84. *Archives of Maryland* 58: 486; 46: 19; 56: 47, 49, 132; AACo Judgments, ISB #2, ff. 429, 761.

85. Earle, 175-81.

86. John Davis, *Travels of Four Years* (London, 1785): 213. Although Ronald Hoffman's *A Spirit of Dissension: Economics, Politics and the Revolution in Maryland* (Baltimore, 1973) contains much of the information on Baltimore, the primary citations are repeated here for the convenience of interested students.

87. Thomas W. Griffith, *Annals of Baltimore* (Baltimore, 1824), 14. For a genuinely clever and perceptive essay on the port of Baltimore's growth, see C. P. Gould, "The Economic Causes of the Rise of Baltimore," in *Essays in Colonial History Presented to Charles McLean Andrews by His Students* (New Haven, 1931): 225-51.

88. Thomas Scharf, *Chronicles of Baltimore* (Baltimore, 1874): 56.

89. Governor Horatio Sharpe to Secretary Cecil Calvert, August 22, 1764, *Archives of Maryland* 61: 567.

90. William Lux to Isaac and John Simon, January 15, 1767, William Lux Letterbook, New York Historical Society, New York, N. Y. (cited hereafter as WLLB).

91. Ibid.

92. William Lux to Mrs. S. Lux, July 15, 1768, WLLB.

93. "Petition against Removal of County Seat of Baltimore from Joppa to Baltimoretown 1768," *Archives of Maryland* 61: 567.

94. Ibid.

95. "Commissioners of Customs in America Respecting a Controversy between the Collectors of Patuxent and Chester, September 28, 1772," Fisher Transcripts, Maryland Historical Society, Baltimore (cited hereafter as MHS).

96. For yearly totals on Maryland port exports, see appendices in Ronald Hoffman, "Economics, Politics and the Revolution in Maryland" (Ph.D. dissertation, University of Wisconsin, 1969).

97. *Maryland Gazette,* April 2, 1767.
98. William Lux to Isaac and John Simon, January 15, 1767, WLLB.
99. James Weston Livingood, *The Philadelphia-Baltimore Trade Rivalry, 1780-1860* (Harrisburg, 1947), 5.
100. Charles H. Lincoln, *The Revolutionary Movement in Pennsylvania, 1760-1776* (Philadelphia, 1901): 59-62.
101. Livingood, 5-10.
102. John Flexner Walzner, "Transportation in the Philadelphia Trading Area" (Ph.D. dissertation, University of Wisconsin, 1968): 57.
103. Clarence P. Gould, *Money and Transportation in Maryland, 1720-1765* (Baltimore, 1915): 127-29.
104. Griffith, 41.
105. *Maryland Gazette,* October 23, 1760.
106. William Molleson to Charles Ridgely, March 25, 1765, Ridgely Papers, MHS. William Lux to James Russell, July 3, 1765, WLLB.
107. Henry Dillon to Hollingsworth and Rudulph, April 18, 1770; Isaac Grist to Zebulon Hollingsworth, August 18, 1771; Samuel Purviance to Levi Hollingsworth, March 14, 1774; Jesse Hollingsworth to Thomas Hollingsworth, April 23, 1776, all in Hollingsworth Correspondence, Historical Society of Pennsylvania, Philadelphia; the Hollingsworth collection extensively documents the influential commercial and fiscal role of Philadelphia throughout the Atlantic seaboard.
108. John Smith to Warnbull and Co., December 3, 1774, Smith Letterbook, MHS; for more information concerning this competition, see George Woolsey to George Salmon, October 13, 1774, Woolsey and Salmon Letterbook; and Thomas Ringgold to John Galloway, October 21, 1774, Galloway Papers, both in Library of Congress, Washington, D. C.
109. Robert Gilmore, "The Autobiography of Robert Gilmore," Gilmore Papers, MHS.

Chapter Three
David R. Goldfield
Pursuing the American Urban Dream: Cities in the Old South

1. See Douglas C. North, *The Economic Growth of the United States, 1790-1860* (Englewood Cliffs, N. J., 1961); see also Louis B. Schmidt, "Internal Commerce and the Development of the National Economy before 1860," *Journal of Political Economy* 47 (December 1939): 798-822.
2. See David L. Smiley, "The Quest for a Central Theme in Southern History," *South Atlantic Quarterly* 62 (summer 1972): 307-25.
3. See, for example, D. Clayton James, *Antebellum Natchez* (Baton Rouge, 1968); David G. McComb, *Houston: The Bayou City* (Austin, 1969); Merl E. Reed, *New Orleans and the Railroads: The Struggle for Commercial Empire* (Baton Rouge, 1966); Kenneth W. Wheeler, *To Wear a City's Crown: The Beginnings of Urban Growth in Texas* (Cambridge, Mass., 1968); Blaine A. Brownell, "Urbanization in the South: A Unique Experience?" *Mississippi Quarterly* 26 (spring 1973): 105-20; Leonard P. Curry, "Urbanization and Urbanism in the Old South: A Comparative View," *Journal of Southern History* 40 (February 1974): 43-60; Lyle W. Dorsett and Arthur H. Shaffer, "Was the Antebellum South Antiurban? A Suggestion," *Journal of Southern History* 38 (February 1972): 93-100. The three articles contain extensive bibliographic references on the literature of the urban South.
4. Statistical references helpful to studies of the urban South include the U. S. Bureau of the Census, *Compendium of the Census* (1850 to 1870 for the antebellum era); "Progress of the Population in the United States," *Hunt's Merchants' Magazine and Commercial Review* 32 (February 1855): 191-95; Donald B. and Wynelle S. Dodd, *Historical Statistics of the South, 1790-1970* (University, Ala., 1973).
5. Curry, 43-60.
6. *Baltimore American,* n. d., quoted in *Alexandria Gazette,* May 9, 1859.
7. See Wyatt W. Belcher, *The Economic Rivalry between St. Louis and Chicago, 1850-1880* (New York, 1947); Julius Rubin, *Canal or Railroad: Imitation and Innovation in Response to the Erie Canal in Philadelphia, Baltimore, and Boston* (Philadelphia, 1961).
8. Charles W. Dabney to Robert L. Dabney, January 31, 1855, Charles W. Dabney MSS, Southern Historical Collection, University of North Carolina; *Richmond Enquirer,*

August 28, 1855; B. M. Jones, *Railroads: Considered in Regard to Their Effects upon the Value of Land in Increasing Production, Cheapening Transportation, Preventing Emigration and Investments for Capital* (Richmond, 1860).

9. Charles Sumner, "Influence of Railroads," *Hunt's* 26 (April 1852): 506-507; "Moral View of Railroads," *Hunt's* 27 (November 1852): 173.

10. See, for example, Eugene Genovese, *The Political Economy of Slavery* (New York, 1965); Fred Bateman, James Foust, and Thomas Weiss, "The Participation of Planters in Manufacturing in the Antebellum South," *Agricultural History* 48 (April 1974): 277-97; Alfred H. Conrad et al., "Slavery As an Obstacle to Economic Growth in the United States: A Panel Discussion," *Journal of Economic History* 27 (December 1967): 518-60.

11. See, for example, "Inventory and Appraisement of the Estate of William Massie, 1862," William Massie Notebooks MSS, Duke University Library; "Annual Meeting of the Stockholders of the Orange and Alexandria Railroad," *Alexandria Gazette,* October 23, 1857; see also Bateman et al., 277-97.

12. Reed, 88-89; Henry Varnum Poor, "Effect of Railroads on Commercial Cities," *Hunt's* 27 (August 1852): 249; George Fitzhugh, *Sociology for the South, or, The Failure of Free Society* (New York, 1854): 141-42.

13. *Charleston Courier,* August 31, 1836; Thomas D. Clark, "The Lexington & Ohio Railroad; A Pioneer Venture," *Register of the Kentucky Historical Society* 31 (1933): 9-28; Reed, 9; W. K. Wood, "The Georgia Railroad and Banking Company," *Georgia Historical Quarterly* 57 (winter 1973): 544-61.

14. *Portsmouth* (Va.) *Daily Pilot,* August 17, 1850; speech of Senator R. M. T. Hunter in U. S. Senate, quoted in *Richmond Enquirer,* April 5, 1850; *Lynchburg Virginian,* October 19, 1848; "Baltimore: Her Past and Present," *De Bow's Review 29* (September 1860): 291-93.

15. "Contests for the Trade of the Mississippi Valley," *De Bow's Review* 3 (February 1847): 98; George Fitzhugh, *Cannibals All! or, Slaves without Masters* (New York, 1857), 59; *Richmond Enquirer,* February 27, 1854.

16. William M. Burwell, "Virginia Commercial Convention," *De Bow's Review* 12 (January 1852): 30; John Y. Mason, "Letter to D. H. London, Esq.," *Southern Literary Messenger* 18 (October 1852): 588-92; "Contests," *De Bow's Review,* 98-108.

17. Reed; *Norfolk Southern Argus,* September 29, 1851.

18. U. S. Bureau of the Census, *Compendium of the Eighth Census: 1860: Mortality and Miscellaneous,* 4: 331.

19. "Railroads of the United States," *Hunt's* 28 (January 1853): 110-15; 41 (August 1859): 241.

20. *Portsmouth* (Va.) *Daily Pilot,* July 8, 1850.

21. "Foreign Trade of Virginia and the South," *De Bow's Review* 13 (November 1852): 493-503; "Baltimore," *De Bow's Review* 13 (November 1852): 291-93.

22. John A. Eisterhold, "Savannah: Lumber Center of the South Atlantic," *Georgia Historical Quarterly* 57 (winter 1973): 526-43; "Exports of Flour to South America," *Hunt's* 40 (March 1859): 351.

23. Quoted in Schmidt, 802.

24. Clement Eaton, *The Growth of Southern Civilization, 1790-1860* (New York, 1961): 173; Randall Miller, "Daniel Pratt's Industrial Urbanism: The Cotton Mill Town in Antebellum Alabama," *Alabama Historical Quarterly* 34, (spring, 1972): 5-35.

25. See Richard C. Wade, *The Urban Frontier: The Rise of Western Cities, 1790-1830* (Cambridge, Mass., 1959); Allan R. Pred, "Manufacturing in the American Mercantile City, 1800-1840," *Annals of the American Association of Geographers* 56 (June 1966): 307-25.

26. *Norfolk Southern Argus,* September 20, 1851.

27. Herbert Wender, *Southern Commercial Conventions, 1837-1859* (Baltimore, 1930).

28. *Mobile Register,* quoted in Miller, 7; *Richmond Enquirer,* December 17, 1850.

29. Richard W. Griffen, "The Origins of the Industrial Revolution in Georgia: Cotton Textiles, 1810-1865," *Georgia Historical Quarterly* 42 (December 1958): 355-75.

30. Fisher & Co. to James Thomas, Jr., June 7, 1855, Beale-Davis Family MSS, Southern Historical Collection, University of North Carolina; *Richmond Enquirer,* November 4, 1853; *Richmond Daily Dispatch,* September 22, 1859; see also Kathleen C. Bruce, *Virginia Iron Manufacture in the Slave Era, 1800-1860* (New York, 1931); Joseph C.

Robert, *The Tobacco Kingdom: Plantation, Market and Factory in Virginia and North Carolina, 1800-1860* (Durham, N. C., 1938); Thomas S. Berry, "The Rise of Flour Milling in Richmond," *Virginia Magazine of History and Biography* 78 (October 1970): 387-408.

31. *Compendium of the Ninth Census: 1870,* 798-99.
32. See Wade, 314-17.
33. "Commercial, Agricultural, and Intellectual Independence of the South," *De Bow's Review* 29 (September 1860): 467.
34. Reed, 81-83; S. Bassett French, "Biographical Sketches," MSS, 160, Virginia State Library.
35. See Walter S. Glazer, "Participation and Power: Voluntary Association and the Functional Organization of Cincinnati in 1840," *Historical Methods Newsletter* 5 (September 1972): 151-68; Clyde Griffen, "Occupational Mobility in Nineteenth-Century America," *Journal of Social History* 5 (spring 1972): 310-30; Edward Pessen, "Who Governed the Nation's Cities in the Era of the Common Man?" *Political Science Quarterly* 87 (December 1972): 591-614.
36. Data obtained from the following sources: U. S. Bureau of Census, "Seventh Census of Virginia: 1850: Free Inhabitants" *MSS,* 11; "Slave Schedule" MSS, 4; "Eighth Census of Virginia: 1860: Free Inhabitants" MSS, 12; "Slave Schedule" MSS, 4; William L. Montague, *Richmond Directory and Business Advertiser for 1852* (Baltimore, 1852); James Butter, *Butter's Richmond Directory, 1855* (Richmond, 1855); French; *Richmond Daily Dispatch,* 1852-61, passim.
37. *Norfolk Southern Argus,* December 29, 1853; Fitzhugh, 145-46.
38. *Richmond Daily Dispatch,* September 23, 1860; Montague, 102.
39. *Richmond Daily Dispatch,* April 19, 1860; *New Orleans Bee,* quoted in Reed, 22.
40. Gail Borden, quoted in Wheeler, 70; quoted in R. W. Griffen, 365.
41. Quoted in Jonathan Lurie, "Private Associations, Internal Regulation and Progressivism: The Chicago Board of Trade, 1880-1923, As a Case Study," *American Journal of Legal History* 16 (July 1972): 215.
42. See ibid., 215-38; Wade, 185; Wheeler, 72; Richard D. Brown, "The Emergence of Urban Society in Rural Massachusetts, 1760-1820," *Journal of American History* 61 (June 1974): 29-51.
43. "Trade of the Mississippi," 291-93; *Richmond Daily Dispatch,* June 15, 1855; September 23, 1853.
44. "The Cities of Georgia: Savannah," *De Bow's Review* 28 (January 1860): 20-28; Richard Irby, "Recollection of Men, Places, and Events, 1845-1900," Richard Irby MSS, Alderman Library, University of Virginia; *Richmond Daily Dispatch,* March 18, 1857.
45. *Richmond Enquirer,* October 20, 1857; "Banking at the South with Reference to New York City," *Hunt's* 42 (March 1860): 312-23.
46. *Richmond Enquirer,* May 26, 1858.
47. Ibid., June 11, 1858.
48. See Peter R. Knights, *The Plain People of Boston, 1830-1860: A Study in City Growth* (New York, 1971), 7; Montague, introduction.
49. Brown, 50; see also Carl Abbott, "Civic Pride in Chicago, 1844-1860," *Journal of the Illinois State Historical Society* 63 (winter 1970): 421; J. Christopher Schnell and Patrick E. McLear, "Why the Cities Grew: A Historiographical Essay on Western Urban Growth, 1850-1880," *Bulletin of the Missouri Historical Society* 27 (April 1972): 162-77.
50. The manuscript census schedules for 1850 and 1860 provide information on the occupation and property holdings of immigrants; see also Earl F. Niehaus, *The Irish of New Orleans* (Baton Rouge, 1965); Wheeler; M. Ray Della, Jr., "An Analysis of Baltimore's Population in the 1850s," *Maryland Historical Magazine* 68 (spring 1973): 20-35; George P. Marks, III, "The New Orleans Screwmen's Benevolent Association," *Labor History* 14 (spring 1973): 259-63.
51. R. W. Griffen, 355-75; "White Girls in Tobacco Factories," *Hunt's* 40 (April 1859): 522-23; *Alexandria Gazette,* May 6, 1852; March 2, 1854; *Norfolk Southern Argus,* March 17, 1854.
52. Quoted in W. E. B. Du Bois, *The Philadelphia Negro: A Social Study* (New York, 1899): 370.
53. See Ira Berlin, *Slaves without Masters; The Free Negro in the Antebellum South* (New

York, 1974); David M. Katzman, *Before the Ghetto: Black Detroit in the Nineteenth Century* (Urbana, Ill., 1973); Leon F. Litwack, *North of Slavery: The Negroes in the Free States, 1790-1860* (Chicago: University of Chicago Press, 1961); see also Donnie D. Bellamy, "Free Blacks in Antebellum Missouri, 1820-1860," *Missouri Historical Review* 67 (January 1973): 198-225; Della, 20-35; Dorothy Provine, "The Economic Position of Free Blacks in the District of Columbia," *Journal of Negro History* 62 (January 1973): 61-72.

54. *Richmond Daily Dispatch,* January 26, 1853; Governor's Message to the General Assembly, December 13, 1859, Virginia House of Delegates, 1859-60, document 1: 44.

55. *Norfolk Southern Argus,* July 25, 1853; see also *Alexandria Gazette,* February 15, 1853; *Richmond Daily Dispatch,* November 25, 1859.

56. Virginia, Board of Public Works, *Thirty-Ninth Annual Report* (1855), cxx.

57. See Robert S. Starobin, *Industrial Slavery in the Old South* (New York, 1969); Richard C. Wade, *Slavery in the Cities: The South, 1820-1860* (New York, 1964); Charles B. Dew, "Disciplining Slave Ironworkers in the Antebellum South: Coercion, Conciliation, and Accommodation," *American Historical Review* 79 (April 1974): 393-418; Clement Eaton, "Slave-Hiring in the Upper South: A Step toward Freedom," *Mississippi Valley Historical Review* 46 (March 1960): 663-78.

58. Robert Russell, *North America: Its Agriculture and Climate* (Edinburgh, 1857): 152.

59. Robert, passim; for advertisements of owners and agents with tobacco factory hands for hire, see *Richmond Daily Dispatch,* January 4, 1853, January 3, 1855; for advertisements of coal mines seeking to hire slave labor, see January 1, 1853, January 1, 1854; "Forge Wages to Negro a/c," in Tredegar Journal MSS, 1850, 1852, Virginia State Library; see also "Eighth Census of Virginia: 1860: Slave Schedule" MSS, 4.

60. "Eighth Census of Virginia: 1860: Slave Schedule" MSS, 1: 322, 326, 327, 328.

61. R. Lewis to Dr. A. G. Grinnan, December 29, 1860, Grinnan Family MSS, Alderman Library, University of Virginia; N. B. Hill to Mr. Atkinson, February 7, 1855, James Southgate MSS, Duke University Library; "Eighth Census of Virginia: 1860: Slave Schedule" MSS, 4.

62. *Alexandria Gazette,* February 29, 1856; *Richmond Daily Dispatch,* April 15, 1859; "Hiring Negroes," *Southern Planter* 12 (December 1852): 376-77.

63. *Norfolk Southern Argus,* April 27, 1857; A. A. Campbell, "Capital and Enterprise: The Bases of Agricultural Progress," *Southern Planter* 20 (January 1860): 36-39; Edmund Ruffin, "The Effects of High Prices of Slaves," *Southern Planter* 19 (August 1859): 472-77.

64. Fitzhugh, *Sociology* 87; J. D. B. De Bow, "Address to Railroad Convention," *De Bow's Review* 12 (September 1852): 557-59; 18 (April 1855): 350-51.

65. *Wheeling Daily Intelligencer,* May 28, 1858; Claudia D. Goldin, "Urbanization and Slavery: The Issue of Compatibility," in Leo F. Schnore (ed.), *The New Urban History* (Princeton, 1975): 231-46.

66. See Charles N. Glaab and A. Theodore Brown, *A History of Urban America* (New York, 1967), ch. 7.

67. See Eaton, *Southern Civilization,* 249; Brown, 29-51; Curry, 43-60.

68. See John Little, *History of Richmond* (Richmond, 1933): 292; James, 79-82; Reed, 82; Wade, *Urban Frontier,* 270; see also Robert A. McCaughey, "From Town to City: Boston in the 1820s," *Political Science Quarterly* 88 (June 1973): 191-213.

69. *Alexandria Gazette,* March 18, 1860; James, 79-82; see also Wade, *Urban Frontier,* 273.

70. *Wheeling Daily Intelligencer,* April 28, 1856; see W. D. Overdyke, *The Know Nothing Party in the South* (Baton Rouge, 1950).

71. Charles E. Rosenberg, *The Cholera Years* (Chicago, 1962): 13-37; Joseph I. Waring, "Asiatic Cholera in South Carolina," *Bulletin of the History of Medicine* 40 (September, October 1966): 462.

72. *Norfolk Southern Argus,* December 16, 1848.

73. Rosenberg, 27-37.

74. *Savannah Daily Morning News,* April 28, 1851; James J. Waring, *The Epidemic of Savannah* (Savannah, 1879): 16-17.

75. *Richmond Enquirer,* June 8, 1854; *Alexandria Gazette,* June 23, 1854.

76. *Norfolk Southern Argus,* January 16, 1856.

77. Baltimore Board of Health *Report,* December 30, 1860 (Baltimore, 1860).

78. *Alexandria Gazette,* April 7, 1856; June 10, 1856; *Boston Herald,* May 13, 1856.

79. Quoted in Samuel Mills Hopkins, *Letters Concerning the General Health* (New York, 1805), 2.

80. *Alexandria Gazette*, June 8, 1849; *Richmond Enquirer*, October 2, 1855.

81. *Charleston Courier*, August 26, 1858; November 11, 1858; *Savannah Daily Morning News*, September 22, 1852; November 6, 1852.

82. Committee of Physicians, *Report on the Origins of the Yellow Fever in Norfolk during the Summer of 1855* (Richmond, 1857).

83. Richard H. Shryock, *Medicine in America* (Baltimore, 1966), 50; see also John Duffy, *Sword of Pestilence: The New Orleans Yellow Fever Epidemic of 1853* (Baton Rouge, 1966).

84. David R. Goldfield, "Disease and Urban Image: Yellow Fever in Norfolk, 1855," *Virginia Cavalcade* 23 (autumn 1973): 34-41.

85. Robert Lebby, *Digest of Acts of the Assembly of South Carolina and Ordinances of the City of Charleston Relative to the Health Department from 1763 to 1867* (Charleston, 1870), June 24, 1853.

86. See David Grimsted, "Rioting in the Jacksonian Setting," *American Historical Review* (April 1972): 77, 361-97; John C. Schneider, "Community and Order in Philadelphia, 1834-1844," *Maryland Historian* 5 (spring 1974): 15-26.

87. See Wheeler, 54.

88. *Wheeling Daily Intelligencer*, February 25, 1860.

89. *Norfolk Southern Argus*, June 18, 1850.

90. Eaton, *Southern Civilization*, 251; George C. Rogers, Jr., *Charleston in the Age of the Pinckneys* (Norman, Okla., 1969): 167.

91. *Norfolk Southern Argus*, January 9, 1856; July 21, 1857.

92. *Alexandria Gazette*, June 8, 1854; December 5, 1854; March 29, 1855; March 11, 1858.

93. Williams O. Stevens, *Charleston* (New York, 1940).

94. See Glaab and Brown, 97; Eaton, *Southern Civilization*, 257.

95. "Mobile: Its Past and Present," *De Bow's Review* 28 (March 1860): 305; *Alexandria Gazette*, April 10, 1857; *Wheeling Daily Intelligencer*, November 13, 1858; January 5, 1859; "Commercial and Industrial Cities of the United States: Richmond, Virginia," *Hunt's* 40 (January 1859): 61-62.

96. "Fires in Cities: London and New York," *Hunt's* 35 (July 1856): 300-301.

97. "Savannah," *De Bow's Review* 28 (January 1860): 20-28; James, 84; Eaton, *Southern Civilization*, 254; "Richmond," *Hunt's* 40 (January 1859): 61-62; see also Nelson M. Blake, *Water for the Cities: A History of the Urban Water Supply Problem in the United States* (Syracuse, N. Y., 1956).

98. See Wade, *Urban Frontier*, 276, 282-85.

99. *Boston Courier*, January 8, 1849; Frederick Law Olmsted, *A Journey through the Seaboard Slave States* (New York, 1856), 132; *Alexandria Gazette*, April 18, 1858; January 26, 1858.

100. *Alexandria Gazette*, March 8, 1859.

101. *Lynchburg Virginian*, April 21, 1851.

102. Eaton, *Southern Civilization*, 257-58.

103. Quoted in McComb, *Houston*, 17; quoted in Lyle W. Dorsett, "The Early American City," in Harold Woodman (ed.), *Forums in History* (St. Louis, 1973), 2.

104. John W. Reps, *The Making of Urban America: A History of City Planning in the United States* (Princeton, 1965): 325-47; Curry, 43-60.

105. "Savannah," *De Bow's Review*, 20-28; Reps, 331-39; *Alexandria Gazette*, January 27, 1854; August 7, 1855; *Norfolk Southern Argus*, December 4, 1852.

106. *Norfolk Southern Argus*, November 14, 1849; *Alexandria Gazette*, May 21, 1851; quoted in James, 83; "Savannah," *De Bow's Review*, 20-28.

107. See Robert H. Bremner, *From the Depths: The Discovery of Poverty in the United States* (New York, 1956); Raymond A. Mohl, "Poverty, Pauperism, and Social Order in the Preindustrial American City, 1780-1840," *Social Science Quarterly* 52 (March 1972): 934-48.

108. "Mobile," *De Bow's Review*, 305; *Norfolk Southern Argus*, November 27, 1848; December 6, 1848.

109. "The Almshouse Experience," in *Poverty, U. S. A.: The Historical Record* (New York, 1971), 1101-1104; "Richmond: 1859," *Hunt's* 61-62; *Alexandria Gazette*, August 3, 1855; August 21, 1855.

110. Overseers of the Poor, "Annual Report," 1859, in *Alexandria Gazette*, December 15, 1859.
111. Wade, *Urban Frontier*, 185; Eaton, *Southern Civilization*, 258; James, 221.
112. Quoted in *Richmond Enquirer*, September 10, 1850; February 6, 1857; Fitzhugh, *Sociology*, 144-48.
113. *Norfolk Southern Argus*, January 29, 1849; May 12, 1855; January 31, 1856; June 15, 1857; October 13, 1857.
114. Eaton, *Southern Civilization*, 259; "Baltimore Mercantile Library Association," *Hunt's* 18 (March 1848): 230-31; Eaton, *Southern Civilization*, 259-60; *Richmond Enquirer*, January 7, 1859.
115. *Richmond Daily Dispatch*, July 28, 1857.
116. *Wheeling Daily Intelligencer*, January 20, 1854; *Richmond Daily Dispatch*, March 27, 1857.
117. McComb, 71-72; James, 87-91.
118. "Richmond: 1859," *Hunt's*, 61-62.
119. Wheeler, 73; James, 87-91; Mobile, *Code of Ordinances* (Mobile, 1859); *Charleston Courier*, February 26, 1816; February 29, 1816.
120. *Alexandria Gazette*, April 12, 1855; May 22, 1855; June 14, 1856.
121. Wade, *Urban Frontier*, 280.
122. On the centralization of the national economy at New York, see Allan R. Pred, *Urban Growth and the Circulation of Information: The United States System of Cities, 1790-1840* (Cambridge, Mass., 1973); Thomas C. Cochran, "The Business Revolution," *American Historical Review* 79 (December 1974): 1449-66; Peter G. Goheen, "Industrialization and the Growth of Cities in Nineteenth-Century America," *American Studies* 14 (spring 1973): 49-65; see James A. Ward, "A New Look at Antebellum Southern Railroad Development," *Journal of Southern History* 39 (August 1973): 409-420.
123. "The Removal of Commerce from Boston to New York," *Hunt's* 30 (April 1854): 391.
124. "Export Trade of Charleston, South Carolina," *Hunt's* 33 (November 1855): 604-605.
125. *Savannah Evening Express*, March 31, 1860; Virginia Board of Public Works, "Annual Report," 1858, 68-69.
126. Quoted in Wender, 3; quoted in Schmidt, 803; see also North.
127. Letter from "Linsey-Woolsey" to *Alexandria Gazette*, March 6, 1860.
128. Fitzhugh, *Cannibals All!*, 248.
129. See Ollinger Crenshaw, "Urban and Rural Voting in the Election of 1860," in Eric F. Goldman (ed.), *Historiography and Urbanization: Essays in American History in Honor of W. Stull Holt* (Baltimore, 1941): 55-60.
130. "Proceedings of the Virginia State Convention," quoted in *Richmond Enquirer*, February 22, 1861; February 28, 1861; see also William W. Freeling, "The Editorial Revolution: Virginia, and the Coming of the Civil War: A Review," *Civil War History* (April 1972): 64-72.
131. See Fitzhugh, *Sociology*, 211; James F. W. Johnston, *Notes on North America: Agricultural, Economical, and Social*, 2 vols. (Boston, 1851), 2: 356. In his calculations Johnston, a British traveler, used the extremely conservative estimate of $300 for a prime field hand. Thus, he probably understated the actual figure.
132. Speech of George W. Brent of Alexandria, "Proceedings...," quoted in *Alexandria Gazette*, March 18, 1861; see speech of Samuel McD. Moore of Rockbridge County, "Proceedings...," quoted in *Richmond Enquirer*, February 26, 1861; speech of Thomas M. Branch of Petersburg, "Proceedings...," quoted in *Richmond Enquirer*, March 19, 1861; see also *Norfolk Southern Argus*, December 11, 1860; William C. Rives, *Letter from the Hon. William C. Rives to a Friend on the Important Questions of the Day* (Richmond, 1860).
133. *Alexandria Gazette*, August 31, 1852; *Norfolk Southern Argus*, April 18, 1854; *Richmond Enquirer*, May 25, 1858; *Wheeling Daily Intelligencer*, May 13, 1858; Jere W. Roberson, "The South and the Pacific Railroad, 1845-1855," *Western Historical Quarterly* 5 (April 1974): 163-86.
134. Speech of George W. Brent, "Proceedings...," quoted in *Alexandria Gazette*, March 18, 1861.
135. "Cities of the South: Richmond," *De Bow's Review* 18 (February 1860): 187-201; *Richmond Enquirer*, March 23, 1861; *Montgomery Advertiser*, quoted in *Christiansburg* (Va.) *New Star*, November 24, 1860.
136. "Richmond," *De Bow's Review*, 18 (February 1860): 187; William M. Burwell, "The

Commercial Future of the South: Theory of Trade Lines, or, Commercial Magnetism Applied to a Direct Intercourse between the City of Memphis and the Market Cities of Europe," *De Bow's Review* 30 (February 1861): 129-56; *Charleston Mercury*, quoted in *New York Herald*, November 4, 1860.

137. *Buffalo Republic*, c. 1856, quoted in Bayrd Still, *Urban America: A History with Documents* (Boston, 1974): 114-15.

138. *Charleston Mercury*, quoted in *New York Herald*, November 4, 1860; *Norfolk Southern Argus*, March 16, 1858; *Richmond Enquirer*, July 25, 1851; *Norfolk Southern Argus*, February 12, 1852.

139. *Richmond Enquirer*, October 7, 1856; *Alexandria Gazette*, December 15, 1859; *Richmond Enquirer*, January 28, 1859.

140. Virginia State Library, *Journals and Papers of the Virginia State Convention of 1861*, 3 vols. (Richmond, 1966), 1: 31-32 (appendix); William H. Gaines, Jr., *Biographical Register of Members: Virginia State Convention of 1861* (Richmond, 1969).

<h3 style="text-align:center">Chapter Four
Howard N. Rabinowitz
Continuity and Change: Southern Urban Development, 1860-1900</h3>

1. As used in this essay, the term "South" refers primarily to the eleven states that comprised the Confederate States of America. I believe that the forces that led to secession, together with the impact of the war and Reconstruction, set these states apart from Kentucky and Oklahoma, the other two states that are normally included in discussions of the postbellum South.

2. E. Merton Coulter, *The South during Reconstruction, 1865-1877*, vol. 8 of *A History of the South*, ed. Wendell Holmes Stephenson and E. Merton Coulter, 10 vols. (Baton Rouge, 1947), 3; Thomas J. Wertenbaker, *Norfolk: Historic Southern Port* (Durham, N. C., 1931): 271.

3. T. Lynn Smith, "The Emergence of Cities," *The Urban South*, ed. Rupert B. Vance and Nicholas J. Demerath (Chapel Hill, N. C., 1954): 28-29, 33.

4. Number of urban places and percentages computed from U. S. censuses 1830 to 1870, and Smith, 28. If Kentucky is included, the percentage of the South's share of urban places declines from 20% in 1830 to 19.1% in 1840, 17.4% in 1850, 15.8% in 1860, and 12.1% in 1870. The share of urban places with over 10,000 people drops from 21.5% to 14.3%.

5. Percentages computed from U. S. censuses for 1860 and 1870, and Smith, 33. If Kentucky is included, the increase in the percentage of urban population is from 7.2% to 9.4%.

6. Kenneth W. Wheeler, *To Wear a City's Crown: The Beginnings of Urban Growth in Texas, 1836-1865* (Cambridge, Mass., 1968): 150-60; Harold D. Woodman, *King Cotton and His Retainers: Financing and Marketing the Cotton Crop of the South, 1800-1925* (Lexington, Ky., 1968): 219; Gerald M. Capers, Jr., *The Biography of a River Town: Memphis: Its Heroic Age* (Chapel Hill, N. C., 1939): 162. Raleigh and Augusta were two other cities that came through the war largely unscathed. See Richard Yates, "Governor Vance and the End of the War in North Carolina," *North Carolina Historical Review* 18 (October 1941): 328-31; Richard Henry Lee German, "The Queen City of the Savannah: Augusta, Georgia, during the Urban Progressive Era, 1890–1917" (Ph.D. dissertation, University of Florida, 1971): 1-7.

7. Grigsby Hart Wotton, Jr., "New City of the South: Atlanta, 1843–1873" (Ph.D. dissertation, Johns Hopkins University, 1973): 90; James M. Russell, "Atlanta, Gate City of the South, 1847 to 1885" (Ph.D. dissertation, Princeton University, 1971): 126; Sidney Andrews, *The South since the War, As Shown by Fourteen Weeks of Travel and Observation in Georgia and the Carolinas* (Boston, 1866): 339.

8. John A. Eisterhold, "Charleston: Lumber and Trade in a Declining Southern Port," *South Carolina Historical Magazine* 74 (April 1973): 61-72; Merl E. Reed, *New Orleans and the Railroads: The Struggle for Commercial Empire, 1830-1860* (Baton Rouge, 1966); John F. Stover, *The Railroads of the South, 1865-1900* (Chapel Hill, N. C., 1955): 39; Woodman, 270-72; Wertenbaker, 298-303.

9. Stover, 57-58.

10. Woodman, 328-29.

11. A. C. Greene, *Dallas: The Deciding Years: A Historical Portrait* (Dallas, Tex., 1973): 18; Russell, 169-70.
12. Woodman, passim.
13. Russell, 30.
14. Ibid., 195-206; *Montgomery Daily State Sentinel,* April 10, 1868; *Montgomery Alabama State Journal,* November 24, 1868. For support of public and private subscription for the Montgomery County Railroad, see *Montgomery Daily Advertiser,* February 28, 1872.
15. Greene, 22-24.
16. Russell, 47.
17. Stover, 58.
18. *Atlanta Daily New Era,* October 23, 1866, quoted in Wotton, 149.
19. Whitelaw Reid, *After the War: A Southern Tour, 1865-1866,* ed. with intro. by C. Vann Woodward (repr. New York, 1965): 355.
20. Russell, 153-54, 88.
21. German, 23-25, 365.
22. For examples of newspaper boosterism, see *Nashville Republican Banner,* August 8, 1871, and *Montgomery Alabama State Journal,* April, 1872, passim.
23. Wotton, 372, 374.
24. Ernest S. Griffith, *The Modern Development of City Government* (London, 1927), 64.
25. David G. McComb, *Houston: The Bayou City* (Austin, 1969): 73; Wotton, 377; *Montgomery Daily Advertiser,* August 8, 1873; Wertenbaker, 271-74; *Montgomery Alabama State Journal,* June 17, 1874; Russell, 175, 282.
26. Arthur J. Krim, "The Innovation and Diffusion of the Street Railway in North America" (M. A. thesis, University of Chicago, 1967): 103.
27. Ibid., 100.
28. U. S. Bureau of the Census, *Ninth Census of the United States: 1870, Population,* 1: 102, 262, 280; *Nashville Dispatch,* August 16, 1865; V. T. Barnwell (comp.), *Barnwell's Atlanta City Directory and Stranger's Guide* (Atlanta, 1867): 16; W. R. Handleiter (comp.), *Handleiter's Atlanta City Directory* (Atlanta, 1870): viii.
29. *Montgomery Daily Ledger,* September 23, 1865; *Raleigh Daily Sentinel,* April 24, 1866.
30. This discussion is based on examination of local newspapers, city reports, and board of education and city council minutes. For fuller documentation, see Howard N. Rabinowitz, "From Exclusion to Segregation: Health and Welfare Services for Southern Blacks, 1865-1890," *Social Service Review* 48 (September 1974): 327-32; Rabinowitz, "Half a Loaf: The Shift from White to Black Teachers in the Negro Schools of the Urban South, 1865-1890," *Journal of Southern History* 40 (November 1974): 570-72.
31. Otis Singletary, *Negro Militia and Reconstruction* (Austin, 1957); Rabinowitz, "Health and Welfare Services," 332-34; Rabinowitz, "Half a Loaf," 572-74; Louis R. Harlan, "Desegregation in New Orleans Public Schools during Reconstruction," *American Historical Review* 67 (April 1962): 663-75.
32. Writers' Program of the Works Progress Administration in the State of Virginia (comp.), *The Negro in Virginia* (New York, 1940): 241-42; *Richmond Dispatch,* May 9, 1867; January 29, 1870; letter of "A Colored Man" to the editor, *Nashville Daily Press and Times,* June 26, 1866; June 18, 25, 28, 1867; *Mobile Nationalist,* July 25, 1867; April 29, 1870; for Charleston, see ibid., May 9, 1867; Roger A. Fischer, "A Pioneer Protest: The New Orleans Street Car Controversy of 1867," *Journal of Negro History* 53 (July 1968): 219-33.
33. For documentation and a discussion of the problems involved in determining the extent of segregation, see Rabinowitz, "From Exclusion to Segregation: Southern Race Relations 1865-1890," *Journal of American History* 43 (September, 1976). The system of race relations was most fluid in New Orleans, but even there widespread segregation existed by the early 1870s. Two studies of New Orleans which implicitly support the Woodward thesis are Dale A. Somers, "Black and White in New Orleans: A Study in Urban Race Relations, 1865-1900," *Journal of Southern History* 40 (February 1974): 19-42, and John W. Blassingame, *Black New Orleans, 1860-1880* (Chicago, 1973). Cf. Roger A. Fischer, *The Segregation Struggle in Louisiana, 1862-1877* (Urbana, Ill., 1974). For the thesis itself, see C. Vann Woodward, *The Strange Career of Jim Crow* (3rd ed., New York, 1974).
34. Wotton, 323, 218, 321.
35. *Montgomery Daily Advertiser,* October 25, 1871; April 21, 1875.

36. For the situation in Richmond, Nashville, Montgomery, Raleigh, and Atlanta, see Rabinowitz, "From Reconstruction to Redemption in the Urban South," *Journal of Urban History* 2 (February 1976): 169-94. For the experience of the other cities, see Wertenbaker, 268-70; Robert E. Perdue, *The Negro in Savannah, 1865-1900* (New York, 1973): 43; Capers, 173; Vernon Lane Wharton, *The Negro in Mississippi* (Chapel Hill, N. C., 1947): 168; Joy J. Jackson, *New Orleans in the Gilded Age* (Baton Rouge, 1969), 28; for Chattanooga, see *Nashville Banner,* February 29, October 10, 1889; McComb, 77-81.

37. See, for example, Montgomery City Council minutes, August 15, 24, October 19, November 2, 1868; May 3, 1869; September 5, 1870 (Alabama Department of Archives and History, Montgomery); Clarence A. Bacote, "William Finch, Negro Councilman, and Political Activities in Atlanta during Early Reconstruction," *Journal of Negro History* 40 (January 1955): 341-64; *Raleigh Daily Standard,* July 14, 1868; January 5, 1869; *Raleigh Register,* March 27, 1878; Elaine Joan Nowaczyk, "The North Carolina Negro in Politics, 1865-1876" (M. A. thesis, University of North Carolina, 1957).

38. Russell, 209.

39. Stover, 124.

40. Ibid., 124, 125, 129, 153.

41. See, for example, Harold Lawrence Platt, "Urban Public Services and Private Enterprise: Aspects of the Legal and Economic History of Houston, Texas, 1865-1905" (Ph.D. dissertation, Rice University, 1974): 20-21, 29.

42. See, for example, *Nashville Daily American,* December 7, 1875, which lists Kercheval as owing $11.75; Platt, 17-22; *Montgomery Alabama State Journal,* November 30, 1873; January 6, 1875; *Montgomery Daily Advertiser,* December 22, 1874.

43. Samuel Millard Kipp III, "Urban Growth and Social Change in the South, 1870-1920: Greensboro, North Carolina as a Case Study" (Ph.D. dissertation, Princeton University, 1974): 47-50, 56.

44. See, for example, *Nashville Republican Banner,* June 8–July 1, 1873; *Montgomery Alabama State Journal,* October, 1873, passim.

45. C. Vann Woodward, *Origins of the New South, 1877-1913,* vol. 9 of *A History of the South,* ed. Wendell Holmes Stephenson and E. Merton Coulter, 10 vols. (Baton Rouge, 1951): 108; David Paul Bennetts, "Black and White Workers: New Orleans 1880-1900" (Ph.D. dissertation, University of Illinois at Urbana-Champaign, 1972): 14-15.

46. Capers, 182-205; quotation, 204.

47. Individual city populations for 1870 and 1880 from the U. S. census. All future city population figures cited in this essay are derived from the federal census unless noted otherwise. Regional and nationwide figures computed from censuses and table in Smith, 33. If Kentucky is included, the percentage of urban dwellers in the South remains unchanged at 9.4% by 1880.

48. *Montgomery Alabama State Journal,* May 6, 1875; *Nashville Daily American,* June 30, 1876; Platt, 41.

49. U. S. Bureau of the Census, *Report on the Social Statistics of Cities,* part 2: The Southern and the Western States (Washington, D. C., 1887): 99, 272.

50. Coulter, 263.

51. Woodward, *Origins of the New South,* 107.

52. Russell, 209-11, 278-87; George Campbell, *White and Black: The Outcome of a Visit to the United States* (London, 1879): 369.

53. Percentages computed from the 1880, 1890, and 1900 U. S. censuses and the table in Smith, 33. If Kentucky and Oklahoma are included, the percentage of urban dwellers rises to 13.4% in 1890 and 15.2% in 1900.

54. Stover, 150-52, 186; quotation, 152.

55. Ibid., 190.

56. U. S. Bureau of the Census, *Eleventh Census of the United States: 1890: Report on Transportation Business of the United States, part 1: Transportation by Land,* 4.

57. Stover, 196, 255.

58. Ibid., 207-208, 274-75, 279-80, 282.

59. Smith, 36.

60. Stover, 187. Atlanta, however, suffered throughout the period because of freight rate discrimination. Russell, 39.

61. Wertenbaker, 308; Stover, 261-62.

62. Stover, 218.
63. Ibid., 193-94.
64. Paul B. Worthman, "Working Class Mobility in Birmingham, Alabama, 1880–1914," *Anonymous Americans: Explorations in Nineteenth-Century Social History*, ed. Tamara K. Hareven (Englewood Cliffs, N. J., 1971): 174-75.
65. William D. Miller, *Memphis during the Progressive Era, 1900–1917* (Memphis, 1957): 43-48.
66. Bureau of the Census, *Social Statistics of Cities, part 2:* 80-81.
67. Durward Long, "The Making of Modern Tampa: A City of the New South, 1865–1911," *Florida Historical Quarterly* 49 (April 1971): 333-45; quotation, 334.
68. H. G. McCall (comp.), *A Sketch, Historical and Statistical of the City of Montgomery* (Montgomery, 1885): 40, 51-60.
69. Stover, 192-93.
70. *Raleigh Daily Constitution,* July 9, 1875, quoted in Sarah McCulloh Lemmon, "Raleigh: An Example of the New South," *North Carolina Historical Review* 43 (July 1966): 265; *Raleigh State Chronicle,* February 2, 1888, quoted ibid., 266. Even a large city like Memphis resisted efforts to support a mill. See W. D. Miller, 54.
71. Woodward, *Origins of the New South,* 140.
72. Wotton, 416; Russell, 243-44; R. David Weber, "Urbanization, Ethnicity, and Occupational Status in the Rising American City, 1870–1900," paper delivered at the sixty-eighth Annual Meeting of the Pacific Coast Branch, American Historical Association, August 21, 1975, Berkeley, Cal., Miscellaneous Tables on Composition of the Work Force in the Largest American Cities.
73. Weber, table 3 and miscellaneous tables. Weber nevertheless emphasizes the similar composition of the work force in all major cities.
74. Capers, 217-18; 224, German, 17; Long, passim.
75. Mayer N. Zald and Thomas A. Anderson, "Secular Trends and Historical Contingencies in the Recruitment of Mayors: Nashville as compared to New Haven and Chicago," *Urban Affairs Quarterly* 3 (June 1968): 53-68; *Nashville Daily American,* October 11, 1878; October 2, 1882.
76. Platt, 171; Kipp, 343; Carl V. Harris, "Annexation Struggles and Political Power in Birmingham, Alabama, 1890–1910," *Alabama Review* 27 (July 1974): 169. See also Eugene John Watts, "Characteristics of Candidates in City Politics: Atlanta, 1865-1903" (Ph.D. dissertation, Emory University, 1969).
77. Platt, 117.
78. U. S. Bureau of Census, *Statistics of Cities Having a Population of Over 25,000 in 1902 and 1903,* Bulletin 20 (Washington, D. C., 1905): 443-45.
79. Ibid., 104-105; W. D. Miller, 69.
80. Letter of "A. F." to a friend in Ohio, reprinted in *Nashville Banner,* July 10, 1890.
81. John H. Ellis, "Business and Public Health in the Urban South during the Nineteenth Century: New Orleans, Memphis, and Atlanta," *Bulletin of the History of Medicine* 44 (May-June 1970): 197-212; (July-August 1970): 346-71. See also Richard J. Hopkins, "Public Health in Atlanta: The Formative Years, 1865–1879," *Georgia Historical Quarterly* 53 (September 1969): 287-304.
82. W. D. Miller, 68; J. J. Jackson, 153.
83. Long, 337; U. S. Bureau of the Census, *Statistics of Cities, 1902 and 1903,* 114.
84. Richmond, *Annual Report of the Superintendent of Public Schools of the City of Richmond, Virginia, for the Scholastic Year Ending July 31, 1881* (Richmond, 1882): 4; ibid., 1890-1891, 23; W. W. Clayton, *History of Davidson County, Tennessee* (Philadelphia, 1880): 249-50; Nashville, *Annual Report of the Board of Education of Nashville for the Scholastic Year 1889–1890* (Nashville, 1890): 37; Wertenbaker, 280; U. S. Bureau of the Census, *Statistics of Cities, 1902 and 1903,* 93-94.
85. U. S. Bureau of the Census, *Statistics of Cities, 1902 and 1903,* 93-94, 479-81, 101.
86. See, for example, Eugene J. Watts, "The Police in Atlanta, 1890-1905," *Journal of Southern History* 39 (May 1973): 165-82; *Souvenir History of the Richmond Police Department* (Richmond, 1901); *Souvenir History of the Montgomery Fire and Police Departments, 1819-1902* (Montgomery, 1902); Wertenbaker, 278, 280; *The Richmond, Virginia, Fire Department: Its Organization and Equipment, with an Account of Its Precursors* (Richmond, 1894); Jackson, 101-107; McComb, 80, 128. Compare, for example, Watts, 176-82, and James F. Richardson, *The New York Police: Colonial Times to 1901* (New York, 1970).

87. U. S. Bureau of the Census, *Social Statistics of Cities, 1880*, 67, 137, 201, 100, 144, 274-75; *Statistics of Cities, 1902 and 1903*, 114-19; W. D. Miller, 79-83.
88. U. S. Bureau of the Census, *Statistics of Cities, 1902 and 1903*, 104-105.
89. Platt, 238; Kipp, 368-69.
90. See, for example, Platt, 54, 104-105, 124, 129-30; Jackson, 316-17; German, passim. For a similar shift in the North, see David P. Thelen, *The New Citizenship: Origins of Progressivism in Wisconsin, 1885-1900* (Columbia, Mo., 1972).
91. Jackson, 165-67; Platt, 136; Long, 337-38.
92. Jackson, 168.
93. Krim, 93, 100; John Anderson Miller, *Fares Please! A Popular History of Trolleys, Horsecars, Streetcars, Buses, Elevateds, and Subways* (New York, 1941): 55-69; quotation, 69; J. J. Jackson, 164; Wertenbaker, 318; the estimate of 51 cities with electric streetcars is from Arthur M. Schlesinger, *The Rise of the City* (New York, 1933): 92.
94. W. D. Miller, 72; McComb, 106-107; Long, 338.
95. *Nashville Banner*, August 31, 1882; June 18, 1883.
96. *Richmond Dispatch*, January 1, 1891; *Nashville Banner*, March 30, 1889; Wertenbaker, 318; Platt, 134. For the impact of the streetcar on a northern city, see Sam Bass Warner, Jr., *Streetcar Suburbs: The Process of Growth in Boston, 1870-1900* (Cambridge, Mass., 1962).
97. *Birmingham Age-Herald*, September 26, 1900, quoted in Harris, 163.
98. *Nashville Daily American*, December 17, 1879; *Nashville Banner*, March 30, 1889; *Birmingham Age-Herald*, October 14, 1900, quoted in Harris, 172.
99. *Nashville Daily American*, February 8, 1880; Bennetts, 6; Wertenbaker, 286-87; McComb, 143; Capers, 214; Kipp, 294, 377.
100. Harris, passim.
101. W. D. Miller, 17; William Waller (ed.), *Nashville, 1900 to 1910* (Nashville, 1972): 10; Wertenbaker, 323.
102. See, for example, Capers, and W. D. Miller; Joseph P. O'Grady, "Immigrants and the Politics of Reconstruction in Richmond, Virginia," *Records of the American Catholic Historical Society of Philadelphia* 83 (June 1972): 87-101; George M. Reynolds, *Machine Politics in New Orleans, 1897-1926* (repr. New York, 1968). See also James Joseph Flanagan, "The Irish Element in Nashville, 1810–1890" (M. A. thesis, Vanderbilt University, 1951).
103. *Atlanta Constitution*, May 6, 1890; *Montgomery Alabama State Journal*, April 8, 1875. For useful studies of two of the South's most important Jewish communities, see Steven Hertzberg, "The Jewish Community of Atlanta from the End of the Civil War until the Eve of the Frank Case," *American Jewish Historical Quarterly* 62 (March 1973): 250-85, and Mark H. Elovitz, *A Century of Jewish Life in Dixie: The Birmingham Experience* (University, Ala., 1974).
104. J. J. Jackson, 17-19.
105. Bayrd Still, *Urban America: A History with Documents* (Boston, 1974): 118-19, 264-65.
106. Alwyn Barr, "Occupational and Geographic Mobility in San Antonio, 1870–1900," *Social Science Quarterly* 51 (September 1970): 396-403; Worthman, passim; Richard J. Hopkins, "Occupational and Geographic Mobility in Atlanta, 1870–1896," *Journal of Southern History* 34 (May 1968): 200-13.
107. See, for example, Kipp, 272; Russell, 264-65.
108. U. S. Bureau of the Census, *Negro Population, 1790-1915*, 90-91, 93. This definition of the South includes Delaware, Maryland, District of Columbia, Oklahoma, Kentucky, and West Virginia. The percentage of blacks in the urban population of the former Confederate states ranged from 22.9% in Texas to 49.3% in South Carolina, while a much smaller percentage of the blacks in the eleven states were urban.
109. See, for example, Gilbert Osofsky, *Harlem: The Making of a Ghetto: Negro New York, 1890-1930* (New York, 1963); Allan H. Spear, *Black Chicago: The Making of a Negro Ghetto, 1890-1920* (Chicago, 1967).
110. U. S. Bureau of the Census, *Eleventh Census of the United States: 1890: Population: I: part 2*, 696.
111. *Richmond Dispatch*, January 2, 1888; Bennetts, passim; quotations, 548, 553.
112. Wotton, 326.
113. W. E. B. Du Bois (ed.), *The Negro in Business*, Atlanta University Publications, no. 4, ed. W. E. B. Du Bois (Atlanta, 1899): 7, 68.

114. Alrutheus Ambush Taylor, *The Negro in the Reconstruction of Virginia* (Washington, D. C., 1926), 135; James T. Haley (comp.), *Afro-American Encyclopedia, or, The Thoughts, Doings and Sayings of the Race* (Nashville, 1896): 212; *Nashville Banner*, December 18, 1886.
115. Conclusions based on examination of city directories in Raleigh for 1886, Atlanta and Richmond for 1891, and Montgomery for 1895. For Negro sections of other cities, see Greene, 18; German, 37; Kipp, 312-13.
116. U. S. Bureau of the Census, *Eleventh Census of the United States: 1890: Report of Farms and Homes,* 29.
117. Annual Reports of the City Departments of Richmond, Virginia, for the Year Ending January 31, 1886, 8; *Atlanta Constitution,* June 25, December 23, 1887; Richard Mendales, "Sic Transit Richmond," typescript, Twentieth Century Urban Negro Project, Center for Urban Studies, University of Chicago, July, 1969, 2-3; J. J. Jackson, 164.
118. See Rabinowitz, "Health and Welfare Services," 343-47; Rabinowitz, "Half a Loaf," 577-88. As late as 1889 there were only 23 Negroes among New Orleans public school teachers. Bennetts, 217. The delay in hiring black teachers in New Orleans may have been due to the failure of the system to expand and thus to provide jobs for white teachers in Negro schools; this was evidently the case in Charleston, where in 1902 there were still only six public schools. U. S. Bureau of the Census, *Statistics of Cities, 1902 and 1903,* 93-94. For the persistence of white teachers in Charleston's black schools despite Negro protests, see George Brown Tindall, *South Carolina Negroes, 1877-1900* (Columbia, 1952): 220-21.
119. *Nashville Banner,* May 1, 1888; Franklin M. Garrett, *Atlanta and Environs: A Chronicle of Its People and Events,* 3 vols. (New York, 1954): 2: 175; letter of Eliza Bowers to the editor, *Atlanta Constitution,* July 28, 1889. Miss Bowers, an Atlanta white, remembered entering the Negro car in Montgomery by mistake three years earlier; Gilbert Thomas Stephenson, *Race Distinctions in American Law* (London, 1910): 227-33.
120. For Raleigh, Nashville, and Richmond, see Rabinowitz, "From Reconstruction to Redemption"; for Jackson, see Wharton, 167-68; for North Carolina cities, see Helen G. Edmonds, *The Negro and Fusion Politics in North Carolina, 1894-1901* (Chapel Hill, N. C., 1951): 124-35; for Jacksonville, see Akin, passim.
121. See, for example, Nashville City Council minutes, December 13, 1883 (Office of the Metropolitan Clerk, Davidson County Building and Nashville City Hall); *Nashville Banner,* May 26, 1882; November 8, 1884; January 8, 9, 1885; Akin, 136; Luther Porter Jackson, *Negro Office-Holders in Virginia, 1865-1895* (Norfolk, Va., 1945): 83; Richmond Common Council minutes, May 7, 1888 (Office of the City Clerk, Richmond City Hall). Black councilmen, however, failed to achieve one of their major goals: the purchase of land for a city park in Jackson Ward. See, for example, Richmond Council minutes, August 18, October 3, 1887; June 7, August 6, 1888; June 3, 1889; April 7, 1890.
122. Woodward, *Origins of the New South,* 230; Edmonds.
123. See Rabinowitz, "The Search for Social Control: Race Relations in the Urban South, 1865-1890" (Ph.D. dissertation, University of Chicago, 1973): 774-81; *Richmond Dispatch,* December 1, 1885; Report of the United States Senate Judiciary Committee, repr. in *Atlanta Constitution,* August 2, 1888.
124. *Nashville Banner,* September 18, 1889; *Atlanta Constitution,* January 22, 1890.
125. *Nashville Banner,* April 3, 1889; August 5, 8, 1890.
126. Akin, 140.
127. Paul Lewinson, *Race, Class, and Party: A History of Negro Suffrage and White Politics in the South* (New York, 1932); J. Morgan Kousser, *The Shaping of Southern Politics: Suffrage Restriction and the Establishment of the One-Party South, 1880-1910* (New Haven, 1974); Edmonds, 158-77; J. J. Jackson, 20.
128. Woodward, *Origins of the New South,* 139.
129. Number of urban places and percentages computed from U. S. censuses of 1860 and 1900, and tables in Smith, 28-29, 33. If Kentucky and Oklahoma are included, the percentage of urban dwellers in the South rises from 7.2% in 1860 to 15.2% in 1900, and the South's share of the nation's urban places grows from 15.8% to 18.4%. The region's share of places over 10,000 inhabitants increases from 16.1% to 19.5%.
130. Woodward, *Origins of the New South,* 139.
131. Ibid., 371.

Chapter Five
Blaine A. Brownell
The Urban South Comes of Age, 1900-1940

1. Ellen Glasgow, *One Man in His Time* (Garden City, N. Y., 1922): 57.
2. The 12 largest cities were selected on the basis of the 40-year period. Charleston and Savannah ranked 6th and 7th, respectively, among southern cities in 1900; but Charleston dropped to 13th and Savannah to 12th in 1910, and both cities were no longer among the 12 largest in the region by 1920. The elimination of Charleston and Savannah, and the inclusion of rapidly growing cities like Birmingham and Fort Worth, tend to overemphasize the overall growth rate of the largest southern cities between 1900 and 1940, but not to any significant degree. The rate of population increase for the 12 southern cities in table 2—plus Charleston and Savannah—was 219.8%. And the population growth rate for the largest 25 cities in 1900 (see table 5) over the 40-year period was 196.9%. In addition, the cities in south Florida are eliminated from consideration here since their origins and patterns of development—especially Miami's—were quite different from those of other southern cities. (These cities are included, however, in the considerations of rank order distribution, specifically in tables 5 and 6.)
3. George B. Tindall, "Business Progressivism: Southern Politics in the Twenties," *South Atlantic Quarterly* 62 (winter 1963): 95. Statistics on the southern economy, unless otherwise noted, are taken from volumes of the U. S. Census; Howard W. Odum, *Southern Regions of the United States* (Chapel Hill, N. C., 1936); and Donald B. Dodd and Wynelle S. Dodd, *Historical Statistics of the South, 1790-1970* (University, Ala., 1973).
4. Information on the economies of specific cities is taken from: Charles G. Summersell, *Mobile: History of a Seaport Town* (Tuscaloosa, Ala., 1949): 52-53; Thomas J. Wertenbaker, *Norfolk: Historic Southern Port*, ed. Marvin W. Schlegal (Durham, N. C., 1962), 300; William D. Miller, *Memphis during the Progressive Era, 1900-1917* (Memphis, 1957): 44, 46-47; Gilbert E. Govan and James W. Livingood, *The Chattanooga Country, 1540-1962: From Tomahawks to TVA* (rev. ed., Chapel Hill, N. C., 1963): 405.
5. See Oliver Knight, *Fort Worth: Outpost on the Trinity* (Norman, Okla., 1953): 175, 178, 199; and James Howard, *Big D is for Dallas: Chapters in the Twentieth-Century History of Dallas* (Austin, 1957): 18, 55-56.
6. *Fifteenth Census of the United States: 1930: Distribution*, vol. 1, *Retail Distribution* (Washington, D. C., 1934), part 2: 67, 538, 967; part 3: 1021, 1031. These figures do not include dealerships specializing in used cars, or the large number of repair shops and accessory stores.
7. Wertenbaker, 290.
8. Statistics on automobile registration are uneven and in many cases not especially reliable, but approximations are nevertheless possible. For additional information, see B. A. Brownell, "A Symbol of Modernity: Attitudes toward the Automobile in Southern Cities in the 1920s," *American Quarterly* 24 (March 1972): 20-44.
9. John A. Beeler, *Report to the City of Atlanta on a Plan for Local Transportation, December, 1924* (Atlanta, 1924): 6.
10. Howard L. Preston, "A New Kind of Horizontal City: Automobility in Atlanta, 1900-1930" (Ph.D. dissertation, Emory University, 1974).
11. Elizabeth Anne Mack Lyon, "Business Buildings in Atlanta: A Study in Urban Growth and Form" (Ph.D. dissertation, Emory University, 1971): 483, 485.
12. Gerald M. Capers, "Memphis: Satrapy of a Benevolent Despot" in Robert S. Allen (ed.), *Our Fair City* (New York, 1947): 216.
13. *Atlanta Life*, November 27, 1926.
14. Paul B. Worthman, "Working Class Mobility in Birmingham, Alabama, 1880-1914" in Tamara K. Hareven (ed.), *Anonymous Americans: Explorations in Nineteenth-Century Social History* (Englewood Cliffs, N. J., 1971): 205.
15. J. Paul McConnell, "Population Problems in Nashville, Tennessee . . ." (manuscript, Y. M. C. A. Graduate School, Nashville, 1933).
16. Harlan W. Gilmore, "The Old New Orleans and the New: A Case for Ecology," *American Sociological Review* 9 (August 1944): 385-94.
17. Worthman, 175.
18. W. E. B. Du Bois, "Of the Wings of Atlanta" in *The Souls of Black Folk* (Fawcett ed., Greenwich, Conn., 1961): 68.

19. *Richmond Planet,* March 29, 1924.
20. Gerda Lerner, "Early Community Work of Black Club Women," *Journal of Negro History* 59 (April 1974): 163-67.
21. August Meier and Elliott Rudwick, "The Boycott Movement against Jim Crow Streetcars in the South, 1900-1906," *Journal of American History* 55 (March 1969): 756-75.
22. Data on social and geographic mobility are taken from recent studies of Atlanta and Birmingham. While conditions doubtless varied from city to city, it is assumed that the most general patterns in these two urban areas were *roughly* representative of those in other large regional cities. Obviously, many more specific and comparative studies need to be done. See Richard J. Hopkins, "Are Southern Cities Unique? Persistence As a Clue," *Mississippi Quarterly* 26 (spring 1973): 121-41; Hopkins, "Status, Mobility, and the Dimensions of Change in a Southern City: Atlanta 1870-1910" in Kenneth T. Jackson and Stanley K. Schultz (eds.), *Cities in American History* (New York, 1972): 216-31; Hopkins, "Patterns of Persistence and Occupational Mobility in a Southern City: Atlanta, 1870-1920" (Ph.D. dissertation, Emory University, 1972); Paul B. Worthman, "Black Workers and Labor Unions in Birmingham, Alabama, 1897-1904," *Labor History* 10 (summer 1969): 375-407; Worthman, "Working Class Mobility."
23. *Memphis Commercial-Appeal,* February 5, 1922.
24. See Carl V. Harris, "Economic Power and Politics: A Study of Birmingham, Alabama, 1890-1920" (Ph.D. dissertation, University of Wisconsin, 1970).
25. *Nashville Tennessean,* April 25, 1927.
26. Ward Greene, *Ride the Nightmare* (New York, 1930): 72, 198; *Nashville Tennessean,* March 13, 1925.
27. *Birmingham Age-Herald,* May 23, 1920.
28. Figures on the homicide rates are available in U. S. Census, *Mortality Statistics: 1930* (Washington, D. C., 1930): 50. See Miller, "Myth and New South City Murder Rates," *Mississippi Quarterly* 26 (spring 1973): 143-44; and Sheldon Hackney, "Southern Violence," *American Historical Review* 74 (February 1969): 906-25.
29. The urban counterpart of the rural lynch mob was the race riot, or massacre, which occurred infrequently but with brutal force in some cities. One example is the Atlanta "riot" of 1906, in which about 10,000 whites assaulted blacks throughout the city, killing 25, seriously wounding 150, and driving more than 1,000 black people from the city in fear for their lives. See Charles Crowe, "Racial Massacre in Atlanta, September 22, 1906," *Journal of Negro History* 54 (April 1969): 150-73.
30. For information on some aspects of these policies, see Carl V. Harris, "Reforms in Government Control of Negroes in Birmingham, Alabama, 1890-1920," *Journal of Southern History* 38 (November 1972): 567-600.
31. Kenneth T. Jackson, *The Ku Klux Klan in the City, 1915-1930* (New York, 1967).
32. See B. A. Brownell, "Birmingham, Alabama: New South City in the 1920s," *Journal of Southern History* 38 (February 1972): 38-39; Harris, "Economic Power and Politics: A Study of Birmingham, Alabama, 1880-1920," 437, 439, 440-41.
33. Quoted in *Nashville Christian Advocate* 71 (July 16, 1920): 900.
34. *Digest of the Ordinances and Resolutions of the City of Nashville* (Nashville, 1917), 467; Nashville City Council minutes 21: 48.
35. Memphis Board of Commissioners minutes, book G, 23, 27, 282, 298; John M. Dean, "To Show, or Not to Show," *Memphis Chamber of Commerce Journal* 5 (March 1922): 1.
36. See John J. Duffy, "Charleston Politics in the Progressive Era" (Ph.D. dissertation, University of South Carolina, 1963): 249-51, 265.
37. See George M. McReynolds, *Machine Politics in New Orleans, 1897-1926* (New York, 1936): 158-59; New Orleans Commission Council, "Report on Commercial Prostitution in the Vice and Gambling Investigation," 1927 (typescript in the City Archives, New Orleans Public Library), 1-2 and passim.
38. Miller, *Memphis During the Progressive Era,* 88.
39. For a perceptive presentation and analysis of this urban, business-oriented "progressivism" in a single southern state, see Sheldon Hackney, *Populism to Progressivism in Alabama* (Princeton, 1969).
40. See James Weinstein, "Organized Business and City Commission and Manager Movements," *Journal of Southern History* 28 (May 1962): 166-82.
41. William J. Robertson, *The Changing South* (New York, 1927): 208.

42. See William D. Miller, *Mr. Crump of Memphis* (Baton Rouge, 1964).
43. *Atlanta City Builder* 16 (February 1932): 11.
44. For a compilation of information on Texas cities during the depression, see Robert C. Cotner et al., *Texas Cities and the Great Depression* (Austin, 1973).
45. See Mark B. Lapping, "The Emergence of Federal Public Housing: Atlanta's Techwood Project," *American Journal of Economics and Sociology* 32 (October 1973): 379-85.

Chapter Six
Edward F. Haas
The Southern Metropolis, 1940-1976

1. See Blaine A. Brownell, "The Urban South Comes of Age, 1900-1940," above.
2. Donald B. Dodd and Wynelle S. Dodd, *Historical Statistics of the South, 1790-1970* (University, Ala., 1973): 17, 75; Raymond A. Mohl and James F. Richardson (eds.), *The Urban Experience: Themes in American History* (Belmont, Cal., 1973): 249.
3. Numan V. Bartley, *From Thurmond to Wallace: Political Tendencies in Georgia, 1948-1968* (Baltimore, 1970), 14-15; Edward F. Haas, "New Orleans on the Half Shell: The Maestri Era, 1936-1946," *Louisiana History* 13 (summer 1972): 284-87.
4. John M. Maclachlan and Joe S. Floyd, Jr., *This Changing South* (Gainesville, Fla., 1956): 44.
5. George B. Tindall, *The Emergence of the New South, 1913-1945* (Baton Rouge, 1967): 694-701; Brownell, "Urbanization in the South: A Unique Experience?" *Mississippi Quarterly* 26 (spring 1973): 113-14; Jack B. McGuire, "Andrew Higgins Plays Presidential Politics," *Louisiana History* 15 (summer 1974): 274.
6. Tindall, 701-703.
7. Gary A. Bolding, "New Orleans Commerce: The Establishment of a Permanent World Trade Mart," *Louisiana History* 8 (fall 1967): 356-59; David G. McComb, *Houston: The Bayou City* (Austin, 1969): 176.
8. For a thorough discussion of the Maestri-Morrison era in New Orleans, see Haas, *De Lesseps S. Morrison and the Image of Reform: New Orleans Politics, 1946-1961* (Baton Rouge, 1974).
9. Neal R. Pierce, *The Deep South States of America* (New York, 1972): 318, 338-40, 348, 350, 354-56, 447, 450, 482; Brownell, *The Urban South in the Twentieth Century* (St. Charles, Mo., 1974): 12; McComb, 227, 241, 243, 253-56; Haas, *De Lesseps S. Morrison*, 26-27, 33, 223-24.
10. Dodd and Dodd, 74-76.
11. Leonard Reissman, "Urbanization in the South," in John C. McKinney and Edgar T. Thompson (eds.), *The South in Continuity and Change* (Durham, N. C., 1965): 84.
12. Brownell, *Urban South*, 15.
13. Ibid., 18, 21-22.
14. Ibid., 20; McComb, 203-205; Pierce, 272, 341-42; Reissman, 84-85; New Orleans *States-Item*, April 13, 1970; *Atlanta Constitution*, April 24, 1975.
15. Brownell, *Urban South*, 19-21.
16. Pierce, 489; McComb, 173; Reissman, 86; *Shreveport Times*, June 2, 1975.
17. See Sam Bass Warner, Jr., *The Urban Wilderness: A History of the American City* (New York, 1972): 115-18, 121; Brownell, "Urbanization in the South," 114, 116-17.
18. Warner, 39-40; McComb, 199, 207; Brownell, *Urban South*, 16-17; Bayrd Still, *Urban America: A History with Documents* (Boston, 1974): 357-58; Malcolm A. Murray, *Atlas of Atlanta: The 1970s* (University, Ala., 1974), map 9.
19. Reissman, 92-96.
20. See Perry H. Howard, *Political Tendencies in Louisiana* (rev. ed., Baton Rouge, 1971): 16-17; *New Orleans Times-Picayune*, January 12, 1975.
21. Warner, 122.
22. Pierre V. De Gruy, "Fat Tuesday in Fat City," *Dixie Roto Sunday Magazine*, February 9, 1975, 16, 18; Brownell, *Urban South*, 16-17.
23. See McComb, 252-56; New Orleans *States—Item*, April 13, 1970; Pierce, 344.
24. New Orleans *States-Item*, April 13, 1970; McComb, 248-50; Pierce, 120.
25. Haas, *De Lesseps S. Morrison*, 233-34; Pierce, 291-92, 332; *Shreveport Times*, May 11, 1975; *Shreveport Journal*, May 9, 1975.
26. For a thorough discussion of the civil rights movement in the South, see Numan V. Bartley, *The Rise of Massive Resistance: Race and Politics in the South during the 1950s* (Baton Rouge, 1969); Hugh Davis Graham, *Crisis in Print: Desegregation and*

the Press in Tennessee (Nashville, 1967); Haas, *De Lesseps S. Morrison;* August Meier and Elliott Rudwick, *From Plantation to Ghetto* (rev. ed., New York, 1970); John Hope Franklin, *From Slavery to Freedom* (4th rev. ed., New York, 1974); Neil R. McMillen, *The Citizens' Council: Organized Resistance to the Second Reconstruction, 1954-1964* (Urbana, Ill., 1971).

27. Haas, *De Lesseps S. Morrison,* 265-66.
28. Pierce, 241-42, 284-88.
29. Brownell, 28.
30. Ibid., 29.
31. *New Orleans Times-Picayune,* September 22, 1974; Murray, map 10. See also Kenneth T. Jackson, "The Crabgrass Frontier: 150 Years of Suburban Growth in America," in Mohl and Richardson, 211.
32. Larry L. King, "Bright Lights, Big Cities," *Atlantic Monthly* 235 (March 1975): 84-88; *Shreveport Times,* March 9, 1975. See also Robert Coles, "Our Hands Belong to the Valley," *Atlantic Monthly* 235 (March 1975): 73.
33. See Pierce, 107-108. See also *Shreveport Journal,* November 14, 1972.
34. Pierce, 110, 286-87, 356-58; Brownell, *Urban South,* 29; David Chandler, "Slicing Up the Cake," *New Orleans* 8 (June 1974): 56-58.
35. Pierce, 110-11, 113-14; "A Mayor Learning on the Job," *Time,* April 21, 1975, 33; *New Orleans Times-Picayune,* April 22, 1975. See also Murray, maps 11, 12, 13, 14, 16, 19, 26, 36, 37.
36. Pierce, 101, 359; Ramsey Clark, *Crime in America: Observations on Its Nature, Causes, Prevention and Control* (New York, 1970): 50-51; "Murdertown, USA," *Time,* February 3, 1958, 17; "A Mayor Learning on the Job," 33; McComb, 215; *New Orleans Times-Picayune,* March 1, 1975.
37. McComb, 215-17; Clark, 50-51; Murray, maps 28-31; William D. Miller, "Myth and New South City Murder Rates," *Mississippi Quarterly* 26 (spring 1973): 143-53; Sheldon Hackney, "Southern Violence," *American Historical Review* 74 (February 1969): 906-925.
38. Pierce, 106-107; "Second Thoughts," *Newsweek,* June 23, 1975, 56; *New Orleans Times-Picayune,* April 22, 1975.
39. *New Orleans Times-Picayune,* November 30, 1972, November 8, 1974, February 5, March 1, 1975.
40. Numan V. Bartley and Hugh Davis Graham, *Southern Politics and the Second Reconstruction* (Baltimore, 1975): 111, 189; Pierce, 109n, 111. See also J. Harvie Wilkinson, III, *Harry Byrd and the Changing Face of Virginia Politics, 1945-1966,* Charlottesville, Va., 1968).
41. Bartley and Graham, 191-92.
42. Brownell, *Urban South,* 29; Pierce, 272-73.
43. *Shreveport Times,* October 25, 1974, March 17, June 12, 1975; *Shreveport Journal,* June 12, 1975.
44. McComb, 199-203.

INDEX

Aaron, Henry, 182
ACCL, 180
"Agrarian feudal myth," 146, 186
Agrarians, 145
Agricultural processing industries, 57-58
Agriculture, 12, 22
Air pollution, 154
Alabama, University of, 179
Alabama and Chattanooga Railroad, 107
Alcorn, Richard S., 9
Alexandria: committees, 68; fire
protection, 74; foreign trade, 56; garbage
cart law, 70; labor force, 64; night watch,
73-74; parks, 77; poor relief, 79; popula-
tion, 93; refuse disposal in, 70; slave
trade in, 88; standing committees, 68;
streets, 75, 76; taxes, 82-83; trees, 78;
Unionist sentiment, 90; women
workers, 64
Algiers (La.), 115, 119
Allen, E. A., 114
Allen, Ivan, Jr., 172
American Municipal Association, 164
Anderson, Joseph R., 58, 88
Annapolis, 28, 31-32, 42
Annexation, 115-16, 125, 126, 134, 135-36,
151, 156, 172, 189
Anniston (Ala.), 107
Architecture, 11
Arlington (Tex.), 178
Arson, 73
Arts, 179
Ashe, Arthur, 182
Assassinations, 186
Association of Citizens' Councils of
Louisiana, 180
Associations, civic, 142-43
Athens (Ga.), 54, 64

Atlanta, 91, 104, 105, 111, 172; air
pollution, 154; annexation, 136, 189;
"Atlanta spirit," 7; automobiles in,
135; banks, 96; benefits from railroad,
97; black boycotts, 140; black businessmen, 118; black mayor, 185; black
neighborhoods, 100; black officeholders,
101; black population, 99, 138, 183;
black property owners, 101; black
schools, 100; board of health, 111;
boosterism in, 11; branch offices in,
175; building in, 98; censorship of
public amusements, 148; chamber of
commerce, 157; education in, 179;
financial condition of, 186, 189; as
financial hub, 133; fire protection in,
119; government, 152; housing project,
158; illicit liquor in, 150; importance of,
128, 132; invested capital, 107; Jews in,
116; Ku Klux Klan in, 147; leaders of,
121; manufacturing, 109; metropolitan
growth, 176, 177; migration to, 137;
mobility in, 141; murder rate, 146;
Neighborhood Union, 140; parks, 112;
period of change, 136; planning commission, 156; poor whites, 116, 117;
population, 53, 92, 93, 106, 126, 127,
173; postwar conditions, 104; prohibition
referenda, 120; rapid transit, 189;
recovery, 95, 97; schools, 112, 187;
segregation, 118, 119; services decline,
104; sit-ins, 180; sports, 178, 179;
streetcars, 98, 114, 119; streets, 111;
taxes, 189; tax receipts, 98; trolley
patrons, 135; war damage, 94; waterworks,
98; workers, 129
Atlantic City (Va.), 115
Atlantic Coast Conurbation, 177

215

CONTRIBUTORS

Blaine A. Brownell is Chairman of the Department of Urban Studies and Director of Urban Affairs at the University of Alabama in Birmingham, and editor of the *Journal of Urban History*. A Senior Fellow in the Institute of Southern History at The Johns Hopkins University (1971-72), he is author or editor of a number of books and articles—including *The Urban Ethos in the South, 1920-1930* and *Bosses and Reformers: Urban Politics in America.*

Carville Earle, a native Baltimorean, teaches geography at the University of Maryland, Baltimore County. He received his Ph.D. in geography from the University of Chicago. His major work, *The Evolution of a Tidewater Settlement System*, was published in 1975. His current research interests include an analysis of staple economies and colonial urban development.

David R. Goldfield, born and raised in Brooklyn, New York lives on a small farm outside of Blacksburg, Virginia. He received his Ph.D. in history from the University of Maryland in 1970 and is currently Associate Professor of Environmental and Urban Systems, Virginia Polytechnic Institute and State University. His most recent book, *Urban Growth in the Age of Sectionalism: Virginia 1847-1861* will be published in spring, 1977. He is working on an urban history text.

Edward F. Haas, a native of New Orleans, received his Ph.D. from the University of Maryland, College Park. He resides in Shreveport, Louisiana where he is Associate Professor of History at Centenary College of Louisiana. His current research interests lie in the field of contemporary politics in urban Louisiana, a sequel to his book, *De Lesseps S. Morrison and the Image of Reform: New Orleans Politics, 1946-1961*, published in 1974.

Ronald Hoffman was born, raised, and currently resides in Baltimore. He received his Ph.D. in history from the University of Wisconsin at Madison and is currently Associate Professor of History, University of Maryland, College Park. His major work, *A Spirit of Dissension: Economics, Politics and the Revolution in Maryland,* published in 1973 reflects his current interest in Revolutionary-era politics in the southern colonies.

Howard N. Rabinowitz left his suburban New York residence to receive his Ph.D. in history from the University of Chicago. Moving westward, he settled in Albuquerque where he is Assistant Professor of History at the University of New Mexico. He recently completed a book, *From Exclusion to Segregation: Race Relations in the Urban South, 1865-1890.*